A SHORT HISTORY OF
YUGOSLAVIA

A SHORT HISTORY OF YUGOSLAVIA

FROM EARLY TIMES TO 1966

BY

H. C. DARBY, R. W. SETON-WATSON,
PHYLLIS AUTY, R. G. D. LAFFAN AND
STEPHEN CLISSOLD

EDITED BY

STEPHEN CLISSOLD

CAMBRIDGE
AT THE UNIVERSITY PRESS
1966

Published by the Syndics of the Cambridge University Press
Bentley House, 200 Euston Road, London, N.W. 1
American Branch: 32 East 57th Street, New York, N.Y. 10022
West African Office: P.M.B. 5181, Ibadan, Nigeria

© Cambridge University Press 1966

Library of Congress Catalogue Card Number: 66–20181

Printed in Great Britain
at the University Printing House, Cambridge
(Brooke Crutchley, University Printer)

CONTENTS

List of Maps   *page* vi

Publisher's Note   viii

Introduction   1

 1   Historical Origins   *by H. C. Darby*   8

 2   Slovenia   *by H. C. Darby*   13

 3   Croatia   *by H. C. Darby*   23

 4   Dalmatia   *by H. C. Darby*   43

 5   Bosnia and Hercegovina   *by H. C. Darby*   58

 6   Montenegro   *by H. C. Darby*   73

 7   Serbia   *by H. C. Darby*   87

 8   Macedonia   *by H. C. Darby*   135

 9   The Formation of the Yugoslav State   154
     by H. C. Darby and R. W. Seton-Watson

10   Yugoslavia between the Wars   170
     by R. W. Seton-Watson and R. G. D. Laffan

11   Occupation and Resistance   *by Stephen Clissold*   208

12   The Post-War Period   *by Phyllis Auty*   236

     Short Bibliography   265

     Sources of the Maps   267

     Index   271

v

LIST OF MAPS

1	The Socialist Federal Republic of Yugoslavia	*page* 2
2	Zones of cereal production	5
3	The Balkan Peninsula, about A.D. 800	10
4	The territories of Samo and Ottokar	14
5	The Slovene lands (pre-1918 frontiers)	20
6	Roman Frontiers and the Eastern Church	24
7	Croatia about A.D. 1070	26
8	The northern frontiers of the Ottoman Empire, 1699–1739	28
9	The 'military frontier' of Austria and Hungary	29
10	The ethnography of Croatia-Slavonia, 1910	39
11	Venice in Dalmatia	45
12	The territory of Ragusa	50
13	The Illyrian provinces, 1809–14	53
14	Medieval Bosnia	61
15	The growth of Montenegro	83
16	The Balkan peninsula, A.D. 910–1265	88
17	The Balkan peninsula, A.D. 1340–55	91
18	Serbia in the tenth and eleventh centuries	92
19	Serbia under the Nemanjid dynasty	97
20	Serbia under Prince Lazar (1371–89)	101
21	A Serbian view of the ethnography of the Vojvodina, 1910	102
22	Serbia under George Branković (1427–56)	104
23	The patriarchate of Peć, 1557	107
24	The growth of Serbia, 1817–1913	117
25	The Balkans in 1878	125
26	The 'contested zone', 1913	128
27	The Balkans in August 1913	132
28	Conflicting claims in Macedonia, 1912	137

29 The Bulgarian exarchate, 1870–1912   *page* 143
30 Yugoslavia in relation to Austria-Hungary   156
31 The Treaty of London, 26 April 1915   161
32 The territorial formation of Yugoslavia   166
33 Istria: Languages and Frontiers   167
34 The Klagenfurt plebiscite, 10 October 1920   168
35 Albania and the Albanian minority in Yugoslavia,
        1913–43   169
36 The boundaries of the *banovine*, 1929–41, and the
        boundaries of the autonomous *banovina* of
        Croatia, 1939–41   198
37 The dismemberment of Yugoslavia, 1941   210
38 The rising in Serbia, summer 1941   214
39 The Fourth Enemy Offensive against the Partisans   225
40 The Fifth Enemy Offensive against the Partisans   227
41 Italo-Yugoslav boundaries   234

PUBLISHER'S NOTE

Most of the material and maps in this book were originally published by the Naval Intelligence Division of the Admiralty as part of a Handbook on Yugoslavia, in three volumes, for service use. By arrangement with the Controller of Her Majesty's Stationery Office, the original owner of the copyright, the historical sections are now reissued in this shorter form. The original contributors were Professor R. W. Seton-Watson and Professor H. C. Darby. A chapter on the history of Yugoslavia during the war has been added by Stephen Clissold, who has also revised and edited the present volume, whilst post-war Yugoslavia has been described by Miss Phyllis Auty.

Place-names normally appear in the form and spelling currently in use, unless the historic context makes the retention of the older names advisable. Alternative forms of nomenclature can be identified from the index.

Four companion volumes have already been published: *A Short History of Germany, 1815–1945*, by E. J. Passant, with contributions by C. J. Child, W. O. Henderson, and Donald Watt; *A Short History of France*, by H. Butterfield, D. W. Brogan, H. C. Darby and J. Hampden Jackson, with contributions by Sir Ernest Barker, A. Ewert, and I. L. Foster; *A Short History of Italy*, by C. M. Ady and A. J. Whyte, revised and edited by H. Hearder and D. P. Waley; and a *Short History of Greece*, by W. A. Heurtley, H. C. Darby, C. W. Crawley and C. M. Woodhouse.

INTRODUCTION

The territory comprising what is now the Socialist Federal Republic of Yugoslavia straddles the complex system of mountain and river valleys which, through the centuries, have served both as bastion and gateway to the south-east of Europe. The fertile provinces watered by the Danube and the Sava bind Yugoslavia to Central Europe; the narrow coastal strip and the offshore islands of Dalmatia link her to the Mediterranean world; in between rise the intricate and rugged mountain ranges which occupy two-thirds of the area of the state and contain more than half its population. Traversing or skirting these highlands lie the valleys along which the migrating peoples and invading armies have passed, from time immemorial, now in one direction, now in another. They lead from Austria along the Sava, Drava, and Danube basins to the Black Sea; from the plains of Central Europe southwards along the Morava and Vardar line to Salonica and the Aegean, or veering eastwards through Bulgaria, to Istanbul and the Bosphorus; in the north, by shorter thrusts, from Vienna to the upper Adriatic at Trieste and Rijeka (Fiume). or through lesser gaps in the Dinaric Alps down to the more southerly parts of the coast.

The history of Yugoslavia is thus to a large extent that of those stronger powers which have, at one time or another, controlled the component parts of the present state, and sought further expansion through these natural gateways. But it is also the story of the resistance offered by those components to attacks on their independence and individuality, and, at the same time, of the efforts they have made to strengthen their own position by absorbing, dominating, or uniting with each other. The national character of each unit has been deeply coloured by the relationship in which it has lived for so long with the stronger alien powers; a relationship basically of opposition, but at the same time one of developing cultural, psychological and religious

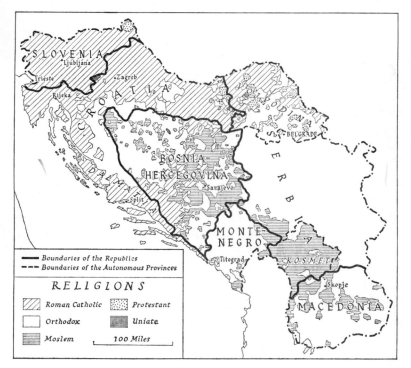

Fig. 1. The Socialist Federal Republic of Yugoslavia.

affinities. This has meant that, in their urge to absorb or unite with each other, the components of the Yugoslav state have found themselves marked by differences of outlook and tradition. The central event of Yugoslav history had been the Turkish invasion, resulting in the destruction of the medieval Serbian state, the conversion to Islam of most of Bosnia and Hercegovina, and the dependence of Croatia and Dalmatia on the Catholic powers, Hungary, Austria, and Venice, for survival. When at last Turkey was driven from Europe, Serbia and Montenegro re-emerged with a national consciousness forged by a tradition of successful recourse to arms and loyalty to their Orthodox Church, to unite with a Slovenia and Croatia proud of their Catholic and Central European character and attached to the

2

constitutional niceties with which they had so often safeguarded
their national individuality. The union between such disparate
partners, in the inter-war years, proved a troubled one, which
the axis powers quickly and brutally dissolved. Its reaffirma-
tion by the Partisans, in the bloodshed of enemy occupation
and civil war, and its formal re-establishment under the stern
guidance of Marshal Tito's Communist regime, have been a
notable achievement.

Other historic factors have added to the complexities of the
Yugoslav scene. The component units have not themselves remained homogeneous. They have been stamped by an intricate
pattern resulting from the movement of population from one to
another as the resulting of a variety of causes; Christian *rajas*
fleeing the exactions and reprisals of their Turkish masters,
colonists brought in to repopulate areas devastated by war or
to defend an important frontier, highlanders migrating to the
more favoured valleys or urban centres. These movements have
left an ethnic and cultural mosaic from which have sprung many
of the endemic disputes of the Balkans; Bosnia-Hercegovina,
Vojvodina, Macedonia.

The national struggle has profoundly affected the economic
and social development of the Yugoslavs. In natural resources
their homeland is well favoured. It possesses a variety and
abundance of mineral wealth: copper, bauxite, chromium,
nickel, gold, and the silver which helped the Serbian empire
to rise to prosperity in the Middle Ages. It produces lignite, coal,
and latterly, oil. Its forests provide the timber which is a valuable
item in the country's exports, and its mountains are a splendid
potential source of hydroelectric power. Yet it is only now that
the state is making a serious attempt to turn most of these assets
to account; in some areas, such as Macedonia, industry is being
built up from scratch. In the past, economic development has
been too often restricted by political considerations. The provinces which fell to the Turks were left with little scope for
economic growth. In Dalmatia, Venice subordinated the cities
to her own commercial advantage. Though Slovenia was per-

3

mitted by Austria to make some industrial progress, that of Croatia was subordinated to the interests of Hungary.

These policies tended to accentuate the predominantly rural character of the Yugoslav peoples. When their first unified state was formed in 1918, nearly four-fifths of the population was engaged in agriculture. The peasant character of the new state was looked upon as right and natural, since the peasantry had been the guardians of the national consciousness and traditions after the old ruling classes had been for the most part either destroyed by the Turkish invasion, converted to Islam, or subjected to strong Germanic, Hungarian, or Venetian influence. Only in the tiny Republic of Ragusa did the ruling patrician caste, with its distinctive blend of Slav and Venetian culture, present a significant exception to this trend. Elsewhere, the nation became almost synonymous with the peasantry. Hence the emergence, during the inter-war period, of strong Peasant Movements. This was particularly the case in Croatia, where the Peasant Party founded by the Radić brothers grew to such an extent that it claimed the exclusive right to represent Croatian interests, and even sacrificed to Serbia its share of industrial development for fear of detracting from the distinctive 'peasant' character of Croatia. Such an attitude offered little scope to the politically important intelligentsia, which tended to polarize into extreme nationalist or extreme Left.

The economic standing of the peasantry showed wide regional variations. Yugoslavia's agricultural structure falls into three broad zones; the fertile plains comprising the Vojvodina and Slavonia to the north-east, which produce most of the nation's surplus food and ensure a relatively high standard of living to its inhabitants; the intermediate zone, where the land normally provides enough food for the local population, and the 'deficiency' areas comprising Montenegro and the sterile Karst country of the Dinaric Alps (see Fig. 2). The tough and often highly gifted people of these mountain regions have proved an important element in the population, but the problem of integrating them into the national economy is a formidable one.

4

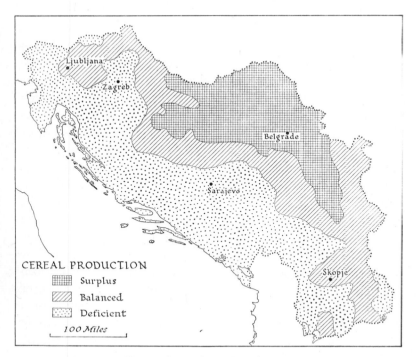

Fig. 2. Zones of cereal production.

The scanty soil offers no support for their increasing numbers[1] and they have traditionally been compelled to migrate overseas or to seek a livelihood in valleys or lowland cities. Hardy and fiercely independent, the resistance they offer to an invader is proverbial. The character of the people, no less than that of the inhospitable terrain, lends itself readily to guerrilla warfare. The harshness of these 'deficiency areas' bred heroism, desperation, and extremism. They were the scene of the fiercest ordeals and triumphs of the Partisans during the last war, but also of the most pitiless brutality and fanaticism.

If the peasantry has embodied the national character and consciousness, the towns have too often proved alien enclaves

[1] The birthrate in Yugoslavia, though now falling, is still one of the highest of Europe.

in their midst. Townsfolk and peasants have differed from each other in their way of life, their scale of values, and their economic interests. The peasant tends to look with hostility on the towns which send out officials to collect taxes from him and impose government orders, take his produce at unjust prices, and enslave him through his indebtedness. Even the 'progress' which the town claims to offer him in the way of new farming techniques, sanitary improvements, education, or political indoctrination are often resented as unwelcome intrusions. This dichotomy between town and country reaches its most acute form when an enemy invasion occurs. The towns, administered by the occupying power and garrisoned by his troops and the local quislings, declare war on the surrounding countryside and strive to subdue it. The countryside reacts by passive resistance, the withholding of food-supplies, and in extreme cases, by waging guerrilla warfare. The fighting in Yugoslavia between 1941 and 1945 was not only resistance to the axis invaders, or clashes between different national and religious groups, or a radical protest against the old order; it was not least a movement of the countryside against the enemy-held towns. The triumph of the Partisans resulted in the 'men of the woods' taking over the towns. Peasants from the 'deficiency areas' took control in large numbers; the Montenegrins were particularly in evidence in Belgrade, men from the Lika in the Croatian towns, where they showed markedly less aptitude as urban administrators and officials than as guerrilla fighters. The towns thus received a strong infusion of peasant blood, and the social revolution has meant the eclipse of the urban middle classes by a radical peasantry rather than by an industrial proletariat, which was too weak to play much part in the Partisan war. Only now, as industrialization gets into its stride, are the workers increasing in numbers and prestige, and the 'workers and peasants' alliance' is starting to overlay the traditional antagonism between town and country.

The task on which Yugoslavia is engaged today is that of harmonizing disparate elements, of finding a working equilibrium. More exactly, it is a problem of equilibrium coupled with momentum, for the state is in the position of a cyclist who cannot move forward until he has learnt to keep his balance, and yet can only find his balance by moving. A right balance has to be struck between the differing needs of town and country, agriculture and industrialization, local or individual initiative and central control; in the international sphere, between East and West. Sometimes the equilibrium is lost, or maintained only at a cost which seems excessive; the curbing of potentially disruptive regional aspirations, limitations on individual liberties and democratic processes, the substitution (according to the indictment of a former Partisan leader) of a 'new class' of party profiteers and bosses, in place of the old oligarchy. Yet, though the cost may be high, the momentum of the new Yugoslav state is undeniable. Achievement has been great. Post-war Yugoslavia is of tougher texture than the inter-war state. It cannot easily be disrupted by internal friction or by external pressure, as Stalin was to discover after he had boasted: 'I have only to raise my little finger, and there will be no more Tito.' The pattern of the new state is distinctive and clearly defined. It has been woven together from many different strands which it will be the aim of the following chapters to trace.

CHAPTER I

HISTORICAL ORIGINS

Comparatively little is known of the peoples occupying the territory now included within Yugoslavia before the coming of the Slavs. It is clear, however, that already in these regions there was a considerable population of varied origins whose history extends back at least a thousand years before the main Slav infiltrations took place.

That the area was peopled even at the time of the early Iron Age (Hallstatt period), long before the dawn of history, is attested in many localities by archaeological remains, but the first historical references to the descendants of these primitive peoples are those made by the ancient Greeks, who, about the fifth century B.C., referred collectively to the various tribes inhabiting the western and central Balkan peninsula as the Illyrians and Thracians. As far as Yugoslav territory is concerned, the Illyrians occupied the area west of the Vardar and north of Epirus (i.e. mainly the lands that physically have been described as the Dinaric region). The Thracians occupied the area to the east of this, including the territory that in later history was to become Serbia.

The characteristics and mode of life of these peoples are obscure, but it is thought that, of the two, the Illyrians were the later comers who drove the Thracians eastward into the central Balkan regions. By some authorities the modern Albanians are thought to represent the only relic of the ancient Illyrian population that has survived to the present day.

Over a period from about 770–550 B.C. the coastlands and islands of the eastern Adriatic were influenced by the spread of Greek trading colonies. These were most frequent in the central coastal districts where there were important colonies at Vis (Issa), Korčula (Korkyra nigra), Hvar (Pharos), Trogir (Tragurion) and Split (Salona). The Greek colonization was, however, never very strongly felt and it had little influence on the life of the peoples inland.

At about the same time, at the beginning of the fourth century B.C., there was a marked infiltration in the north and north-west, in Illyria, of the so-called 'Celtic' peoples from central Europe. Though these peoples have left a record of their influences in the place-names of Dalmatia and elsewhere, they represent a strain in the population that was quickly assimilated by the Illyrians.

THE ROMANS

It was not until well on into the third century B.C. that Roman influence began to be important in the area. Pirates from the Illyrian coasts interfered with the commerce of the Adriatic, and the result was two Roman expeditions in 229 and 219 B.C. By this time, the Illyrian tribes had formed a kingdom with its capital at Skodra (Scutari, Skadar) in Albania; and during the next two centuries, especially after 168, there were intermittent Roman expeditions demanding tribute. In A.D. 9, the whole area was finally annexed and incorporated by Tiberius as part of the Roman empire under the name of 'Illyricum'. The term, however, was used in widely different senses, and places as far apart as Vienna and Athens formed part of an 'Illyricum' at different times.

From this time onward, Latin civilization spread rapidly over much of the area. Gold, silver and copper were mined in the interior, and flourishing commercial cities were to be found along the coast. The area played an important part in the Roman empire, especially in relation to the defence of the Danube frontier. It became a great recruiting ground for Roman soldiers, and many Illyrians rose to high office in the empire, even to the purple itself. Five natives of Illyria became emperors—Claudius, Aurelian, Probus, Diocletian and Maximilian—and all were sons of Illyrian peasants.

In A.D. 285 the Roman empire was divided into two by Diocletian—an eastern and a western half. Constantine reunited

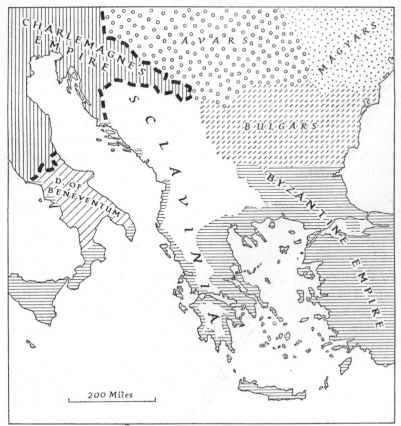

Fig. 3. The Balkan Peninsula, about A.D. 800.

the two halves, but soon the empire was divided again, and, after various changes, what had started as an administrative division became, after A.D. 395, a final and more fundamental separation. The line of this ultimate division ran northward from near Lake Scutari to the river Sava. It seems to have corresponded broadly with the linguistic frontier between the Latin-speaking and the Greek-speaking worlds, and, roughly speaking, it agreed with the line that later separated Latin from Greek Christianity in the Balkan peninsula (Fig. 3).

THE COMING OF THE SLAVS

During the fifth century, the invasions associated with the break-up of the Roman empire greatly affected the Illyrian lands. Visigoths, Huns and Ostrogoths, together with many lesser groups, either passed through or controlled all or part of the area. The coastal fringes of Dalmatia, too, were reconquered for the Eastern Roman empire by Justinian about A.D. 535. Soon after the middle of the sixth century the whole area was devastated by the Avars, raiding from their centre in the Danube plain; but, while Avar supremacy was soon over, a new people, who also appeared in the sixth century, were destined to make Illyria their own. These were the Slavs. Their movement into Illyria, and southwards even to the Pelopponese, was part of the great dispersion of the Slavs that took place during the sixth and seventh centuries in eastern Europe. They seem to have been driven southward by the Avar menace. Unlike their predecessors, they formed permanent settlements, and were in full occupation of Illyria by about A.D. 650.

The Slavs who thus entered the western Balkan lands comprised three groups.[1] To the north were the Slovenes, who seem to have been the first to arrive; to the south were the Croats and the Serbs. The early distinctions between them are obscure, but they were soon accentuated by historical and cultural differences. The Slovenes and the Croats of western Illyria came under western and Roman Catholic influence, whilst the Serbs of eastern Illyria underwent that of Constantinople and the Orthodox Church. The Slovenes spoke a language which came to differ from that spoken by the Croats and the Serbs. The latter speak the same language (known by the convenient label of Serbo-Croat) though the Croats use the Latin and the Serbs the Cyrillic alphabet, and considerable differences of vocabulary, construction, and dialect have developed in different parts of the country. Macedonian, which has affinities with

[1] The Bulgars, who are basically of Slav stock with Ural-Altaic peoples superimposed, also belong strictly speaking to the South Slav group, but are not considered here.

Bulgarian as well as with Serbo-Croat, is now regarded as a separate language.

The newcomers absorbed most of the existing Romanized population. The greatest exception was the coastal area where the wealthy city-states were able to maintain their distinctive Latin character, thus making of Dalmatia 'a Slavonic land with an Italian fringe'. Elsewhere, the scattered and nomadic remnants of the Roman provincials were known as 'Mavrovlachs', 'Morlachs', or 'Vlachs', and they preserved their separate identity and language for many centuries until they became completely slavonicized; northern Dalmatia and maritime Croatia were known as 'Morlacchia' in the eighteenth century. There was also a 'Major Vlachia' in the region where the frontiers of Bosnia, Dalmatia and Croatia meet, and a 'Minor Vlachia' as far north as Požega between the Sava and the Drava.[1] To the south, there were still some tribes who had escaped romanization, and who now escaped slavonicization; these became the Albanians of later times. With the exception of the Italians, the Morlachs and the Albanians, the whole area became Slav in language and culture, and the name of 'Illyria' disappeared from history until it was revived in quite different contexts in the eighteenth and nineteenth centuries.

An important factor in the subsequent history of the Slavs was the arrival of the Magyars in the plain of Hungary about the year 900. This Finno-Ugrian people inserted, so to speak, a wedge between the South Slavs on the one hand, and the Czechs, Poles, Slovaks and the Russians on the other. The history of the South Slavs developed, therefore, quite separately from that of their kindred folk in the rest of Europe, though there were many sentimental and cultural ties which were later emphasized.

Since, during some thirteen centuries, the South Slavs were subject to differing destinies, it will be necessary to consider the individual history of the chief groups and territorial divisions.

[1] One of the regions of Serbia is still known as 'Stari Vlah', i.e. Old Wallachia.

CHAPTER 2

SLOVENIA

SLAVS AND GERMANS UP TO THE FIFTEENTH CENTURY

The Slovenes first appeared in the upper valley of the Sava and the surrounding regions during the latter half of the sixth century. They appear to have been under the subjection of the Avars for a time, and a little later they formed part of the Slavonic empire of Samo, A.D. 627–58 (Fig. 4). After his death, they fought against the Bavarian and Friulian dukes and also against the Avars, and in due course they submitted to the Franks (748). Under the Frankish kings, especially under Charlemagne, the work of conversion to Christianity was carried on from the patriarchate of Aquileia and the archbishopric of Salzburg, and the Slovenes have ever since formed part of the Western, as distinct from the Eastern, Church. With this missionary work was associated German colonization and the increase of German influence generally in the area. The ascendancy of the Slovene nobles was replaced by that of Frankish officials. The area of Slovene speech, too, in time became restricted more or less to the area south of the Drava, though place-names to the north of the river still remain as relics of the earlier Slovene advance.

There is not much record of the Slovenes throughout the Middle Ages. Their district formed a large part of the duchy of Carantania, created in A.D. 952 by the Holy Roman Emperor, Otto I, to protect his realm against Magyar raids. From this large duchy, Carniola and then Styria broke off, in the tenth and eleventh centuries respectively, to form separate marcher counties, and, ultimately in the case of Styria, a separate duchy (Fig. 5). During the eleventh, twelfth and thirteenth centuries, the three units were held by various families and ecclesiastical princes; their boundaries, and their allegiance, changed from

13

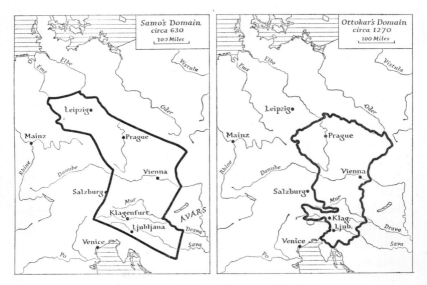

Fig. 4. The territories of Samo and Ottokar.

time to time, and their history is both obscure and complicated. In the thirteenth century, they came to form part of the realm of Ottokar of Bohemia who tried, as Samo had done before, to build up a Slav empire in this part of Europe (Fig. 4).

After the defeat of Ottokar by the Holy Roman Emperor, on the Marchfeld in 1278, Styria fell into the hands of the Habsburg family, who four years later acquired Austria itself, and so started a process of territory-building that was to last over six centuries. Carinthia and Carniola were bestowed by the Emperor Lewis upon the Habsburgs in 1335. The result of the close connexions with the Holy Roman Empire in general, and now with Austria in particular, was increased German influence in the area; though, in the thirteenth century, the Slovene language was still recognized and given a legal standing at Vienna, and documents of the period show many Slovene names amongst the nobility. But German influence was in the ascendant, and, in the following century, Rudolf IV of Austria settled a large number of Germans at Gottschee (Kočevje), where their descendants remained to form a feature of the linguistic map of Slovenia. In 1374, the county of Istria was added to the Habsburg domains, and in 1382 the city of Trieste, thus securing an outlet on to the Adriatic.

THE REFORMATION AND COUNTER-REFORMATION

From the fifteenth to the seventeenth centuries all three provinces of Carniola, Carinthia and Styria suffered from Turkish raids, and many areas were depopulated. These depredations added to the distress of the peasantry and fanned their resentment against the feudal landowners who exploited but failed to protect them. A series of peasant revolts occurred between 1478 and 1573 and were cruelly suppressed.

Social unrest was further embittered by religious strife. The doctrines of the Reformation found considerable support among the Slovenes during the early part of the sixteenth century. The new religion was accepted by most of the nobles and townsmen; many churches were in Protestant hands, and Protestant schools appeared everywhere. An important feature of the Reformation here was the use of the Slovene language. Primož Trubar, a native of Carniola, translated the New Testament into Slovene (1555), and published a variety of Slovene hymn books, catechisms and other religious works. These were printed at the German Protestant centre of Tübingen and at Ljubljana itself; they appeared not only in German and Latin script, but also in Cyrillic and in the older Glagolitic script. Collaborators gathered around Trubar from Istria, Croatia, Dalmatia and Serbia, giving to this early work a 'Yugoslav' character. At one time it seemed as if the doctrines of the Reformation might spread to neighbouring Croatia. The result of all this activity was a greater interest in the study of the Slovene language, and, in 1584, Adam Bohorič produced a small grammar; a Slovene dictionary also appeared about the same time. The whole Bible, too, was translated by J. Dalmatin, and it was accompanied by a vocabulary to make the translation intelligible to Croats.

The new movement was supported by the provincial 'Estates' or parliaments, clamouring for some measure of independence from Austrian centralization. But the Counter-Reformation suppressed the movement with ruthless energy. The policy of the Austrian rulers, and the vigour of the Jesuits, brought about a complete victory of the old religion. Much of the Slovene Protestant literature was burnt because it was heretical; and many works perished completely. The use of Bohorič's grammar was prohibited; the power of the 'Estates' was lessened; the Protestant leaders were exiled; many thousands of Protestant townsmen went elsewhere with their industries; and the region became, and has remained, an almost exclusively Roman Catholic area. Still, despite this persecution, the result of the Protestant movement was not only to revive Slovene language and literature, but also to stimulate Slovene self-consciousness which was to flower into a national movement some three and a half centuries later.

THE SEVENTEENTH AND EIGHTEENTH CENTURIES

After the Catholic victory, there was nothing outstanding in Slovene history during the seventeenth century. There is, however, a very interesting description of affairs in Carniola at this time in a book written by Freiherr von Valvasor—*Die Ehre Krains* (1689). The industries of the province included the production of steel at Jauerburg, of leather at Neumarktl, of lead at Assling and of cloth at Bischoflack. The province also had important trading relations with Germany and Italy. To Germany it sent honey, quicksilver and copper; and it received in return leather, wool and household goods. To Italy it sent iron, wool, corn and cattle; and it received in return silk, cloth, spices and fish. German was the official language spoken by the upper and middle classes, but Slovene was the language of the mass of the people. Italian also was spoken by many of the nobles and merchants.

During the eighteenth century, the reigns of Maria Theresa (1740–80) and Joseph II (1780–90) were noted for their centralizing tendencies. Many of the rights of the provincial 'Estates' were absorbed by the Crown, but this centralization was not extended to linguistic matters. Maria introduced a Slovene catechism into the schools, and Joseph II, despite his general Germanizing policy, was zealous for the enlightenment of his people, and promoted the translation of educational books into Slovene. In short, Slovene literature, under a cloud since the Counter-Reformation, began to recover something of its position in the life of the area. There also was economic advance. An agricultural school was founded in Carniola in 1771, and agricultural societies began to be active. The cultivation of maize and potatoes was introduced, and the draining of the great moor of Ljubljana was undertaken. The linen and silk industries, too, were encouraged.

Joseph's centralization was followed by a period of reaction, and the provincial 'Estates' regained something of their former autonomy; but, in the midst of these changes, the Slovene people became involved in the wars of the French revolution.

THE NAPOLEONIC EPISODE, 1797–1814

Towards the end of the eighteenth century, the Romantic Movement in Europe was leading many groups of peoples on the continent to a study of their own customs, legends, folklore and dialects. It was a feeling that was widespread, for example, among the Slavs; and the Slovenes, like the Czechs, felt an impulse towards the preservation and cultivation of their own language. A number of people in the Slovene lands were drawn increasingly to write 'in the tongue of the people, and for the people'; and, under the patronage of the wealthy mineowner, Baron Zois, the movement grew apace. The leader of the new Slovene awakening was Valentin Vodnik (1758–1819), a priest of Carniola. He was a poet, a scholar and a journalist, and he devoted his life to working on the history and language of the Slovenes. In 1797 he founded the first Slovene newspaper at Ljubljana, and he also wrote a local history and a popular grammar.

The new feeling of self-consciousness soon allied itself with the liberal tendencies spread by the French Revolution. What is more, the course of the French campaigns against Austria brought French troops into the Slovene lands in 1797, in 1800, in 1805 and again in 1809. The French proclamations were issued in Slovene as well as in French and German, and Napoleon promised to respect the local customs of the country. After the last of these campaigns, the Treaty of Vienna incorporated into the French empire the units of Carniola, western Carinthia, Görz, Istria, part of Croatia, Dalmatia and Ragusa. With the capital at Ljubljana, these became the 'Illyrian Provinces', giving the French a contact between Italy and the Balkans, and guarding the route to the Near East (Fig. 13).

Under French rule, the material condition of the provinces greatly improved. Roads were built; the administrative system was reorganized; the 'Code Napoleon' was introduced; a postal system was created; and trade was fostered. But more important than these material benefits was the intellectual stimulus of the new regime. The Slovene language was encouraged in schools, and an academy or high school was founded at Ljubljana, where Vodnik himself became a teacher. Native officials were employed in local administration, and Slovene was introduced for official purposes. The glory of the new order was celebrated by Vodnik in one of his most famous poems, 'The Resurrection of Illyria'; here he praised the work of Napoleon in awakening the consciousness of the Illyrian Slavs as a whole, for Slovenes, many Croats and some Serbs alike gained advantages from finding themselves included in one political unit. Something of the same stimulus was found even outside the Illyrian Provinces, for in 1810, at Graz in Styria, a Slovene society was founded, and in 1812 a chair of Slavonic was created at the University of Graz.

The new political unit proved, however, to be short-lived. After the disastrous Russian campaign of 1812, the French were forced to abandon the Illyrian Provinces, and, at the Congress of Vienna, 1814–15, the area was restored to the Austrian

18

empire. Dalmatia (with Ragusa) was incorporated with Austria. Istria, Carinthia, Carniola and Görz became the 'kingdom of Illyria', also forming part of Austria, and this remained until 1849 (see p. 20). Finally, the connexion of Croatia and Slavonia with Hungary was renewed, except that the Military Frontier was revived (see p. 33).

SLOVENE CONSCIOUSNESS IN THE NINETEENTH AND TWENTIETH CENTURIES

The Austrian restoration put an end to liberal political trends in the Slovene lands, and any local autonomy they possessed became quite nominal. German influence and speech once more dominated all education. But the strong impulse towards self-consciousness did not die away. It even received encouragement from German scholars themselves, amongst whom the writings of Goethe and Grimm had aroused an interest in local traditions and customs. The work of the Slovene poet and scholar Jernej Kopitar (1780–1844) in developing a Slovene literary idiom out of the numerous debased and germanized local dialects was important. In 1808 he published the first scientific Slovene grammar. He had been deeply stirred by the 'Illyrian' experiment of Napoleon, and later worked in close association with the great Serbian scholar Vuk Karadžić, who was responsible for the development of the Serbo-Croat literary idiom (see p. 118). Kopitar wished to see Karadžić's orthographic reforms adopted amongst his own people; but this met with opposition from the more particularist Slovene writers like the great poet Prešeren (1800–49). But, even so, much had been done to turn Slovene into a standard literary language.

The government at Vienna had hoped to confine the awakening national patriotism within safe literary channels, but the movement inevitably developed beyond merely literary expression. In 1843, after twenty years of agitation, Janez Bleiweis (1808–81) at Ljubljana founded a journal called *Novice*, devoted to agricultural and economic affairs; but its scope was soon enlarged to include more general and political topics. The

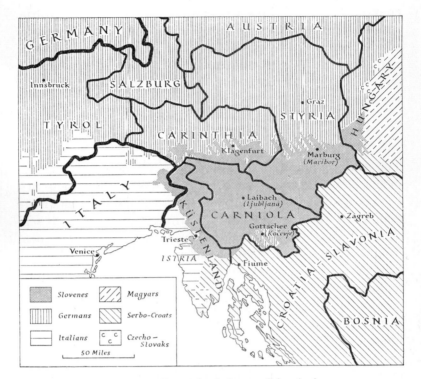

Fig. 5. The Slovene lands (pre-1918 frontiers).

Slovene movement was now extending far beyond a few literary intellectuals.

Amid the crisis in the Austrian empire in 1848–9, various and conflicting proposals were put forward for the autonomy of Carniola and Carinthia, and for their union with other Slav provinces of the empire. Thus, 'Slovenija', a Slovene society recently founded at Vienna, formulated a demand for the creation, under Habsburg rule, of an autonomous kingdom of Slovenia, to include Carniola and all the Slovene portions of Carinthia, Styria and the Littoral—but these proposals came to nothing. There were some changes, however; and among them were the abolition of the title 'kingdom of Illyria', and the institution of Carniola, Carinthia and the other Austrian provinces as separate crown-lands, each with its own Diet or parliament. But what autonomy these possessed was extremely limited; and for the next ten years the centralizing policy of Bach (the Austrian Minister of the Interior during 1849–59) pressed hard on the Slovene and the other provinces of the empire alike. The society of St Hermagor, however, founded in 1852, did much to keep Slovene literature alive by issuing books in Slovene each year. Of the many men of letters who chose to write in their native tongue, Slovenia produced one at least of outstanding genius—the poet France Prešeren.

The new Austrian constitution of 1861 brought no advantage to the Slovenes. The reconstitution of the local Diets still left the Slovene (as opposed to German) members in a minority even in the Diet of Carniola; and a request that the minutes of the Carniolan Diet should be kept in Slovene as well as in German was firmly refused. In 1867 the 'Ausgleich', which secured the supremacy of Germans in Austria and of Magyars in Hungary, was very unpopular with the Slovenes; and in 1868–9 there was further agitation for a kingdom of Slovenia, and for the use of Slovene as the language of education and government. Against this rising Slav feeling, all German parties in Austria were united in wishing to maintain the special position of the Germans in the empire, with German as the official language of the state. Moreover, the construction of the Vienna–Trieste railway, and industrial developments in the towns, greatly strengthened the German element. The Imperial Government, however, especially under Count Taaffe (1878–93) made considerable cultural concessions to the Slovenes as to the other Slavs of the Austrian monarchy. In 1882, too, the Slovenes obtained, for the first time, a majority in the Diet of Carniola and in the town council of Ljubljana. For the rest of the century, Slovene discontent centred around the need for a university in Ljubljana, around the general question of education, and around the inadequacy of Slovene representation in the *Reichsrat* or central Austrian Parliament. But, on the other hand, this discontent never reached the high pitch of feeling to be found among some other South Slav peoples; economic conditions in Slovenia were relatively favourable, and the Slovene group was small and scattered through six Austrian provinces.[1]

But, with the twentieth century, Slovene feeling gained much in intensity from increasing contacts with the Croats; and the local problem of Slovene rights soon became part of the wider issue of the 'South Slav question in the Habsburg Monarchy' (see p. 154). In 1907 the introduction of manhood suffrage in the Austrian lands enabled the Slovene cause to become more vocal. The Agram (Zagreb) trials in 1908 caused much indignation among the Slovenes, and the annexation of Bosnia and Hercegovina in 1908 led to riots at Ljubljana and elsewhere. Finally, the introduction of a democratic regime in Serbia (1903), together with the Serbian victories in the Balkan Wars of 1912–13, aroused enthusiasm everywhere. The Clerical party, it is true, was distrustful of any association with the Orthodox Serbs; but, in some minds, the idea of union with the Croats was even becoming Yugoslav in its scope.

[1] The Slovene population was estimated (c. 1910) as follows:

In Austria

Carniola	490,978	(93 % of the total population)
Styria	409,684	(29 % of the total population)
Carinthia	82,212	(21 % of the total population)
Görz-Gradisca	154,564	(62 % of the total population)
Trieste	56,916	(30 % of the total population)
Istria	55,134	(14 % of the total population)
Total	1,249,488	

Elsewhere

Hungary	102,000
Italy	35,000
America	100,000
Other countries	20,000

(The figures for Austria are taken from the Austrian census for 1910; the other figures are estimates from L. Niederle, *La Race Slave* (Paris, 1916), p. 142. The Hungarian Census for 1910, however, put the number of Slovenes in Prekomurje at about 67,000, and there were very few Slovenes in Hungary apart from these. There were some 2,000 Slovenes in Fiume.

CHAPTER 3

CROATIA

EARLY HISTORY TO 1091

The history of the Croats from their arrival in the seventh century up to the tenth century is obscure. During this little-known period the foundation was laid for the dualism in religion, alphabet and outlook that has ever since marked the South Slav lands. Along the Adriatic seaboard, Roman influence remained important until the rise of Venice, and it was from the bishoprics of the Adriatic cities as well as from those of north-western Italy that the Croats were converted to western Christianity. But during the ninth century, the great work of the Slav missionaries, Cyril and Methodius (before A.D. 880), changed the ecclesiastical geography of the Balkan peninsula. They not only evolved the Cyrillic alphabet, but spread the Slavonic rite of the Eastern Church through the interior of the peninsula, with the result that, while the Croats retained their allegiance to Rome and with it their western alphabet, the Serbs became attached to the Eastern Church and wrote in Cyrillic characters (Fig. 6).

The Croats, under a loosely-knit tribal organization, had for long acknowledged no outside authority, but gradually those of the north passed under the influence of the Frankish empire, while the southern Croats came under that of the Byzantine empire. The ninth century was a period of confusion, and, during its last years, much of the area was temporarily conquered by the Byzantine emperor (A.D. 877). Soon, however, the Croats threw off this allegiance, and emerged as a unit about A.D. 924 when Tomislav, one of the župans of Nin, to the north of Zara (Zadar), assumed the title of chief or king. Whatever his exact status, he was the first of a series of rulers who governed an independent country for nearly two hundred years. The main arsenal and centre of these early Croat rulers was at Biograd on the Dalmatian coast.

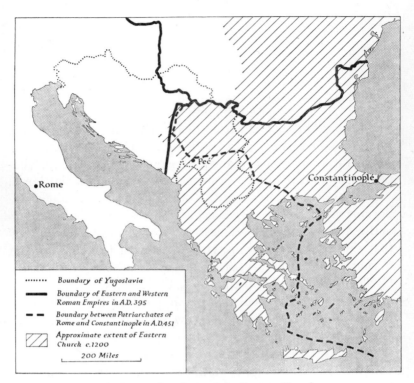

Fig. 6. Roman frontiers and the Eastern Church.

Records from this period are extremely scanty, and the extent of this early kingdom of Croatia has been disputed. The Croatian view is that Croats occupied the whole region south of the Drava down to the Drina and the Neretva. The inhabitants of this kingdom took an active part in the trade and piracy of the Adriatic, and were at times engaged in warfare with Venice. Krešimir Peter (1058–74), who at one point restored the naval power of the Croats, is the hero of numerous national legends, and many Croats long continued to look back upon these early centuries as the golden age of their country. One of Krešimir Peter's successors, Zvonimir (1076–89), was crowned by the legate of Pope Gregory VII.

24

CROATIA AND HUNGARY

The death of Zvonimir in 1089 was followed by disputes between rival claimants to the throne, and, amidst the confusion, appeal was made to Ladislas I, king of Hungary, who was related to the royal house of Croatia. He took control of Croatia in 1091, and in 1094 he founded the bishopric of Zagreb (Agram), which soon became the main ecclesiastical centre of the Croat lands. After his death in 1095, insurrection again broke out in Croatia, but this was successfully put down by his successor Koloman, who was crowned king of Croatia and Dalmatia in 1102. Thus began the connexion between Croatia and Hungary which, apart from occasional interruption, was to last for over eight hundred years. The exact nature of this connexion is a matter of dispute. Magyar historians have regarded the work of Koloman as amounting to the annexation of Croatia; while Croat historians have thought of it merely as establishing a personal link between the two countries. Probably 'the original relationship was incapable of definition by modern terms. Certainly it varied greatly from time to time. At some moments Croatia acted as a completely sovereign State; at others she was treated as a vassal. She always, however, retained a large degree of internal independence.'[1] Koloman reorganized the administration of his new kingdom, leaving it autonomy in domestic affairs, and placing it under a viceroy or 'Ban' who was sometimes a member of the royal house and sometimes a Croat noble.

The history of Croatia from the twelfth to the sixteenth century is compounded of the general history of Hungary with its domestic crises, the rivalry of the feudal lords within Croatia itself, resistance to the constant Turkish menace, and the ferment, produced by these factors, of peasant unrest. The latter came to a head in 1573 in a general rising, linked to a similar movement amongst the Slovenes, under the Croat peasant leader Matija Gubec. The rebels demanded the abolition of the landowners' unjust economic privileges, the lifting cf crip-

[1] C. A. Macartney, *Hungary and her Successors* (Oxford, 1937), p. 357.

Fig. 7. Croatia about A.D. 1070.

pling taxes, and a general recognition of political rights. For a time it seemed that the peasants might gain control of Zagreb and force satisfaction of their demands. But the rising was eventually put down and its leaders executed, leaving behind a legacy of resentment between the peasants and their masters, and the memory of Matija Gubec as a tragic folk-hero. The turbulent Croat nobles were free to continue their feuds and ambitions, some of them pursuing independent policies of their own in the Adriatic and in Bosnia. Thus the Šubić family of Zrin and Bribir, for a short period early in the fourteenth century, united parts of Croatia, Slavonia, Bosnia and Dalmatia under their own rule. A little later, about 1340, instigated by the papacy, they were carrying on a campaign against the Bogomils of Bosnia.

The extent of medieval Croatia is also difficult to estimate. In the north, it does not always appear to have included Slavonia,

26

between the Sava and the Drava, and this strip of territory seems at times to have been more closely attached to Hungary. The extreme eastern portion of the strip (Syrmia) was certainly Hungarian territory which had been incorporated in 1127 after long dispute with the Byzantine empire. In the south, the limits of Croatia were restricted in the fourteenth and fifteenth centuries. To the south-east, Bosnia under Stephen Tvrtko (1353–91) was virtually independent and expanding momentarily to include parts of Croatia proper (see p. 61). To the south-west, the greater part of Dalmatia passed under Venetian control (c. 1420) and was henceforward to remain separate from Croatia for many centuries (see p. 48). But already, by this time, the advancing power of the Ottoman Turks had begun to transform the political geography of the northern Balkan lands.

THE TURKISH STRUGGLE AND THE 'MILITARY FRONTIER'

After the defeat of the Christians of the Balkan peninsula at Kosovo in 1389, the Turks were soon raiding northward, but the full Turkish impact did not come upon Croatia until the fall of Bosnia in 1463. Throughout the fifteenth century, the Hungarians continued to keep the Turks at bay, and the Croat nobles helped in the reorganization of the frontier defence. But at length, in 1526, the Magyar army was routed at the battle of Mohacz; the Hungarian king was killed, and all effective Hungarian resistance was virtually at an end for the time being. The death of the king was followed by a struggle between rival claimants to the throne of Hungary. The kingdom was divided between the Catholic Ferdinand of Austria and the Protestant John Zapolya, the first of a line of independent Transylvanian princes. Faced by this division, the Turks found it easy to become masters of the greater part of the Hungarian plain, together with most of the lands between the Sava and the Drava. By the middle of the century, the whole of Hungary had fallen into three parts: a narrow strip of Austrian Hungary in the west, the principality of Transylvania in the east, and Turkish

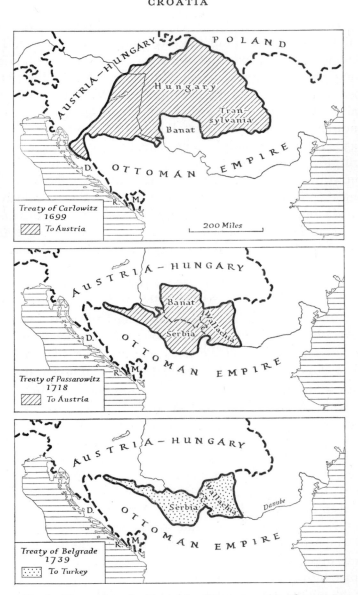

Fig. 8. The northern frontiers of the Ottoman empire, 1699–1739.
D, Dalmatia (Venetian); M, Montenegro; R, Ragusa.

28

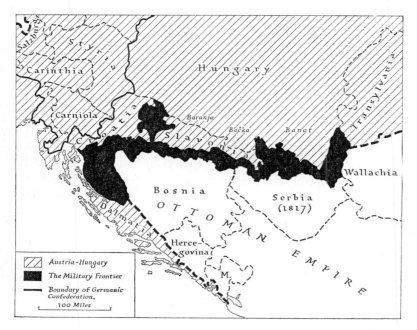

Fig. 9. The 'military frontier' of Austria and Hungary. M, Montenegro.

Hungary set between these two. It was a division that lasted for one hundred and fifty years.

Amidst the confusion following the battle of Mohacz, the Croatian Diet elected Ferdinand of Austria as king in 1527. The Diet of Slavonia at first elected John Zapolya, but it also afterwards declared for Ferdinand. Soon, however, much of Croatia and almost all of Slavonia were in Turkish hands. The little that remained of each region was now united, and Zagreb, up to now in Slavonia, became henceforward the capital of Croatia. The necessity for organizing the southern frontier against the Turk led to the formation, in 1578, of a special marchland, known as the 'Military Frontier' (*Militärgrenze*) under direct Austrian control. This was a land of forts, watch-towers and beacons, and its inhabitants, the 'graničari' or frontiersmen, held their land on a special tenure in return

29

for military service. Turkish raids had greatly depopulated this area, and the problem of defence was partly that of re-peopling. Large numbers of foreigners were accordingly welcomed into the empty lands, particularly into eastern Croatia and into Slavonia. Some of the newcomers were Germans; most of them were Orthodox Serbs, people who had fled northward, and whose descendants were to become a complicating factor in the 'Croat question' of the nineteenth century.

In the meantime, the recovery of the Christian against the Turk had begun. By the Treaty of Carlowitz (Karlovci) in 1699, the Turks ceded practically all Croatia-Slavonia, as well as the greater part of Hungary, to the Habsburg emperor. The Treaty of Passarowitz in 1718 added further territory, though some of these later gains had to be restored in 1739 by the Treaty of Belgrade (Fig. 8). As a result of this Christian advance the area of the 'Military Frontier' was extended and reorganized until it came to comprise the three 'generalates' of Karlovac (Carlstadt), Varaždin and Petrinja (Fig. 9). The Croatian Diet (and that of Hungary too) greatly resented these limitations of territorial sovereignty imposed by Austria, and repeatedly demanded the incorporation of the 'Frontier' within the civil administration of Croatia. But the frontiersmen were against any change in their status, and the imperial government saw in them a useful counterpoise against the unruly nobility of the south. The regime of the 'Frontier', despite Croat opposition and despite the decay of Turkish power, was not finally abolished until 1873–81 (see p. 37). The tradition of the frontier remained long after 1881, and a high percentage of officers in the Austro-Hungarian army continued to be drawn from the old frontier regiments. Even as late as the war of 1914–18, these regiments showed much loyalty to the emperor, despite the great rise of Croat national feeling all around them.

CROATIA, HUNGARY AND AUSTRIA

After 1527, Croat relations were complicated by the fact that they were now concerned with Austria as well as with Hungary. There was indeed one body of opinion that looked to Austria rather than to Hungary. The loyalty of the new settlers in the 'Military Frontier' was, most naturally, given to the emperor; and during the seventeenth century, therefore, it is not surprising that some Croats were in favour of breaking the constitutional connexion with Hungary and becoming attached directly to Austria.

But the links between Croatia and Hungary, both victims of the Habsburgs' centralizing policy, remained strong. The attempt of the Emperor Rudolf II (*d.* 1612) to restrict Croatian autonomy led the Croatian Diet, or *Sabor*, to send delegates to the Hungarian Diet (1591), and the Ban of Croatia, at the request of the Croats themselves, first attended the Hungarian House of Magnates in 1625. An indication of the friendly relations between the two peoples is furnished by the fact that it was a Croat, Count Nicholas Zrinski, who, in the seventeenth century, composed the first great epic poem in Magyar. It celebrated the defence of the castle of Szeged, under his grandfather, against the Turkish army in 1566. Indeed, the Turkish danger provided another cementing influence for Croat and Hungarian interests.

The repressive policy of Leopold I (1657–1705) further drew the nobility of the two peoples together. Thus a member of the Zrinski family and other Croat nobles together with some Magyar leaders, intent on preserving Croat and Hungarian rights, were involved in a conspiracy that culminated in their execution in 1671. But this union of Croat and Magyar interests did not mean that the Croats in any way surrendered their independent status in the seventeenth and eighteenth centuries. When the Croat Diet acknowledged the Pragmatic Sanction in 1712 (that is, twelve years before the Hungarian Diet did so), it asserted its position clearly: 'Neither force nor conquest united us to the Hungarians, but by our spontaneous and free desire we submitted ourselves not to the kingdom [of Hungary] but to their king.'

In 1745 the extent of Croatia proper was increased by the transference of the three Slavonian counties of Syrmia (Srem), Virovitica and Požega from the 'Military Frontier' into the civil administration. Various other administrative changes later in the century show how the destiny of Croatia was swaying between Austria and Hungary. Between 1767 and 1777, Croatia was controlled direct from Vienna, but the Croat and Hungarian nobility used its influence to transfer this control to Hungary in 1779. At the same time, Fiume, joined to Croatia in 1776, was declared an integral part of the Hungarian kingdom. The eagerness of Hungary to annex Fiume reflects the great need of the country for a seaport, and also emphasizes the importance of Croatia in providing an Adriatic seaboard for the inland Hungarian kingdom. The desire of Hungary to control Croatia is thus seen to spring from one of the most fundamental geographical needs of the kingdom.

The centralizing rule of the Habsburg emperor Joseph II (1780–90) left the kingdom of Hungary on the verge of rebellion, and incidentally cemented the bonds between the Croat and Magyar nobles. His successor, Leopold, abandoned the attempt at centralization, and Hungary was declared to be a free and independent kingdom under its own laws. It was in this very year (1790) that the Croat Diet asked that the common affairs of Croatia and Hungary should be regulated by the Hungarian Diet to which three Croat deputies were to be sent. Domestic affairs were, of course, reserved to the Croat Diet itself, though some Croat nobles desired to see Croatia completely incorporated into Hungary. Thus Croatia, although remaining autonomous, strengthened the bonds between itself and Hungary. It was to take over one hundred years to undo this close connexion with Hungary.

THE CROAT NATIONAL REVIVAL

But Croat national feeling was already stirring. Towards the end of the eighteenth century the Hungarians had been agitating with Vienna for the use of Magyar instead of Latin as the language of official business, but even the pro-Magyar Croat representatives of 1790 had made it clear that the Magyar tongue would not be welcome in Croatia. And, in 1805, the bishop of Zagreb had been urging the Croats to make more use of the 'lingua Illyrica', and had encouraged Croat literary endeavour. The awakening national consciousness was then stimulated from an unexpected quarter. In 1809 Austria was compelled to cede to France a large strip of territory which Napoleon constituted into a single unit bearing the ancient name of the 'Illyrian Provinces' (see p. 53). Though the Napoleonic experiment lasted no more than four years, a new energy was visible in almost every sphere of activity, and the common nationality of the Southern Slav peoples began to rouse itself as Croats, Serbs and Slovenes found themselves in the same political unit. The enthusiasm and inspiration that went under the term 'Illyrian' was to count for much in the development of Yugoslav consciousness during the nineteenth century.

After the defeat of Napoleon in 1813 and the disappearance of the 'Illyrian Provinces', the connexion of Croatia and Slavonia with Hungary was renewed, and the Austrian 'Military Frontier' revived. The constitutional position of the two provinces, however, remained vague. The Magyars held that they were subject provinces (*partes adnexae*); the Croats held that they were allied kingdoms (*regna socia*). In any case, the Croats maintained their own elected parliament (*Sabor*) and their local autonomy under their Ban appointed by the emperor; they were also represented by delegates in the Hungarian Diet at Pressburg.

Croat feeling was moreover becoming more articulate, for, during the early decades of the nineteenth century, the Croats, like so many other peoples in Europe, felt the stirrings of that mysterious romantic movement that found expression everywhere in increasing national awareness. The rising national feeling found a champion in Ljudevit Gaj (1809–72), part poet and part publicist, who drew much of his inspiration from the Czech and Polish national movements. The political activity of these years was rooted in a literary revival of the Serbo-Croat language, and was associated with the 'Illyrian' ideal of a union of Croats, Serbs, and Slovenes. Gaj wrote a book on the *Essential Principles of Croat-Slav Orthography*, and in 1835 he founded an anti-Magyar journal called 'Illyrian News' in which he advocated the union of all the South Slavs, and the use of the word 'Illyrian' instead of 'Croat', 'Serb' and 'Slovene'.

The Magyars, too, had been moved by the new stirrings of nationality, and the 'thirties and 'forties were full of demands for constitutional reform, and of social and political reactions against the centralization of Vienna. The replacement in 1840, after much agitation, of Latin by Magyar (not German) as the language of public business in Hungary was but a symptom of their own national revival. What the Magyars demanded from Vienna, however, they were not prepared to concede to Croatia, and they viewed the movement stimulated by Gaj and his associates with the greatest alarm. The name of 'Illyria' was prohibited from being mentioned in public, and in 1843–4 the Hungarian Diet declared that Magyar and not Latin was to become the official language of Croatia after a period of six years. In the storm of protest that followed, one of the Hungarian extremists, none other than the Magyar leader Kossuth, declared himself unable to find Croatia on the map, and stated emphatically: 'I know no Croatian nationality.' In the face of this policy of magyarization, relations between the Croat and Magyar nationalists were rapidly approaching a complete breakdown; but before the six years' respite was over, the situation had been changed by wider events in the Austrian empire.

While the Croat-Magyar breach was developing, the Magyars themselves had been extracting concession after concession from Vienna until the climax came in 1848. In that year, the triumph of the 'February Revolution' in Paris let loose the liberal trends of the century all over Europe. In Vienna itself, the mob was roused to demand a constitution from the emperor; while Hungary, in full revolt, demanded a fully representative government of its own, and moved its parliament from Pressburg to the traditional capital of Budapest. The Habsburg monarchy could only yield to the general onslaught upon its privileges.

But the Magyars in turn were incapable of giving to the Croats that liberty they themselves were demanding from the emperor, and the famous 'March Laws' passed by the Hungarian Diet in 1848 encroached greatly on Croatian autonomy. Their aim was to incorporate Croatia within the administrative system of Hungary, and public opinion in the Croat lands became very incensed. At this moment, too, one of the Croat leaders, Baron Joseph Jelačić, was appointed governor or Ban, and the emperor was able to use Croat forces to subdue the Hungarian revolt. In September 1848, Jelačić, with an army of 40,000 Croats, crossed the Drava, and the Serbs of Bačka and the Banat, too, armed themselves against the Magyars (see p. 122). In the bitter racial war that followed, this Croat-Serb force, together with Russian help, enabled the emperor to overcome the Magyar revolutionaries by August 1849. Thus were the Croats and Serbs driven to ally themselves with the Habsburg monarchy against the Hungarian demand for a more fully representative government.

CROATIA-SLAVONIA UNDER AUSTRIA, 1849–68

The aim of Jelačić was to unite Croatia, Slavonia and Dalmatia with the Serb districts of South Hungary, and so create an Illyrian state under the constitutional rule of the Habsburg emperor. But after the victory of August 1849, both Croats and Serbs looked in vain for their reward from the emperor. It is true that the new Habsburg constitution of 1849 proclaimed Croatia and Slavonia as an Austrian crown-land separate from Hungary, and gave the new unit the port of Fiume. It is true, too, that beyond the Danube the two districts of Bačka and the Banat were formed into an 'autonomous Serb Vojvodina' with its capital at Temesvar. But under the new Austrian regime neither the Croats nor the Serbs got the liberty they wanted. The absolutist centralization of Vienna, directed by Alexander Bach as Minister of the Interior, pressed as heavily on the loyal Croats and Serbs as on the rebellious Magyars. Indeed a contemporary was driven to assert that the Magyars 'received as punishment what the other races received as reward'. Local autonomy was withheld from Croatia on the pretext that the general unrest made it inadvisable.

The 'ten years of reaction', as the Bach period was called, were ended by the defeat of Austria in Italy, and in 1860 the 'October Diploma' promised the restoration of constitutional rights; but, in the following year, the so-called 'February Patent' of 1861 limited all effective power to an executive at Vienna, and so angered both Croats and Magyars. The nationalist Croats, thus antagonized both by Austria and by Hungary, could only continue to agitate in vain for the formation of a 'triune kingdom' of Croatia-Slavonia-Dalmatia.

So matters stood when, faced with defeat by Prussia in 1866, the Habsburg monarchy was forced to reorganize the structure of the state. And so it concluded with Hungary the famous 'compromise', or *Ausgleich*, of 1867. Thus was created the Dual Monarchy whose constitution was to remain unchanged until its disappearance amid the events of 1918. The essence of the compromise was that the Slav peoples of the empire were sacrificed to the two dominant partners, and Croatia was once more affiliated to Hungary. As the Hungarian statesman Andrássy assured the Austrian Chancellor von Beust, 'You look after your barbarians and we will look after ours.'

THE 'NAGODA' OF 1868

It now remained for the Magyars to come to terms with the Croats. The compromise, or *Nagoda*, between Hungary and Croatia in 1868 was the complement of the *Ausgleich*, and it formed the basis of Croat-Magyar relations until the dismemberment of the Hungarian state. The majority of the Croats were against the arrangement, but their press was muzzled and their franchise restricted. Ultimately the *Nagoda* was passed through a Croatian Diet, packed by means of bribery and corruption, and helped by some officials and nobles loyal to Hungary. But even this unrepresentative assembly refused to agree to the cession of Fiume to Hungary, and the Magyars accordingly took possession of it by *force majeure* in May 1870.

The *Nagoda* recognized that Croatia was a 'political nation possessing a special territory of its own', and it provided for provincial autonomy under the Croatian parliament (or *Sabor*) at Zagreb. Croat administration covered Internal Affairs, Justice (including Public Worship), and Education, and the heads of these three departments formed a domestic Croatian cabinet. The official language of the state was recognized as Serbo-Croat. Hungary, moreover, promised to help Croatia to obtain both Dalmatia and the Military Frontier Province, still under Austrian control. The latter territory, after many delays, was incorporated in Croatia in 1881, but Dalmatia remained Austrian until 1918.

Despite this 'Home Rule', the Croats never felt they had achieved adequate self-government. Their Ban was appointed by the Crown (but on the nomination of the Hungarian prime minister) and he was responsible to a Hungarian Minister of State in the Hungarian cabinet. The Croat *Sabor* was represented in the Hungarian Parliament by forty members in the Lower House (out of a total of about 453), and by only three members in the Upper House (out of a total of about 400). The Croat representatives thus always faced an overwhelming majority during disputes, and these were frequent, especially over financial matters. Finally, the joint affairs of the Dual Monarchy were regulated by sixty delegates from Austria and Hungary, and the Croatian share in the Hungarian representation was limited to five members. There was no provision for giving Croatia any access to the central machinery of the Austro-Hungarian monarchy except through the Hungarian Minister of State.

To the Magyars, the *Nagoda* seemed to provide a liberal measure of 'Home Rule' and independence. To the majority of Croats, inflamed by 'managed' elections, and sensitive about the claims of their nationality, it seemed to place undue restriction upon their position in the Austro-Hungarian monarchy, and it was bitterly resented.

CROATIA-SLAVONIA UNDER HUNGARY, 1868–1914

The years after 1868 were marked by continual friction with Hungary, and Croat opinion was repeatedly irritated by evidences of Magyar control which led more than once to out-

37

bursts of rioting. It is true that successive Bans were long supported by a Unionist party in the *Sabor*, but this was because of the very restricted franchise which favoured the landowners and officials inclined to the Magyar cause. Magyar ascendancy reached perhaps its most obnoxious form under the regime of Count Khuen-Héderváry who was Ban from 1883 to 1903. Under these conditions of repression, Croat national feeling became increasingly self-conscious. One of the leading figures in the cultural renaissance of the country was Bishop Stross-mayer of Djakovo (1815–1905), founder of the South Slav (Yugoslav) Academy of Science and Art at Zagreb (1867), whose first president was Franjo Rački, the pioneer of historical research in Croatia. Among other things, it published editions of early Croat poets, and documents dealing with the early history of the Southern Slavs. Strossmayer also founded a national Croatian university at Zagreb in 1874 amidst general rejoicing. He believed that only on the basis of education could the differences between the Catholic Croats and Orthodox Serbs be overcome, and up to his death at the age of ninety, in 1905, he did all he could to encourage the idea of Southern Slav unity.

But the liberal Yugoslav views of Strossmayer were not accept-able to the more extreme Croat nationalists who were deeply suspicious of the Serb element within Croatia-Slavonia. With the incorporation of the 'Military Frontier' in 1881, this Serb element was greatly increased.[1] It amounted to nearly 25 per cent of the total population, but the extreme Croat party under Ante Starčević refused to admit the special claims of the Serbs.

[1] The 1910 Census shows the composition of the population as follows:

Croats	1,638,354	(62·5 %)
Serbs	644,955	(24·6 %)
Slovenes	15,686	(0·6 %)
Other Slavs	61,182	(2·4 %)
Germans	134,078	(5·1 %)
Magyars	105,948	(4·0 %)
Others	21,751	(0·8 %)
Total	2,621,954	

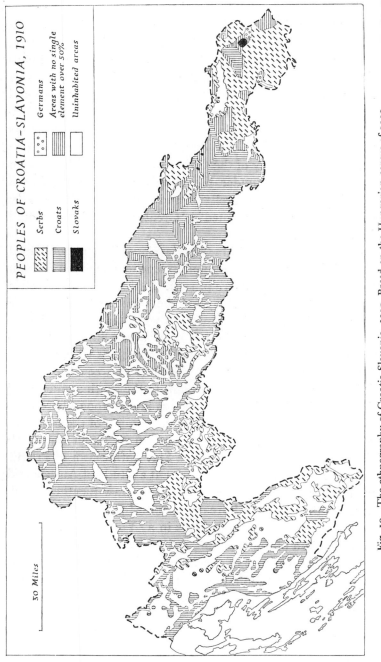

Fig. 10. The ethnography of Croatia-Slavonia, 1910. Based on the Hungarian census of 1910.

It was a strange situation. What Hungary wanted from Austria she refused to Croatia; and what Croatia wanted from Hungary, she in turn refused to the Serbs within her borders. Khuen-Héderváry, however, played off the Serbs against the Croats by insisting on religious toleration, on independent denominational schools, and on Serb freedom to use the Cyrillic alphabet. Serb newspapers were subsidized from Belgrade, while Croat papers were confiscated from day to day. The Serbs were not of one voice. Some, like many of the Croats themselves, wished for an independent Croatia under the Habsburg monarchy, but a Croatia in which their own religion and alphabet would be freely admitted. Other Serbs wanted a 'Greater Serbia' that would include Croatia.

Croat-Serb relations within Croatia-Slavonia were not helped by the rising self-consciousness and independence of the Serbian state to the south in 1878 (see p. 125). In this year, too, Austria occupied Bosnia-Hercegovina, and the Croats, becoming more conscious of their historic connexions with this country, began to dream of a 'Greater Croatia' that might include Bosnia-Hercegovina, thereby antagonizing the Serbians who, too, had designs upon it. These strained relations between the Croats and their own Serbs and the Serbians to the south seemed fatal to the idea of a Yugoslav state, and, as late as 1902, there were anti-Serb riots in Zagreb. But with the coming of the new century feeling changed. A new generation of Croat and Serb leaders had been inspired with the Slav enthusiasm of Prague University. Faced with the intransigent attitude of Austria and Hungary, the Croats and Serbs began to draw together, until, ultimately, the ideal of a 'Greater Croatia' paled before that of the union of all the Southern Slavs in a 'Yugoslavia'.

An indication of the changing attitudes of Croats and Serbs, and a possible way out of the *impasse* with Hungary came in 1904 when a constitutional crisis developed between Hungary and the Emperor. In October 1905, forty Croat deputies from Croatia, Istria and Dalmatia attempted to bargain with the Magyars. In return for support against the Crown, the Croats (all but some extremists) demanded electoral reform, freedom of the press, a Croatian administration on liberal lines, and the union of Dalmatia with Croatia. These demands, stated in the so-called 'Resolution of Fiume', won the support of the Serb party which, ten days later at Zara, declared itself in favour of joint political action between Croats and Serbs (see p. 56). The situation thus created might have had great consequences had it not been for the intransigence of the Magyar politicians, who had come to terms with Austria and did not need the help of the Croats or their Resolution of Fiume. After alienating Croat sympathies by a 'Railway Regulations Act' which required that all railway officials in Croatia should speak Magyar, the Hungarian government sought to discredit the Serbs and play them off against the Croats. In 1908 some fifty-three Serbs of Croatia were arrested on the charge of complicity in a pan-Serb movement in Croatia. The 'Agram treason trials' that resulted won considerable notoriety in the European press. Meanwhile, the famous historian, Dr Friedjung, on the strength of documents supplied by the Austrian government, had written an article in an Austrian newspaper accusing the leaders of the Serbo-Croat coalition of receiving bribes from the Serbian government. The libel action that followed in the Vienna courts developed into a *cause célèbre* that can be compared with the Dreyfus case for the general interest it aroused. The documents were proved to be forgeries; the accusations were shown to be false; and both the nature of the evidence and the conduct of the trial aroused great comment throughout Europe. In Croatia itself, the exposure of the forgeries only served to increase the unrest and to vindicate the Serbo-Croat coalition within the Diet.

Successive Bans tried to deal with the rapidly deteriorating situation in Croatia. Some tried by force, and the constitution was suspended more than once; others tried compromise. But it was too late for concessions; the victories of Serbia in the Balkan wars of 1912–13 roused great enthusiasm throughout Croatia-Slavonia, and the Yugoslav ideal of Bishop Strossmayer was rapidly becoming not only a cultural ideal but a political possibility. By 1914 three schools of opinion were thus to be found in Croatia. A small element wished for the maintenance of the *Nagoda* and association with Hungary. A second body of opinion favoured the creation of a Slav state, within the Habsburg monarchy. This new kingdom would compromise not only Dalmatia and Croatia-Slavonia (with Fiume), but also the Slovene lands of the north and Bosnia-Hercegovina to the south. It would be equal in status to Austria and Hungary themselves, thus converting the Dual Monarchy into a partnership of three elements. This was the 'Trialist' solution, and it was favoured by a party in Austria itself. A third body of opinion wished for a Yugoslav solution and an independent Yugoslav state that would include Serbia as well as the other Southern Slav lands. Common interest and religious conviction favoured the Trialist solution, but racial sentiment and linguistic identity favoured the Yugoslav ideal. As a sergeant of the reserves put it when arrested for desertion: 'the Croats were always loyal to the Emperor, but he did not love them and delivered them over to the Magyars, so that they were forced to turn to the Serbs, who at least spoke their language.'[1]

[1] Quoted in C. A. Macartney, *Hungary and Her Successors* (Oxford, 1937), p. 361.

CHAPTER 4

DALMATIA

THE BYZANTINE PERIOD TO 1102

The Slav immigrants of the early seventh century were able to expel or assimilate the greater part of the existing population over much of the Balkan lands. On the eastern shores of the Adriatic, however, the comparatively wealthy maritime cities were able to withstand the invaders, and so formed places of refuge for the Latin or Italian population. Thus it was that Dalmatia became in Freeman's phrase, 'a Slavonic land with an Italian fringe'[1]; the fringe was far from being continuous, for the Slav settlers reached the sea at many points between Kotor (Cattaro), Zara (Zadar), Dubrovnik (Ragusa) and other Latin cities.

The sovereignty of the coastland at this time was held by the Byzantine emperors, heirs of the Roman dominion. The province had been recovered by Justinian in A.D. 535, and it remained nominally under Byzantine authority until 1102. But long before this, the Byzantine control had become a mere shadow. The political condition of the area was continually changing, and the exact status of cities and tracts of territory was vague and probably incapable of exact definition. In A.D. 806 the northern portion of the region was included within the realm of Charlemagne who agreed, however, that the coastal towns be subject to the Byzantine authority. This distinction between interior and coastal authority was to remain a constant theme throughout Dalmatian history.

For the next three centuries, the main interest of Dalmatia lay, not in the dying shadow of Byzantine authority, but in the repeated attempts of Croatia and Venice to intervene in an area which, by the nature of its coast, favoured independence and

---

[1] E. A. Freeman, *The Historical Geography of Europe* (3rd edition, 1903), p. 115.

4-2

piracy. In the midst of the confusion of the ninth century, the task of policing the sea and of protecting shipping was increasingly taken over by Venice, though not without rebuffs. In the following century, the new kingdom of Croatia made its power felt and disputed Venetian interest in the area. But in the year 1000, the doge of Venice (Peter Orseolo II), after defeating the Croats and crushing the Slav pirates at the mouth of the Neretva, assumed the title of 'duke of Dalmatia', though Byzantine sovereignty was still recognized. Centuries were to pass before Dalmatia finally became Venetian. 'Nevertheless, Peter's expedition was of the highest importance; it raised the prestige of the Venetians, it opened to them a long line of factories down the Dalmatian coast, and it advanced their claim to free trade in the Adriatic.'[1] By the middle of the eleventh century, however, Croatian power had revived; Krešimir Peter (1058–74) restored the naval power of the Croats, and assumed the title 'king of Dalmatia'. The new unit of Croatia-Dalmatia was soon included within the sphere of Hungarian influence, and the twelfth century had hardly dawned when, in 1102, Koloman of Hungary was crowned King of Croatia and Dalmatia (see p. 25). The nominal suzerainty of the Byzantine empire was finally over except for one brief interlude; and, from this time onward, the medieval story of Dalmatia is very largely that of the struggle of Hungary and Venice for dominion in the Adriatic.

HUNGARY AND VENICE IN DALMATIA, 1102–1420

Hungary and Venice were natural adversaries. On the one hand, Hungary, as a rising power in search of a seaboard, could not fail to be interested in the affairs of the Adriatic; and, as kings of Croatia, the rulers of Hungary were well placed for interfering in the affairs of the sea. On the other hand, Venice, with her growing interest in the trade of the Levant, could not but wish to control the sea-routes that led to her markets, and it was

[1] H. F. Brown in *The Cambridge Medieval History*, vol. IV (Cambridge, 1923), p. 406.

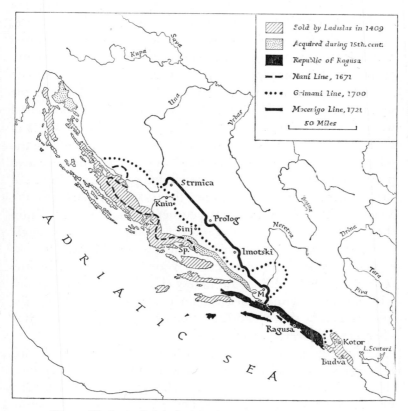

Fig. 11. Venice in Dalmatia. M, Metković; S, Sibenik; Sp, Split.

essential that the piracy, to which the Dalmatian coasts and islands so readily lent themselves, should be kept down. The forests of the seaboard, moreover, provided wood for the building of the Venetian galleys.

During the centuries that followed the Fourth Crusade of 1202–4, Venetian interests in the eastern Mediterranean were greatly increased, and the need for controlling Dalmatia grew correspondingly greater. Structurally, the Venetian empire was coming to consist of a series of strategic points, calling-stations, islands, and merchant quarters in cities, all of which were strung

45

along the greatest of medieval trade routes. A firm grip on the Adriatic was a vital necessity to the economic life of the state.

The Dalmatian cities themselves fought jealously to preserve as much autonomy as possible beneath the nominal sovereignty of Venice or Hungary. Both powers had their partisans. The great Dalmatian historian, Giovanni Lucio, who lived in the seventeenth century, observed that there had always been, and were even in his own day, two classes of men in the cities of Dalmatia—'one living by terrestrial pursuits and industries, the other by navigation and fisheries; from which difference two parties grew up in each state, the landed party attaching itself to the Croats and Hungarians, the maritime party to the Venetians'.[1] These dissensions between jealous factions within the Dalmatian city-states did much to complicate the struggle between Hungary and Venice. And this struggle was further confused by the cross-currents of wider politics, e.g. by the repercussions of the Bogomil heresy, by the conflict of Venice with Genoa and the other Italian trading cities, and by the interference of the Byzantine emperors who for a short time after 1171 recovered Dalmatia.

During the period 1115–1420, there were twenty-one wars between Venice and Hungary.[2] It was only natural, therefore, that some of the Dalmatian cities changed hands repeatedly. Owing partly to these changes, and partly to the very nature of the sovereignty, it is difficult to put on a map the precise limits of Venetian control during any given period, or even at one moment. Thus Spalato (Split), under Hungarian sovereignty since 1105, revolted to Venice in 1327, only to return to the Hungarian allegiance in 1358. The Republic of Ragusa, though recognizing Venetian suzerainty between 1205 and 1358, and thereafter that of Hungary, achieved in fact a very real degree of prosperity and independence, and at times exerted a commercial and diplomatic influence rivalling that of Venice. Zara

[1] Quoted in T. G. Jackson, *Dalmatia, The Quarnero and Istria*, vol. 1 (Oxford, 1887), p. 119.
[2] Count Louis Vojnovitch, *Dalmatia and the Yugoslav Movement* (London, 1920), pp. 64–85.

was a particular object of contention between Hungary and Venice; four outbreaks against Venice are recorded between 1180 and 1345. It was to subdue Zara that the famous Fourth Crusade was diverted at the instance of Venice in 1202; and, on another occasion in the next century, Venice was able to prevent the city from acknowledging the protection of Hungary (1346). By the Treaty of Zara in 1358, however, Venice was forced to give up the title of 'duke of Dalmatia and Croatia' held by the doge, and to abandon her claim to Dalmatia. At the Congress of Turin in 1381, Venice was again forced to renounce her Dalmatian interests, and was even compelled to promise an annual tribute to the king of Hungary.

The affairs of Dalmatia were also complicated by the rise of the inland powers to the south of Hungarian Croatia. About 1196 the early Serbian state under Stephen Nemanja reached the coast from the Neretva south to Kotor (Cattaro) and beyond; the frontiers fluctuated, but the Serbian frontage on the Adriatic continued for the next century and a half until it reached its greatest extent in the reign of Stephen Dušan, c. 1355 (see p. 96). Between Serbia and Croatia, the rise of Bosnia under Stephen Tvrtko (1353–91) also brought the Bosnian frontiers to the sea. By 1390 Tvrtko was able to annex a large stretch of coast; exceptions to his authority were Zara under Venetian suzerainty, and Ragusa under the protection of Hungary (see p. 61). In the confusion following the death of Tvrtko, and amid the internal complications of the Hungarian kingdom, Venice was able to obtain virtual control of almost the whole of the Dalmatian coastline. In 1409 Ladislas of Naples, who claimed the throne of Hungary, sold his potential rights to Venice for 100,000 ducats (Fig. 11). By 1420, Venice had gained all the Dalmatian cities, except for Almissa (which surrendered in 1444) and Ragusa.

The territory which the Venetians now acquired had become increasingly Slav during the preceding centuries. The Latin element in the Dalmatian cities had diminished, and, from the eleventh century onwards, the proportion of Slav names en-

countered in public records increased very rapidly. Nor did the
Venetian victory of the fifteenth century check the ascendancy
of Slav speech, for more Slavs sought refuge here from Turkish
domination in the interior (see p. 63). Even outside the towns,
however, there were still some other Roman provincials left.
These scattered and nomadic tribes were known as 'Mavrovlachs', 'Morlachs', or Vlachs (see p. 12).

THE VENETIAN AND TURKISH REGIME, 1420–1797

From 1420 until the eighteenth century, the history of Dalmatia
is largely a narrative of resistance to the Turk, and is part of the
wider story of the rise and decline of Ottoman power in Europe.
Serbia fell in 1459, Bosnia in 1463, and Hercegovina in 1483,
until the Turkish and Venetian frontiers now marched with one
another. Once more, the clash between hinterland and shore
asserted itself, and during the next two and a half centuries there
were seven periods of warfare between the two powers.[1] The
Venetians did not feel the full onslaught of the Turk until after
the defeat of Hungary at Mohacz in 1526. The peace of 1540
left only the coastal cities to Venice; the interior was under the
control of a Turkish *sanjak-beg* at Klis near Split and, despite
their differences and their periodic warfare, Christian and Turk
settled down to live side by side. The coming of the Turk had,
however, further increased the Slav character of the coastal cities,
for refugees from the interior entered Christian territory. The
pirate community of the Uskoks,[2] at Klis and then at Senj, was
in origin a band of refugees, and it was the piracies of these
fugitives that led to a renewal of war during 1571–3, when a
Dalmatian squadron contributed to Christian victory over the
Turkish navy at the famous battle of Lepanto in 1571. The
reports and diaries of Venetian agents provide an extremely

---

[1] These periods were: 1468–79, 1499–1502, 1538–40, 1571–73, 1644–69, 1684–99,
1714–18.

[2] The Uskoks were later favoured by the Habsburgs on account of the damage
they inflicted on Venetian commerce, and their activities actually provoked a war
between Austria and Venice. This was concluded by the Treaty of Madrid (1617)
which provided that their community should be dissolved and that they should be
resettled in the interior of Croatia.

interesting picture of the relations between Christian and Moslem along the Dalmatian frontier itself at this time—of desultory warfare, of clashes between the Turkish raiders and the townsfolk, of challenges to single combat, of love affairs involving members of both sides, and of the rough courtesy and chivalry to be met with amongst the antagonism of the two faiths, for, as one Venetian wrote, 'no nation are all evil alike'.[1] The peace of 1573 left the Dalmatian frontier more or less as it had been, each party regaining what had been lost.

War between Venice and Turkey did not break out again for over seventy years. In 1645 the pasha of Bosnia entered Dalmatia at the head of a large army, but the Venetians were able to repulse these forces, and, after intermittent warfare in Dalmatia and elsewhere, peace was declared in 1669. Venice lost Crete, but she was able to retain all she had acquired in Dalmatia though there was some dispute before the exact limits of the frontier were agreed to by both parties. The result was the 'Nani line', delimited by 1671, and named after the Venetian delegate (Fig. 11).

Hostilities again broke out in 1684. Turkey was already at war with Austria; repulsed from Vienna in 1683, the Turks continued to lose ground until all Hungary had been recovered by the Christians. To the south, the Morea was taken by the Venetians who were also able to drive the Turks back from the seaboard of Dalmatia into the interior. The war was closed by the Treaty of Carlowitz in 1699, one of the most disastrous treaties suffered by the Turks; in the south, the Venetians gained the Morea, and in Dalmatia the *nuovo acquisto*, delimited in 1700, brought her frontiers up to the 'Grimani line', so called after the Venetian negotiator (Fig. 11). Ragusa, which had had the foresight to conclude a treaty with the sultan assuring her valuable trading privileges in return for an annual tribute, remained independent. In order to prevent disputes with Venice, Ragusan territory was separated from that of Venice by a narrow

---

[1] Long extracts from these reports and diaries for the period 1571–4 are given in Sir J. Gardner Wilkinson's *Dalmatia and Montenegro*, vol. ii (London, 1848), pp. 297–350.

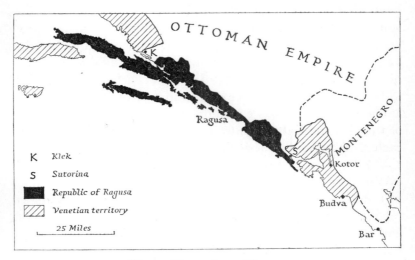

Fig. 12. The territory of Ragusa.

strip of land on either side; the Turks thus reached the sea at Klek and Sutorina, and this curious feature of the frontier remained until the war of 1914–18 (Fig. 12).

The seventh Venetian-Turkish war broke out in 1714 and, while Venice suffered reverses elsewhere, she made small gains in Dalmatia; by the Treaty of Passarowitz in 1718, the Morea to the south was lost, but the *nuovissimo acquisto* in Dalmatia brought the Venetian frontier up to the 'Mocenigo line', delimited in 1721–33, and so called after the Venetian representative (Fig. 11). The threat of the Turkish power in Dalmatia had ceased to be critical; and the province of Dalmatia now remained secure in Venetian hands until 1797.

DALMATIAN CIVILIZATION

It is possible to assess the character of Venetian rule in Dalmatia between 1420 and 1797 in two different ways. On the one hand, the Venetians kept a firm hand on the administration of the province, and were suspicious of any local political vitality. Such municipal autonomy as was allowed was exercised by a small

50

ruling class whose privileges sometimes provoked unrest. One serious manifestation of this was the revolt which broke out on the island of Hvar in the second half of the sixteenth century and dragged on for some years. The province of Dalmatia as a whole was ruled by the 'Proveditore Generale' at Zara, and the 'grand council 'of each town became increasingly the instrument of the resident Venetian agent ('proveditore'). Local industry, too, was suppressed so as to prevent competition with Venetian trade; thus a salt monopoly hindered the fishing industry, and a deliberate attempt was made to ruin the local oil and silk industries by cutting down the olive and mulberry trees. Popular education was also discouraged, and Zara did not possess a printing press until 1796. The Orthodox Serbs of the province were at a disadvantage as compared with the Roman Catholics, and were without civil rights.

Yet, on the other hand, the intellectual life of the Dalmatian cities during the fifteenth, the sixteenth and the seventeenth centuries reached a far higher level than that of the purely Slav lands of the Balkans. Art and architecture flourished in the towns, and the cathedrals at Zara, Šibenik, Korčula, Trogir, and elsewhere, tell their own story of Venetian influence. A remarkable school of writers and scholars flourished, from Marko Marulić (1450–1524), a humanist and theologian of European repute, to Ivan Gundulić (1588–1638) author of dramas and epics, and Rudjer Bošković (1711–87), a scientist of the first order. Both the latter were citizens of Ragusa, where the highest flowering of Dalmatian culture was to be found. Here, the mixture of Latin and Slav resulted in an outstanding development of art and literature from the fifteenth to the seventeenth century, and the city has sometimes been called the 'South Slavonic Athens'. Ragusa, too, provided vigorous competition to the trade of Venice, and the English word 'argosy' is derived from the carracks of Ragusa. The changing trade-routes of the sixteenth century, however, and a great earthquake in 1667, put a check to this prosperity.

The eighteenth century saw a decline in the quality of Dalmatian civilization as a whole. 'As the commercial greatness of Venice declined towards the end of her career, the prosperity of her dependencies naturally passed away at the same time. Decay and torpor set in, shipbuilding declined, the ports were deserted and the trade came nearly to a standstill. The arts were neglected, and the series of architectural works was closed, except at Ragusa, which still preserved its liberties and some remains of its former prosperity. The palaces of the rich Venetian and native merchants were deserted or neglected, and many of them fell into the ruin which now meets the eye at every turn.'[1] Such was the condition of the province when Venetian rule came to an end in 1797.

THE NAPOLEONIC EPISODE, 1797–1814

Before the eighteenth century was over, Dalmatia felt the impact of wider events in Europe. In 1797 Napoleon extinguished the Venetian republic, and Dalmatia, together with the rest of Venetian territory, was ceded to Austria by the Treaty of Campo Formio. There was some confusion when the change-over took place, but order was soon restored on the arrival of Austrian troops and officials.

The Austrians, however, were not long in occupation before there were further changes. After the defeat of Austria at Auster-litz, Dalmatia was ceded to France by the Treaty of Pressburg in December 1805, and the province was incorporated within the ephemeral kingdom of Italy, of which Napoleon himself was king. This acquisition, however, met with disapproval from Russia, who seized the Gulf of Kotor (Bocche di Cattaro), garrisoned Hercegnovi (Castelnuovo) and induced the Monte-negrins to rise in opposition to the French (see p. 78). Ragusa, set between the new French province and the Russian forces, was still independent; indeed it was the only neutral state in the Mediterranean during 1800–5, and its carrying trade greatly prospered from this fact. Now, in 1805, Napoleon seized the city, though the republic was not decreed as having 'ceased to

[1] T. G. Jackson, *Dalmatia, The Quarnero and Istria*, vol. I (Oxford, 1887), p. 181.

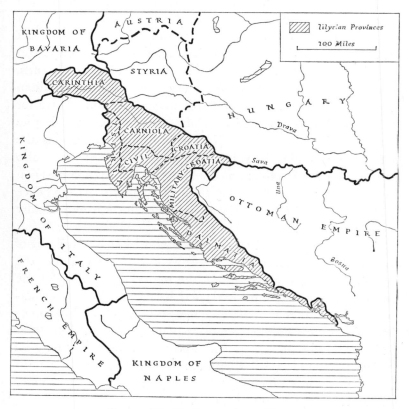

Fig. 13. The Illyrian provinces, 1809-14.

exist' until 1808. In the meantime, much of its territory continued to be raided by Russian and Montenegrin troops until
the Treaty of Tilsit with Russia in July 1807.

The disasters of Austria in 1809 led to the cession of western
Croatia and the complete loss of her seaboard by the Treaty of
Vienna (14 October); France now possessed a large strip of
territory stretching through Carinthia, Carniola, Görz, Istria,
part of Croatia, Dalmatia and Ragusa (Fig. 13). Napoleon then
reconstituted this territory into one unit known as the 'Illyrian
Provinces', and it was incorporated as an integral part of the

French empire (see p. 33). It served both to cut off Austria from Italy and the Mediterranean, and to give France easier communications with the Near East. And so it remained as part of France until the French were driven out by English and Austrian forces. Vis, the outermost of the Dalmatian islands, was occupied by an English naval force under Captain William Hoste in 1811, and the islands became a valuable centre for smuggling English goods into Dalmatia and beyond, despite the blockade instituted by Napoleon. Shortly after this the islands of Korčula, Hvar and Lagosta (Lastovo) were also occupied by the English; and by 1814 the last French garrison had been withdrawn from the whole of Dalmatia. At the peace negotiations that followed the Illyrian Provinces were formally ceded to Austria.

The French occupation, though only a brief interlude, is of considerable importance in the history of Dalmatia. Under the direction of Marshal Marmont, the material condition of the province was greatly improved; new roads were built; agriculture was encouraged; commerce was stimulated; and brigandage was suppressed. The Orthodox population gained in status and an Orthodox bishop was appointed. Both in material achievement, and as an experiment in associating Serbs, Croats and Slovenes in a common 'Illyrian' community, its memory was to act as a powerful stimulus.

THE AUSTRIAN PERIOD, 1815–1914

By the treaties of 1814–15, Dalmatia (with Ragusa) was assigned to Austria; and in 1822 its administration was reorganized, and the political privileges of the Dalmatian nobility were replaced by a bureaucracy dependent upon Vienna. From the small educated class of Italian townsmen, Austria recruited men for the administrative services of Lombardy-Venetia, then under Austrian control. The mass of the Slav people remained without adequate educational facilities, and even by the end of the century, the figures for illiteracy were very high. The 'Illyrian' impetus still found echoes in the province, and found expression too, in the writings of the poet Tommaseo (1802–74). In 1836 a Slav review was started at Zara (Zadar); and in 1849 a politico-literary society was founded, also at Zara, but this was suppressed in 1850.

It was not until 1861 that Slav feeling had a chance to become somewhat more vocal under the new Austrian constitution of that year. The franchise, however, was restricted; thus 15,672 Italian speakers were represented by twenty-six deputies in the Dalmatian Diet, while some 140,000 Slav speakers were represented by only fifteen. But, even so, the next ten years saw a vigorous parliamentary clash between (1) the 'autonomists' who stood for Dalmatian autonomy, and who were increasingly inclined to sympathize with Italian culture, and (2) the 'unionists' who stood for the realization of the Illyrian ideal and for union with Croatia. In 1860–1 Austria had promised to bring about the union of Dalmatia with Croatia; and, in the *Nagoda* of 1868, Hungary expressly promised to support the demand for the union of Dalmatia with Croatia; and the Ban of Croatia included 'Dalmatia' among his titles. Within the province itself feeling in favour of union with Croatia was rapidly gaining ground, and, at the elections of July 1870, the Slav 'unionist' party obtained a majority—25 as against 16. It seemed a turning point in the history of Dalmatia, and the Diet presented an address to the Crown asking to be united to Croatia, but this was met only by vague promises, and the union was destined not to be realized until the formation of Yugoslavia itself.

Indeed, one of the main events preventing the union had already taken place in 1867. In that year the *Ausgleich* between Austria and Hungary, and all it implied, had adjusted an equi-poise that was to remain undisturbed throughout the long reign of Francis Joseph (1848–1916), and it was to the interest of neither member of the new Dual Monarchy to promote union amongst their Southern Slav subjects. Croatia, therefore, remained tied to Hungary, while Dalmatia, though now geographically separate from the Austrian lands, remained subordinate to Vienna (Fig. 30). Hungarian railway policy, moreover, did as much as

55

possible throughout the century to hinder anything that might serve to bring the Southern Slavs together, and any railway project that might connect the Dalmatian seaboard to its hinterland was opposed; thus Split remained without a rail connexion with the interior.

It had often been said that Bosnia and Hercegovina were the head of which Dalmatia was the face, and the occupation of these provinces in 1878 aroused great interest among the Dalmatians. But, as the century drew to a close, relations with Bosnia were overshadowed by the fate of Croatia. The resistance of the Croats to Hungarian repression aroused ever-increasing sympathy in Dalmatia, and, in 1903, the Dalmatian representatives at the central Austrian parliament petitioned Francis Joseph to intervene against the ill-treatment of their compatriots under the Hungarian regime. In October 1905 came the 'Resolution of Fiume', demanding the union of Dalmatia with Croatia, and the 'Resolution of Zara', pledging the support of the Serbian community to this proposal (see p. 41); but no response to these resolutions came from either the Magyar or the imperial authorities. Events were moving to a climax, however, and, after the introduction of manhood suffrage in 1907, the Dalmatian deputies were able to speak on behalf of their Croatian kinsmen with ever greater authority than before. A further step forward was taken two years later when Serbo-Croat was put on an absolute equality with Italian as an official language; a long-delayed reform, seeing that Slav speakers numbered some 96 per cent of the total population.[1]

With the victories of Serbia in the Balkan War of 1912 (see

[1] The Austrian census of 1910 gave the following figures:

Serbo-Croats	610,669
Italians	18,028
Germans	3,081
Others	3,077
Total	634,855

Of the Serbo-Croats, some 80 per cent were Croats. The Italian element had been declining during the preceding thirty years, and the only town now left with an Italian-speaking majority was Zara.

p. 130), there were pro-Serbian demonstrations at many places in Dalmatia, and the Austrian government was forced to resort to repressive measures against the press and against some of the town councils. The fear that Austria might declare war on Serbia at this time brought a protest from the Serbo-Croat party leaders at Zara against the danger of involving 'our people in a civil war', i.e. of making Austrian Slavs fight against Serbian Slavs. Such was the temper of the Dalmatian people when the events of 1914 broke upon them.

CHAPTER 5

BOSNIA AND HERCEGOVINA

EARLY HISTORY

The early history of Bosnia is completely obscure. The country took its name from the river called in classical times *Bosante* or *Bosanius*, and this name came to be applied to those Slav tribes who entered the region during the seventh century. To the north and west were the Croats; to the south and east, the Serbs. Magyar historians have stated that the land of Bosnia was the nucleus of the original kingdom of Croatia, and this seems likely; but, whatever the truth may be, it is clear that the overlordship of the area changed hands may times. Croats, Serbs, Hungarians and Byzantine emperors, all held parts of it at different periods. Divided amongst autonomous tribal units or *župe*, separated by difficult country, and possessing neither well-defined natural frontiers nor a strong nuclear area, the Slavs of Bosnia do not seem to have attained a collective individuality until the close of the twelfth century. From these dim and legendary times, the ruler or 'Ban' named Kulin (1180–1204) stands out as the champion of the national autonomy of Bosnia, and his reign became famous for its prosperity; in good years, the farmers of later centuries used to say 'the times of Kulin are coming back again'. He was the first great figure in Bosnian history (Fig. 14). The trade of his country was developed by the merchants of Ragusa, and Italian craftsmen found plenty of scope for their activities within its frontiers. By this time, the schism between the Eastern and Western Churches had left Bosnia exposed to both influences, and this complication was further increased by the spread of the Bogomil heresy in Balkan lands. The Patarenes or Bogomils, who are said to have taken their name from a Bulgarian priest of the tenth century named Bogomil or 'Beloved of God', held that the material world was created by Satanael or the Devil, and that to escape his domination man must strive to avoid all contact with matter by leading a life of rigid ascetism. The Bogomils rejected the Old Testament, the Incarnation, the Cross, the sacraments and the whole organization of the Christian Church. They formed a 'Bosnian Church' of their own, headed by a 'Bishop' and served by a semi-monastic body of devotees who spread their faith by acting as envoys or missionaries. Bogomilism became the faith not only of the common people but of many land-owners and nobles as well. Kulin himself formally abandoned the Roman Church in order to become a Bogomil, but he was forced to recant later under pressure from the papacy and from Hungary (1203). Despite this, the Bogomil heresy continued to spread throughout the land, and it became a most important factor in the subsequent development of the country.

The century following the death of Kulin in 1204 was a con-fused period, marked by repeated Hungarian attempts to gain control of Bosnia by exploiting its religious differences. But neither religious crusades nor theological concessions were able to win the Bogomils back to the Roman faith. From 1254 on-wards the power of the Bans was much reduced under Hun-garian suzerainty, and the country was divided into two—the southern hilly portion (Upper Bosnia) was allowed to remain under the native Bans, while the northern portion (Lower Bosnia) was placed more directly under Hungarian control. This latter area, joined to a portion of northern Serbia, was known as the duchy of Mačva and Bosnia, and formed a Hun-garian outpost against Bulgaria and Serbia. It was in response to a request from one of its dukes that the Franciscans settled in the region; from the latter part of the thirteenth century on-ward they played an important part in the history of Bosnia. The direct authority of Hungary in Lower Bosnia was replaced in 1299 when the area passed into the hands of the Croatian family of Šubić. These Croat princes, as vassals of Hungary, succeeded in reuniting Upper and Lower Bosnia; but, before the first quarter of the fourteenth century was over, Bosnia had once more regained its independence under a native dynasty.

A native rising in 1322 led to the fall of the Šubić family and to the election of a Bogomil, Stephen Kotromanić, as Ban. It was the beginning of a new epoch in the history of Bosnia. To the east, the Serbian empire had expanded greatly, and the reign of Kotromanić was full of complicated relations with Serbia, with Hungary and its vassal state of Croatia, with Venice and with the papacy—sometimes in alliance with one, sometimes with another. In 1325 he was able to acquire the principality of Hum or Hlum (later called Hercegovina), which had been disputed between Hungarian and Serbian powers. Bosnia was thus in control of the coast between Split and the Neretva, and had gained an outlet to the sea for the first time in its history. In 1340 Kotromanić, persuaded by the king of Hungary, adopted the Roman Catholic faith. The result was considerable internal friction, for the Bogomils had now grown into a powerful organization centred at Janjići in the valley of the Bosna. In the warfare between Kotromanić and Stephen Dušan of Serbia, the Bogomils of Bosnia supported the latter, but Dušan was too occupied with affairs elsewhere to realize any designs he might have had on Bosnia (see p. 97).

STEPHEN TVRTKO, 1353–91

In 1353 Kotromanić was succeeded by his nephew Stephen Tvrtko, a minor, and for nearly seventeen years the history of Bosnia again became disfigured by civil war and foreign interference. It is true that the death of Stephen Dušan removed the danger of a Serbian occupation of Bosnia, but, coming from the north, Hungary occupied Hum and continued to encourage the persecution of the Bogomils. It was not until 1370, and only then after many vicissitudes, that Tvrtko was master of his country.

Having overcome all opposition at home, Tvrtko started upon a career of foreign conquest. He recovered Hum and annexed part of Dalmatia (1374). Moreover, the death of Dušan had left the Serbian empire exposed to attack, and the Serbian knez, Lazar, ceded a large tract to Bosnia in return for help; this

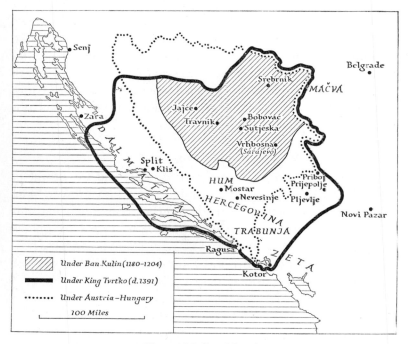

Fig. 14. Medieval Bosnia.

addition included the principality of Trabunja and a strip of coast as far as Kotor. In 1376 Tvrtko was able to have himself crowned 'king of the Serbs, and of Bosnia, and of the Coast'. In 1378 he married the daughter of the last Bulgarian emperor, and some have declared that he hoped to found a state stretching from the Adriatic to the Black Sea. His court at Sutjeska and Bobovac took that of the Byzantine empire as its model, and his officers of state held high-sounding Greek titles. The leadership of the Southern Slavs had, in fact, passed from Serbia to Bosnia; while Tvrtko had become a king, Lazar was merely prince (*knez*) of the diminished state of Serbia. Later in his reign Tvrtko was able to take a large stretch of the Adriatic coast from Hungary; the large islands of Brač, Hvar and Korčula, too, surrendered (Fig. 14). The mainland towns of Zara and Ragusa, however, remained independent. By 1390 he was able to include among his titles that of 'king of Dalmatia and Croatia'. It was the highest point in the power of medieval Bosnia. But before Tvrtko died in 1391, the attempt to stem the Turkish advance by forming an alliance with Serbia was shattered at the battle of Kosovo. Many Serbs now fled northward and westward into Bosnia, though the full effects of the Turkish victory did not react for some time on Bosnian territory itself.

THE TURKISH CONQUEST, 1453

At the death of Tvrtko, disorder broke out, and the power of Bosnia began to disappear as rapidly as it had grown. 'The Bosnian kingdom had been made too fast. Its founder had not lived long enough to weld his conquests into an harmonious whole, to combine Catholic Croats with Orthodox Serbs, Bosnian Slavs with the Latin population of the Dalmatian coast towns, Bogomil heretics with the zealous partisans of Rome.'[1] A disputed succession added fuel to the disorder. For half a century after 1391, the great barons seem to have fought indiscriminately against one another, against the king, against Hungary, and against the Turk. During this confusion, the Turks, aided possibly by Bogomils, were able to make their first invasion of Bosnia (1398), and Venice was able to control the Dalmatian coast (see p. 47).

During the early fifteenth century, the ineffective successors of Tvrtko were overshadowed by three great magnates—Hrvoje Vukčić, Sandalj Hranić and Stephen Vukčić. The first of these was duke of Split; the two latter, uncle and nephew, were successively in control of the land of Hum. In 1448 Stephen was granted the title of 'duke of St Sava' either by the emperor Frederick III, or by the pope, and this title, in its German form of 'Herzog', is the origin of the name Hercegovina.

In the meantime the Turks were becoming more and more involved in the disturbed political life of the country. They frequently had to be bought off with tribute, but even this did

---

[1] W. Miller in *The Cambridge Medieval History*, vol. IV (Cambridge, 1923), p. 559.

not always prevent them raiding for plunder and slaves. Soon this raiding was to end in complete conquest. The accession of Mohammed II started a new period in Balkan history. The fall of Constantinople in 1453, and the complete subjection of Serbia in 1459, left Bosnia open to the Turks. When it was invaded in 1460, no help came from Venice, Hungary or the papacy. Its last king, Stephen Tomašević, surrendered, only to be beheaded by the Turks in 1463. The fierce persecution of Bogomils by Roman Catholics and Orthodox had made the invaders welcome to a large section of the population, and this, together with the rivalries of the nobles, made the Turkish occupation of the greater part of the country a comparatively easy matter.

Some small areas held out. In the south-west, Hercegovina resisted under the successor of Stephen Vukčić until 1483, although Albania (or the greater part of it) had fallen in 1478. In the north, the districts of Jajce and Srebrnik were organized into marchlands for the defence of Hungary against the Turk; the banat of Srebrnik fell in 1520, that of Jajce in 1528. Large numbers of Christians (mainly Roman Catholics) then fled into Croatia-Slavonia and Hungary; others went to Ragusa, and even to Venice and Rome. Many, on reaching the coast, continued to wage war against the Turks in the Adriatic, from Klis in north-west Dalmatia and then from Senj in maritime Croatia. These, known as Uskoks from the Serbo-Croat word for 'refugee', gained considerable notoriety as pirates (see p. 48).

THE TURKISH OCCUPATION, 1463–1878

The arrival of the Turks was the great opportunity of the Bosnian Bogomils—not that they remained Bogomils, for most of them adopted the Moslem faith. 'They had preferred to be conquered by the Sultan than converted by the Pope; and, when once they had been conquered, they did not hesitate to be converted also. The Mussulman creed possessed not a few points of resemblance with their own despised heresy. It conferred, too, the practical advantage upon those who embraced it of retaining their lands and their feudal privileges. Thus Bosnia presents us with the

63

curious phenomenon of an aristocratic caste, Slav by race yet Mohammedan by religion. Hence the country affords a striking contrast to Serbia. There the Mohammedans were never anything more than a foreign colony of Turks; here the Mohammedans were native Slavs, men of the same race as the Christians, whom they despised.'[1]

The Turkish governor of the new province was the *vali* whose residence was shifted from Vrhbosna (Sarajevo) to Banja Luka and then to Travnik, and who interfered but little in local administration. The Bosnian state remained in fact an aristocratic republic, whose nominal head was now a Moslem instead of a Christian. Some governors were native Bosnians, and indeed it was sometimes said that 'one must be the son of a Christian renegade to attain to the highest dignities of the Turkish empire'.[2] Below the governor came the Bogomil nobles changed into Bosnian *begs*. While keeping their own language, they imitated the dress, the titles and many of the customs of the Turkish court; 'they displayed the customary zeal of converts and out-Ottomaned the Ottomans in their religious fanaticism', and indeed they became, at times, 'keener in the cause of Islam than the Commander of the Faithful himself'.[3] This military caste of nobles was headed by the *kapetans* of the forty-eight divisions of the province. They exercised complete control over their subjects, but were obliged to furnish contingents of cavalry for the sultan's armies. As might be expected, they played a great part in the Turkish wars, and rose to high administrative and military office in the Turkish empire, even to that of grand vizier. Below the military caste came the Christian peasants, the *raja*, whose duty was to till the soil and to pay their taxes to their lords. Among their hardships perhaps the greatest was the system by which a proportion of their sons were forcibly recruited into the Turkish corps of janissaries.

But although the foreign yoke pressed hard in many ways, the Turks allowed considerable toleration in religious matters.

---

[1] W. Miller, *Essays on the Latin Orient* (Cambridge, 1921), p. 494.
[2] W. Miller, *op cit.* p. 494.   [3] W. Miller, *op. cit.* p. 495.

To the Turk, social status depended on religion, and, while power had to be restricted to Moslems, the Christians were left free to organize their communal affairs and their private laws as they pleased. At the time of the conquest, in the fifteenth century, the Orthodox element seems to have been relatively unimportant, at any rate, judging from its influence upon affairs of state. But now, under the Moslem regime, the Orthodox Church came to stand for almost all Christians in the eyes of the Turks, and the Bosnian Christians were placed under the Greek Patriarch at Constantinople. This did not mean that Roman Catholic influence disappeared, for, in 1463, the Franciscans received a charter from Mohammed II allowing them the free exercise of their religion. But, even so, Catholicism died out or was expelled over large areas and became restricted very largely to the more barren region of the south-west. Many Catholics had fled into Croatia-Slavonia and Hungary, and large settlements of Serbs, Vlachs and other Orthodox peoples were made in northern Bosnia right up to the limits of the province along the Kupa river. The effects of these movements of population in determining the relative distribution of Roman Catholics and Orthodox remain up to the present day.

From the fifteenth to the nineteenth centuries the Turks were intermittently at war with the surrounding states. Along the Croatian and Montenegrin frontiers, Christians and Moslems were always in dispute without regard to any formal treaties between their respective sovereigns. The Croatian frontier between Hungary and Turkey was particularly important because the Turks regarded Bosnia as the stepping-stone to Hungary, and because the Bosnian nobles were hereditary foes of Hungary and its Roman Catholic faith. During the sixteenth and seventeenth centuries, the Bosnian nobles were continually engaged in Turkish campaigns in Hungary. But after 1683, when the Turks were repulsed from Vienna, the period of Turkish expansion was over and the Bosnians had then to defend their frontiers against the advancing Christians. The Austro-Turkish war continued intermittently for the rest of the century. The forces of the Austrian emperor invaded Bosnia in 1688, and again in 1690 when they retired north of the Sava accompanied by some 3,000 Roman Catholics. There was a third invasion in 1693, and a fourth in 1697; on this last occasion, some 40,000 Bosnian Christians migrated northwards and were settled in Slavonia. After long negotiation, the Treaty of Carlowitz was concluded in January 1699. By this treaty, Austria gained the whole of Transylvania and Hungary except for the Banat of Temesvar, together with the greater part of Slavonia and Croatia (Fig. 8). The decline which had begun with the repulse from Vienna in 1683 was confirmed, and from this time forward the Turkish power began to be a nuisance rather than a danger to the Christian powers of Europe.

War between Turkey and Austria (in alliance with Venice) broke out again in 1715, and, after a series of Austrian victories, the Treaty of Passarowitz was concluded in 1718. Austria retained its conquests, and so acquired the Banat of Temesvar together with a strip of territory south of the Sava and the Danube, and extending east-west from northern Bosnia into northern Serbia. A renewal of war with the Turk in 1737 proved disastrous to Austria, and was ended by the humiliating Treaty of Belgrade in 1739; all the territory gained at Passarowitz was surrendered with the exception of the Banat of Temesvar (Fig. 8).

For the next half-century, no Austrian army again crossed the line of the Sava and the Danube. In 1787, however, Austria and Turkey were again at war; Bosnia and Serbia were once more occupied by Austrian troops, but these gains were restored to the Turk by the Treaty of Sistova in 1791. Thus the Bosnian frontier with Austria remained as it was fixed in 1739 until Bosnia became an Austrian province in fact, if not in name, in 1878.

THE REBELLIONS OF THE NINETEENTH CENTURY

During the nineteenth century the main factors important in the fortunes of Bosnia and Hercegovina were the presence of: (1) a conservative landholding Moslem aristocracy more fanatical than the central Ottoman authorities at Constantinople; (2) an oppressed Christian peasantry subject to heavy taxation. Both these elements gave rise to continual unrest throughout the century.

The Moslem nobles were of the same race and language as the people they oppressed. But, although Slavs, they were 'more Turkish than the Turks in outlook', and were bitterly opposed to the reform of the Ottoman empire attempted by Mahmud II (1808–39). The Bosnian unrest against the 'infidel' or 'giaour' sultan burst into revolt in 1821 during the insurrections in Albania, Greece and Moldavia. A second Bosnian revolt in 1828, at the time of the Russo-Turkish war, was quelled with much bloodshed. Further attempts at reform, after the war was over, produced a third rebellion in 1831, when the Bosnian nobles denounced the sultan as a traitor to Islam, and when their leader, Hussein Aga, 'the dragon of Bosnia', preached a Holy War against the Ottoman authorities. This revolt, like the others, was quelled, but the power of the Bosnian nobles still remained unbroken. The abolition of the kapetanates in 1837 provoked yet another revolt which flared to greater dimensions in 1839 when the sultan promised some measure of legal equality and more equitable taxation to his Christian populations. For the next decade or so, the authority of the central government at Constantinople remained virtually in abeyance in Bosnia. Not until 1850 did a Turkish army under Omer Pasha bring about the downfall of the Moslem aristocracy of Bosnia. Sarajevo, long the stronghold of the nobles, now replaced Travnik as the official capital of the country.

But the downfall of the local aristocracy did not bring much relief to the Christian peasantry of Bosnia. The reforms that had been promised did not get far beyond the paper on which they were written. The corruption of the Turkish officials and the exactions of the tax-farmers continued to make the life of the peasants barely supportable. In 1858 the Christian peasantry of northern Bosnia rose in revolt, and in the following year some definite measures of agrarian reform were promised. In 1861–2 there was another revolt against the Turkish bureaucracy—

this time in Hercegovina. In the meantime, large numbers of Bosnians were leaving for the Slav territories of Austria and Hungary. At length, the Bosnian unrest broke out with consequences that were fatal to the Turkish authority in the province. The harvest of 1874 had been a bad one, and in July 1875 the small town of Nevesinje rose against the local officials. Within a short time, the whole of Bosnia and Hercegovina were in revolt—stimulated by the advantages gained by Serbia in 1867 and by the Cretan insurrection of 1866–9. The agitation spread to all the Balkans, and even beyond to the courts of the great European powers. The insurgents of Nevesinje had set in train a sequence of events that made the Eastern Question, with all its complexities, the centre of European politics for the next three years.

After consultation with Germany and Russia, Count Andrássy, the Austro-Hungarian Foreign Minister, presented a note to the Turkish government (January 1876) enumerating the concessions that should be made to the Christians of Bosnia and Hercegovina. But, while the sultan promised to carry out the reforms, the rebels refused to accept the Andrássy note unless the great powers provided a guarantee that the reforms would really be carried out. The 'Berlin Memorandum' of May 1876 accordingly threatened action by Austria, Russia and Germany if the proposed reforms were not adopted. But, in the meantime, the situation in the Balkans had become worse. Serbia and Montenegro declared war against the Turk, and the Bulgars rose in revolt; all attempts to secure a settlement were fruitless. In April 1877 Russia, the champion of the Slav peoples, entered the war, and defeated the Turkish army by the following January. The Treaty of San Stefano (March 1878) proposed a radical resettlement of Balkan frontiers, and provided for reforms in Bosnia. But these provisions were revised a few months later by the Treaty of Berlin (July 1878) which placed the two provinces under Austro-Hungarian administration. Austria-Hungary, moreover, was allowed to place garrisons at three places (Priboj, Prijepolje and Plevlje) in the sanjak of Novi Pazar—the narrow strip separating Serbia and Montenegro (see p. 126). The

Austrian argument for the occupation of Bosnia and Hercegovina had been the incapacity of the Turkish government and
the inconvenience caused by continual disturbances in the
neighbouring Turkish territory. But it was understood that
the provinces should be returned to Turkey after the restoration
of order and prosperity, and an agreement to this effect was
signed by the Austro-Hungarian and Turkish representatives.
The occupation aroused considerable controversy, but one writer,
who was no advocate of Austria, went so far as to admit that it
was 'the only solution within the sphere of practical politics'.[1]

THE AUSTRO-HUNGARIAN REGIME, 1878–1914

The entry of Austrian troops into the two provinces proved
difficult. The Moslems actively opposed the change, and there
was some guerrilla fighting; Orthodox opinion, too, was very
unfavourable; but by October 1878 the last resistance had
been overcome. The details of the occupation were arranged
by an Austrian-Turkish Convention in April 1879, which
affirmed that the territories were still technically under Turkish
sovereignty despite the Austro-Hungarian control. The administration of the area was then placed under the Austro-Hungarian Joint Ministry of Finance; the provinces were included
within the Austro-Hungarian Customs Union; and conscription
was introduced. These measures resulted in an insurrection in
Hercegovina in 1881–2, and, after this, the administration was
placed under the control of Baron Kállay.

Kállay had long been a student of Balkan affairs, and had
written a *History of the Serbs* in which the racial identity of Serbs
and Bosnians was admitted. He now, however, prohibited the
circulation of his own book in the provinces, lest it might help
pro-Serb tendencies, and he proceeded to create an ordered
administration on somewhat despotic lines. A promise to transfer
the administration to native Bosnians was not fulfilled, and the
number of Austro-Hungarian officials kept increasing. These
officials for the most part were Catholics and included not only

[1] A. J. Evans, *Illyrian Letters* (London, 1878), p. 240.

Germans but Croats, Magyars and even Czechs and Poles. The Catholic element was further increased during the early years of the occupation by the colonization of a belt of land in the north along the right bank of the Sava; the colonists were mainly Catholics brought from other parts of the Empire, and they included Germans, Poles, Czechs and Ruthenians. Their descendants were to form a noticeable feature of the country's linguistic map. Moreover, Kállay's policy in agrarian, educational and ecclesiastical affairs was greatly criticized by various sections of the population. But it must be admitted that the material condition of the two provinces greatly improved under his control. Brigandage disappeared; sanitary measures were undertaken; public works were constructed, though it is true that roads and railways were built to suit the strategic convenience of Austria-Hungary rather than the economic needs of Bosnia— thus rail-connexion with the ports of the Adriatic, except for Metković and Gruž, was forbidden. Still, when he died in 1903, he had managed to convert 'two wild Turkish provinces into a civilized state, even if the subjects did not love their civilizers'.[1] Indeed, Kállay was accused by his opponents of promoting material prosperity at the expense of the ideals of Bosnian culture.

The administration of his successor, Baron Burian (1903–12) was notable for the outright annexation of the two provinces to the Austro-Hungarian monarchy on 7 October 1908. It was a sudden move, made without consulting the other powers, except Russia, and despite the agreement that the two provinces should be returned after the restoration of law and order. But now the reform of the Turkish empire in 1908 was making the Austro-Hungarian government nervous lest the Turks would seek to end the provisional occupation on the grounds of their own improved administration. Moreover, Russia was weak after the war with Japan. It was also a precautionary measure against the possibility of a strong Serbian state that might block the *Drang nach Osten* policy developed by Germany and Austria (see p. 126).

[1] W. Miller, *The Ottoman Empire and its Successors, 1801–1927* (Cambridge, 1936), p. 397.

In the meantime, both Orthodox and Moslems were asking for the introduction of a proper constitution, and in 1910 an imperial decree granted some control of the administration to a legislature elected on the basis of manhood suffrage. The legislative power of the newly elected Parliament, however, was limited, and all bills required approval from the Austro-Hungarian authorities before they could become law. Executive control, moreover, still remained in the hands of the governor and his officials, and there was, consequently, much agitation for the establishment of a ministry responsible to the local parliament.

The new Parliament consisted of seventy-three elected and seventeen *ex officio* members, the various faiths being represented in direct proportion to their numerical strength in the country. The Moslems were apprehensive, especially in view of the decline of Turkish power in the Balkans. The Roman Catholic Croats looked towards Vienna, but even they were increasingly alienated by affairs in Croatia itself. The Orthodox Serbs turned more and more towards the neighbouring state of Serbia; their economic status was, moreover, much worse than that of the other two elements; for while there were few Moslem serfs, and the Croat serfs were roughly in proportion to the total Croat population, the proportion of Serb serfs greatly exceeded that of the Serb population.[1] This agrarian inferiority caused much dissatisfaction among the Orthodox Serbs. It was only natural,

[1] This is clear from the following table showing the religion, parliamentary representation and economic status of the different communities in Bosnia and Hercegovina in 1910:

	Population	%	Elected seats in Parliament	Total seats in Parliament	Percentage of servile tenures
Orthodox	825,418	43·5	32	37	74·0 (Serbs)
Moslems	612,137	32·4	24	29	4·6 (Moslems)
Roman Catholics	434,061	22·8	16	23	21·4 (Croats)
Uniates	8,136	0·4	—	—	—
Jews	11,868	0·6	1	1	—
Protestants	6,342	0·3	—	—	—
Total	1,897,962	100	73	90	100

Based on (1) the Austro-Hungarian Census of 1910; (2) L. von Sudland, *Die Jugoslawische Frage* (Vienna, 1918), p. 211.

71

therefore, that the victories of Serbia in the Balkan Wars of 1912–13 should arouse enthusiasm amongst the Bosnian Serbs, as indeed among all the Slav population of Austria-Hungary. Revolutionary activities were abroad in the provinces, and there was some terrorism caused by the Serb secret society known as the 'Black Hand'. When the Archduke Francis Ferdinand, heir to the Austrian and Hungarian crowns, visited Sarajevo on 28 June 1914, both he and his consort were assassinated in the streets of the city by a young Bosnian revolutionary, Gavrilo Princip. In the following month the Austro-Hungarian government accused the Serbian government of tolerating terrorist organizations directed against Austria-Hungary, and the succeeding train of events soon developed into the war of 1914–18.

CHAPTER 6

MONTENEGRO

'When God finished making the world,' runs an old Montenegrin ballad, 'He found that he had a great many rocks left in
His bag; so He tumbled the whole lot on to a wild and desolate
bit of country—and that is how Montenegro was formed.' This
legend embodies the most important fact about the geography
and history of Montenegro. The barren limestone country
around Cetinje was a very inaccessible fortress, and its caves
and rocks gave ample opportunity for guerrilla warfare. It was
the only corner of the Balkan lands to escape the domination of the
Turk from the fourteenth century onwards; here, a few Christian
shepherds and goatherds always maintained their liberty. It is
true that the Turks sometimes managed to penetrate into the wild
country, but they could never maintain their forces for long.
Montenegro remained a small island of freedom in the great
Turkish sea. That is her essential role in the history of the Balkans.

THE EARLY STATE, 1356–1516

The early history of the area that became Montenegro forms
part of the story of the rise of medieval Serbia (see p. 90); and
it was not until the break-up of Stephen Dušan's realm, after
his death in 1355, that the distinctive unit to be known as
Montenegro emerged as an independent principality. This area
north of Lake Scutari had been known as the 'Zeta'. It had
formed one of the divisions of Dušan's realm, and, in the confusion after his death, a noble named Balša succeeded in found-
ing a dynasty that lasted until 1421. The territory of the Balšas
seems to have reached the Adriatic at Antivar (Bar) and Budva,
and its capital for a time at any rate, was Scutari itself.

The name 'Montenegro', which came into general use early
in the fifteenth century, is the Venetian form of the Italian

'Monte Nero', called 'Crna Gora' in Serbian. This term 'Black Mountain' was derived, according to one view, from the dark appearance, at some seasons of the year, of Mount Lovćen in the country immediately to the north of Lake Scutari. The name itself, then, is an indication of the close relations that existed with the Venetians; the Balšas and Venice were sometimes in dispute about Scutari and other places, and at other times in alliance against the Turk.

When the male line of the Balšas became extinct in 1422, a new dynasty was founded by Stephen Crnojević, who established his capital at Žabljak on the north-eastern edge of Lake Scutari. By this time the Ottoman Turks had advanced well into the Balkan peninsula; and, after the great Christian defeat at Kosovo in 1389, the Zeta in the west had provided a refuge for many who fled before the Turkish conquerors. In the next century it was entirely surrounded by Turkish territory; Bosnia fell in 1463; Albania in 1478; Hercegovina in 1482. Thus it was that Stephen's successor, Ivan the Black, was forced, after a vigorous resistance, to abandon Žabljak, and to withdraw to the more inaccessible country to the north. Here, not far from Mount Lovćen itself, he established his new capital at Cetinje, and this was to remain the capital throughout all the later history of the principality. Deprived of the fertile plains of Lake Scutari, and cut off from the sea-coast, the destiny of the Montenegrins was to wage incessant warfare against the Turk for almost four centuries.

A whole cycle of legends has gathered around the name of 'Ivan the Black', telling of his valorous deeds against the Turks, and of how one day he would arise to drive the Turks from Europe. Amongst his other preoccupations Ivan found time to import a printing press from Venice. It was set up at Obod, to the south of Cetinje, and from here, after 1493, were issued some of the earliest books printed in Cyrillic characters. Ivan built a monastery at Cetinje, and also made it the see of a bishopric. It was into the hands of these bishops, or 'vladikas', that the destiny of the country passed when the descendants of Ivan ceased to rule in 1516.

THE ELECTIVE VLADIKAS, 1516–1696

The Crnojević dynasty came to an end in 1516, when Montenegro was transformed from a temporal into a theocratic state. The details of the change-over are obscure and not easy to explain, but the monks of Cetinje, from among whom the bishop was elected, had always been a powerful influence in Crna Gora. Their fanaticism had supported the struggle against the Turks; and, during the absences of the later Crnojević rulers, who seemed frequently to have gone to Venice, the bishops may have taken control. At any rate, tradition records that the last Crnojević transferred his power to the bishop before leaving finally for Venice. From this time onward until 1851 the Montenegrins were ruled by the bishops of Cetinje. The bishops, or vladikas, were elected by local assemblies, and after 1557 were consecrated by the patriarch of Peć. This union of temporal and spiritual power may well have saved Montenegro. The vladika, as an ecclesiastic, was unlikely to desert to Islam, while his office was by its nature beyond the ambitions of civil chieftains. A civil governor still continued to exist, but his office was entirely subsidiary to that of the vladika.

The seventeenth century was marked by repeated attacks from the Turks; Cetinje itself was captured in 1623 and again in 1687; and it has even been asserted that the Montenegrins were forced to pay tribute for a short time. But the Turks soon withdrew, for, in the mountains of Montenegro, 'a small army is beaten, a large one dies of starvation'. At this time, two Montenegros may be said to have existed—a free Montenegro centred on Cetinje, and an 'unredeemed' Montenegro peopled by Islamized Slavs and Albanians to the south.

THE HEREDITARY VLADIKAS, 1696–1851

The reign of Danilo I, 1696–1737

Before the end of the century a great change took place when Danilo Petrović of Njeguši was elected vladika in 1696. His successors continued to rule the state until it came to an end in the war of 1914–18. The new feature introduced in 1696 was the power of the vladika to nominate a successor from among his relations. As an Orthodox bishop he was perforce celibate, and the succession was usually continued from uncle to nephew. It was in this strange form that the theocratic state adopted the hereditary principle. The central power was thus established upon a more stable basis, and with this new cohesion the state was better able to withstand changes from without.

During the reign of Danilo I, every effort was made to revive the fortunes of Montenegro, and there were important developments both at home and abroad. Some Montenegrins had adopted Islam, and these renegades had given aid to the Turks. In order to strengthen the state, therefore, desperate action was taken, and on Christmas Eve 1702 a wholesale massacre (the 'Montenegrin Vespers') rid the country of all Mohammedan men—whether Turks, Slavs or Albanians. After this, the struggle was continued with fury on both sides. In 1712 the Turks were defeated, but two years later they were able, after many reverses, to occupy Cetinje for a third time. The Turkish army, however, harassed by guerrilla warfare, and suffering from lack of provisions, was forced to leave the desolation of Crna Gora to its hardy inhabitants.

In the meantime, a new factor had entered into Montenegrin history. Russia, under Peter the Great, was in conflict with the Turks, and had become increasingly interested in the Balkan lands. In 1711 Russian envoys came to the Montenegrins, as to other Balkan peoples, and the tsar was hailed as the champion of Montenegrin liberty. In 1715 the vladika visited Peter the Great, who recognized Montenegrin independence and granted a subsidy to enable the Montenegrins to rebuild their devastated villages. It was the first of many subsidies, and each of Danilo's successors repeated his visit to the tsar. From now on, sometimes in conjunction with the Venetians, Danilo was able to win many victories over the Turks, and, by his death in 1737, Montenegrin independence had survived some of its fiercest trials.

The reign of Sava, 1737–82

Danilo was succeeded in 1737 by his nephew Sava, a man of very different temperament, and little suited to be the ruler of a hardy people in stirring times. He was unable to check the feuds and independence of the local chieftains, and it was a confused period. For the greater part of his reign, Sava remained in the background, and the effective power was wielded for a time by his cousin Vasilije (1750–66), and then by an adventurer, Stephen Mali (1768–74), who claimed to be none other than the Russian Emperor Peter III, the murdered husband of Catherine II. Despite these complicated internal politics, the Turks were on several occasions defeated and were never able to subdue Crna Gora.

The reign of Peter I, 1782–1830

A new era dawned in 1782 with the death of Sava and the accession of his nephew Peter I, called by later generations 'the great and holy vladika'. He did much to reconcile the dissensions among the various factions of the state; the administration was reorganized, and in 1798 the first Montenegrin code of laws was established. 'He found a loose coalition of clans and tribes, he left a relatively united state.'[1] Peter, too, took part in the war of Austria and Russia against Turkey, though the Montenegrins gained nothing out of the peace treaties made by their allies in 1791 (Sistova) and 1792 (Jassy) respectively. He was able, however, to inflict a defeat on the Turks, and, in the year 1799, Turkey not only formally recognized the independence of Montenegro, but declared that 'the Montenegrins have never been subjects of our Sublime Porte'—an admission that was to constitute an important precedent. About this time, also, the region of the Brda (to the north-east), whose inhabitants had often acted in concert with those of Crna Gora, was finally incorporated into Montenegro. It was a considerable accession of territory at the expense of Turkey (Fig. 15).

[1] H. W. V. Temperley, *History of Serbia* (London, 1919), p. 154.

During these years, too, the little principality became involved in the complicated affairs of Napoleonic Europe. In 1806 the Montenegrins, in conjunction with the Russians, opposed the French in Dalmatia by contesting Ragusa and occupying the shores of the Gulf of Kotor. The Treaty of Tilsit in 1807, however, left the gulf to the French until 1813, when the Montenegrins, in combination this time with the British fleet under Admiral Fremantle, drove them out. For five months the shores of the gulf became Montenegrin territory, and the capital of Montenegro was even moved to Kotor. But at the Congress of Vienna, 1814–15, the area was handed back to the Austrians, and, on the advice of Russia, Montenegro yielded up the port together with the opportunity of an outlet on the Adriatic; the state remained land-locked until 1878–80.

For the last fifteen years of his life, Peter was at work uniting the various elements of the state in the face of constant threat from the Turks. He attempted to put an end to the blood feuds which, handed down from one generation to another, had divided families and weakened the country. Under his guidance the government was assuming a more stable and consolidated character, and the way was prepared for the reforms of his successors. Turkish invasions were repelled in 1819–21 and again in 1828–9. When he died in 1830, at the age of eighty-one, he was venerated as a saint. He had nearly doubled the area of his country; he had cemented relations with Russia; and he had maintained the integrity of the state in the face both of internal friction and of Turkish peril.

The reign of Peter II, 1830–51

Peter I was succeeded in 1830 by his nephew Peter II, celebrated as a reformer, warrior and poet. His famous epic 'The Mountain Garland' tells of the struggle against the Turk. He set up a printing press at Cetinje, and did much to further the humanizing work of his predecessor. Important changes were made, too, in the administration of the country, in order to increase the central authority at the expense of the unruly chiefs. A permanent senate of twelve members was established at Cetinje in 1831; and a year later the office of civil governor, which had existed since 1516, was abolished; the ecclesiastical power thus completely swallowed the temporal authority,

Abroad, the first half of Peter II's reign was marked by continued struggle against the Turks. The Montenegrins were offered the town of Scutari, and a frontage on the Adriatic together with a part of Hercegovina, if they would but acknowledge Turkish suzerainty. But Peter II refused to accept the bargain, and war broke out in 1832. Although the Montenegrins invaded both Albania and Hercegovina, they were unable to acquire any permanent territory. On one occasion a body of Montenegrins seized Žabljak and held it against the Turks until Peter II ordered its restoration on grounds of expediency (1835). There were also disputes with Austria. The Pastrović clan, along the Adriatic shore between Budva and Spič, sold its territory to Montenegro, always eager for a chance of an outlet to the sea. But Austria objected to this infringement of its sovereignty, and Montenegro had to yield up the territory in return for monetary compensation, and the Austro-Montenegrin frontier was delimited in 1838–40.

The total population of the state at this time was estimated at about 120,000 people. It was not a large number, but there were difficulties towards the end of Peter II's reign when the crops—chiefly potatoes and maize—failed. The famine was so severe that the Crnička district and part of the Brda, already discontented with the centralizing tendencies of the period, attempted to secede, and were reunited only after a short period of civil war (1847). In the following year the Montenegrins, like the Serbians, were stirred by the action of the Austrian Serbs in the revolution of 1848 (see p. 35). Peter offered aid to Jelačić, Ban of Croatia, who, however, did not wish to accept outside help in a civil war with the Hungarians. Peter II died in 1851—the last of the vladikas.

The reign of Danilo II, 1851–60

The reign of Danilo II was marked by a radical change in the ancient constitution of the country—a change which perhaps was inevitable sooner or later. He wished to marry, but the custom which compelled the ruler to be consecrated as bishop would not allow this. He therefore proposed to separate the civil and ecclesiastical offices of his predecessor. In 1852 he assumed the title of 'gospodar' or prince of Crna Gora and of the Brda; the succession was declared to be hereditary in the male line; while the office of bishop was to be held by a member of the Montenegrin aristocracy. Despite these startling changes, and indeed partly because of them, Danilo II was able to continue the work of his predecessor in consolidating the state. In 1855 a new legal code was introduced, providing for civil and religious liberty, and aiming at putting down brigandage. Both in its administration and in its civilization, Montenegro was assuming a more 'western' character.

Parallel with these changes at home, there were various foreign complications. The new constitution of 1852 had been introduced with the approval of both Austria and Russia, but Turkey objected and revived its claim to the suzerainty of the province. In the war that followed, the Turks, after many reverses, were compelled by diplomatic pressure from Austria and Russia to cease fighting. The Austrian delegate, at the peace negotiations of March 1853, made special reference to the Turkish acknowledgement of 1799 that Montenegro was in no sense a vassal state. Thus Austria championed the little state that, within a generation, was to regard her as a deadly foe.

When the Crimean War broke out between Turkey and Russia in October 1853, the latter expected support from Montenegro, but Danilo II refrained from war on the advice of Austria. This peaceful policy produced great discontent which culminated in revolt; the people of the Brda region declared themselves an independent state, and were induced to submit only after civil war. At the Treaty of Paris which ended the Crimean War in 1856, the Russian delegates, under pressure from Austria, disclaimed any special interest in Montenegro beyond that of 'friendly disposition'. Turkey seized the opportunity, however, to state that it regarded Montenegro as 'an integral part of the Ottoman empire', but it was careful to add that it 'had no intention of altering the existing state of affairs'. The Turkish claim was at once denied by Danilo II in a memorandum addressed to the powers. He pointed out that 'for 466 years the Montenegrin people has never been subjected to any power' (i.e. since the battle of Kosovo), and that 'for four and a half centuries it has waged continual warfare with Turkey'. The memorandum, moreover, claimed: (1) the official recognition of Montenegrin independence; (2) an extension of frontiers towards Albania and Hercegovina; (3) proper delimitation of the Turco-Montenegrin frontier; (4) the annexation of Bar, in order to provide an outlet to the sea. But nothing came of these demands, despite a Turkish offer of increased territory in return for a recognition of Turkish sovereignty.

In the years that followed Danilo was anxious to maintain peaceful relations with Turkey, but it was a desire that his subjects did not share. Frontier incidents in 1858 led to war, which was marked by a brilliant Montenegrin victory at Grahovo. It was hailed as the 'Marathon of Montenegro', and was followed by the appointment of an international commission to delimit the Turco-Montenegrin frontier. As a result, the district around Grahovo was added to the principality.

Danilo II died in 1860 after being shot by a Montenegrin rebel whom he had exiled. He left only a daughter, and the throne passed to his nephew Nicholas.

THE REIGN OF NICHOLAS I UP TO 1914

Territorial Expansion, 1860–80

Nicholas was only nineteen years old when he began his long reign (1860–1918). In 1861 the neighbouring Hercegovinians rose against the Turks (see p. 67); and, though the Montenegrin

81

government carefully kept out of the war on the advice of the Powers, individual Montenegrins crossed the frontier to take part in the struggle of their fellow Slavs. Seizing this pretext, Turkey declared war on Montenegro early in 1862, and advanced from Nikšić and Spuž into the short neck of territory (barely twelve miles wide) that connected Crna Gora and the Brda. Despite fierce resistance the Montenegrins were defeated, though the subsequent Convention of Scutari acknowledged the frontier of 1859, and allowed the Montenegrins free trade through the port of Bar (31 August 1862). During the fourteen years that followed Montenegro was at peace, and at one time almost succeeded by negotiation in gaining a direct outlet on to the Adriatic at Novasella near Spič (1866), but this was vetoed by England and France because it would have meant an increase of Russian influence in the Mediterranean.

In October 1874 the murder of twenty-two Montenegrins by the Turks at Podgorica nearly started war again, but the crisis was smoothed over by the great powers. In the following year, however, the revolt of Bosnia and Hercegovina soon started a train of events that could not be smoothed out (see p. 68). The revolt aroused very great sympathy among the Montenegrins, and in July 1876 Nicholas, in concert with Prince Milan of Serbia, declared war on Turkey. Within a few months Montenegrin victories at Danilov Grad, Medun and elsewhere brought an armistice (November); but, in April 1877, Russia declared war on Turkey, and the Montenegrins reopened hostilities. It was a year of great victories, and the Turkish attempt again to separate Crna Gora and the Brda was defeated. Nikšić and Bileća in Hercegovina were taken, and, on the Albanian side, Ulcinj, Bar and the territory south of Lake Scutari were occupied; the seaboard was at last in Montenegrin hands.

The Treaty of San Stefano (3 March 1878) allowed Montenegro to retain her recent conquests, and the state was roughly trebled in area (Fig. 15); the independent status of the country was, moreover, once more formally recognized by the Turks. But the fate of Montenegro was bound up with the wider

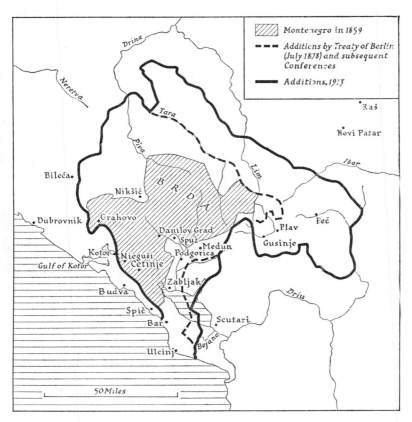

Fig. 15. The growth of Montenegro.

policies of the great powers in Europe, and the Treaty of Berlin
a few months later (13 July 1878), while affirming her independence, reduced her area from 5,272 to 3,680 square miles. In
particular, Ulcinj was restored to Turkey and Spič ceded to
Austrian Dalmatia. Bar was still left to provide an outlet to the
Adriatic, but, in order to prevent this port from becoming a
possible Russian base, the treaty provided that Montenegrin
waters should 'remain closed to the ships of war of all nations';
that Montenegro should have no fleet; and that the maritime
policing of the coast should be undertaken by Austria-Hungary.

The Montenegrin frontier on the Albanian side remained in dispute for some time owing to the lawless independence of the local tribes; and after much negotiation Montenegro, in 1880, gave up the districts of Gusinje and Plav in return for Ulcinj, together with the strip of coast as far as the river Bojana—thus making altogether a seaboard of some thirty miles (Fig. 15). But even after this the frontiers still remained in dispute at some points, partly owing to the restless border tribes; there were further rectifications, and, as late as 1911, there were still some undefined areas along the frontier.

Peaceful development, 1880–1912

As a result of the struggle with the Turk, the tradition of fighting in Montenegro went back for five centuries or so, and it was no easy task to change this Homeric society of mountain chieftains into an organized nineteenth-century state. Despite occasional border unrest, however, the thirty years following 1880 were marked by considerable economic, social and political developments. Motor roads were built, and in 1908 a railway between Bar and Lake Scutari was opened; a bank was founded; agriculture (particularly the cultivation of vines and tobacco) was improved, and an agricultural college was opened at Podgorica. By 1910 there were twenty-one post offices, and before the outbreak of war in 1914 the number had been trebled; and this may be taken as symptomatic of the accelerated progress of the country in general. As might be expected in a country where capital was scarce, much of this development was in the hands of foreigners, particularly Italians, and there was a cry of 'Montenegro for the Montenegrins'. It must be added, however, that all this improvement did not prevent the occasional recurrence of famine and the continual emigration of younger men to Serbia, to the U.S.A. and elsewhere.

Parallel with economic development, there was considerable social and intellectual progress, and a public library, a theatre and a museum were opened in Cetinje. In 1893 the four-hundredth anniversary of the foundation of the printing press at Obod was celebrated amidst many representatives from foreign universities. Theoretically, at any rate, primary education was compulsory, and by 1906 there were 112 primary schools with 150 teachers and 9,756 pupils; there were also secondary schools at Cetinje and Podgorica. Higher education, however, had to be sought abroad, usually at the University of Belgrade, and this Serbian link was not without important political effects, for the younger generation came back with new ideas of democracy that soon clashed with the autocracy of their ruler.

In the third place, there were important political developments. The old legal code of 1855 was revised in 1888; and, to the surprise of Europe, parliamentary institutions were introduced in 1905, and the first Montenegrin parliament met on 19 December. It consisted of fourteen *ex officio* members, and sixty-two elected by manhood suffrage. The experiment, however, was not an unqualified success. Party feeling ran high, and cabinet crises were frequent. There were complaints, too, that the dominant personality of Nicholas was autocratic. The international status of the country had been improved by the marriage of one of the daughters of Nicholas to the heir to the Italian throne; another of his children married the exiled Peter Karageorgević, who was later to become king of Serbia, while four married into German and Russian royal families; indeed, Nicholas was described as 'the father-in-law of Europe'. In 1898 he visited Queen Victoria at Windsor; in 1900 he assumed the style of 'Royal Highness', and finally, in 1910, he took the title of king.

In the meantime, the annexation of Bosnia and Hercegovina by Austria in 1908 had aroused antagonism in Montenegro, but Montenegrin acquiescence was purchased in the following year by the removal of the Austrian restrictions upon Bar and the rest of the Montenegrin coastline.

The Balkan Wars, 1912–13

The generation of peace since 1878 was soon to be shattered by the wider complications of the Eastern Question. In 1912 Serbia, Montenegro, Greece and Bulgaria challenged Turkey, just weakened by the Italian war and the loss of Tripoli (see p. 130). On 8 October Montenegro, claiming a rectification of her frontier, declared war on the Turks, and was joined by her allies. Plav and Gusinje, which had been yielded up in 1880, were occupied; so was Peć, and, after a long siege, Scutari itself (the old residence of the Balšas) surrendered. The great powers, particularly Austria and Italy, were averse to seeing too great a Slav frontage on the Adriatic, and they intended that Scutari should form part of a new Albanian state; it had therefore to be evacuated by the Montenegrins. The Treaty of London (30 May 1913) ceded all Turkish territory west of the Enos–Midia line to the Balkan allies, with the exception of Albania; the division of the spoil and the details of the frontiers were left to be adjusted. In the Second Balkan War, caused by the failure of the allies to agree about the division, Serbia, Greece and Montenegro together with Roumania defeated the Bulgarians. The subsequent adjustment of frontiers gave Montenegro a considerable increase of territory, for the sanjak of Novi Pazar was partitioned between Serbia and Montenegro (Fig. 27). The area of the enlarged state amounted to about 6,250 sq. miles; its population was variously estimated, and probably numbered something under half a million. The greater part of this population was Serb in speech and Orthodox in religion, but it included about 25,000 Roman Catholics and about 105,000 Moslems; the latter were mostly Albanians, and some 80,000 of them lived in the new territory added in 1913 (Fig. 35).

The partition of the sanjak of Novi Pazar had at last brought the two Serb peoples of Montenegro and Serbia into territorial contact; and, early in 1914, proposals for uniting the two countries were discussed. This would have involved a customs union, a fusion of the two armies and a joint foreign policy, but the two states would have retained their separate dynasties. Austria objected to the proposal, but despite this, and despite personal differences between Nicholas and the king of Serbia, the movement for union between the two peoples was rapidly growing when the war of 1914 broke out.

CHAPTER 7

SERBIA

The main fact about medieval Serbia is that the Nemanjid dynasty, from the twelfth century onwards, succeeded in building a substantial state out of the somewhat unorganized Slav communities of the Balkan peninsula. The Nemanjid effort culminated in the great empire of Stephen Dušan (1331– 55), which, however, broke up almost immediately after his death.

But Dušan's achievement became more than a historical memory. It was to constitute a political programme for those Serbs who, early in the nineteenth century, were liberated from over five centuries of Turkish rule. Nineteenth-century British statesmen did not use the affairs of Plantagenet England as an argument in forming their policy, but the memory of Dušan's empire, kept alive by folk-tales and ballads, was an important factor in the 'Eastern Question' and the 'Macedonian Problem'. The aspirations of modern Serbs cannot therefore be appreciated without some knowledge of their medieval history.

ZETA AND RAŠKA TO 1168

The Serbs arrived in the Balkan peninsula during the early part of the seventh century A.D. According to one account, the Byzantine emperor Heraclius (610–41) granted them the territory later known as 'Serblia', but this may only have been a gift of what they had already taken, and Heraclius probably only confirmed them in possession of their territory in return for a formal recognition of his suzerainty. For five centuries after their arrival the history of the Serbs is that of struggles between their various clans, each under a chieftain or *župan*. Sometimes a more powerful župan would absorb his weaker neighbours and take the title of 'grand župan' (*veliki župan*), but such unions

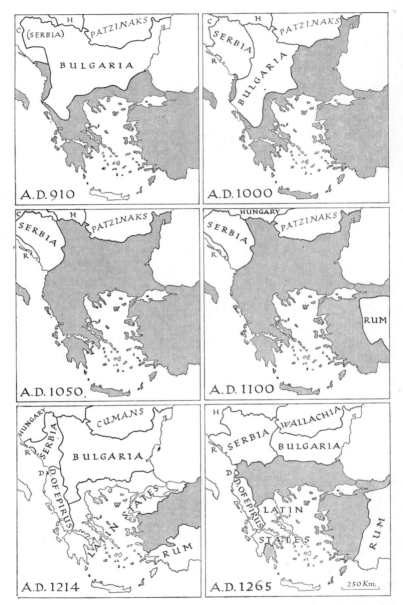

Fig. 16. The Balkan peninsula, A.D. 910–1265. The area included in the Byzantine empire is stippled. C, Croatia; D, Durazzo; H, Hungary; R, Ragusa.

were followed by disruption and regrouping, and the whole period was turbulent and confused.

The internal confusion and lack of cohesion were increased by foreign influences. Just as, in the north and west, Hungary and Venice disputed with the Byzantine empire and complicated the life of Croatia and Dalmatia, so in the south the struggle between the Bulgarian state and the Byzantine empire complicated the life of what was to become Serbia and Montenegro. The arrival of the Bulgars in the Balkan peninsula after the middle of the seventh century created a state that soon threatened the easternmost of the Serb županates. From the eighth to the twelfth centuries almost all the southern Serb area was usually under the suzerainty of either Bulgarian or Byzantine rulers (Fig. 16). About A.D. 850 the Bulgarian danger seems to have led to a union of the southern Serbs under a certain Vlastimir, the nucleus of whose resistance was the upper valleys of the Tara, the Lim and the Ibar—a land of hardy mountaineers. The Serbs strengthened their hand by acknowledging the suzerainty of the Byzantine emperors, and Byzantine influence was extended by the work of the two great Slav missionaries, Cyril and Methodius. Between 871 and 875 the Serbs were won, nominally at any rate, to Christianity, and the interior of the Balkan peninsula was drawn into the orbit of the Eastern Church, while the Dalmatian coast and the north Balkan area were being attached to the western allegiance of Rome.

Towards the end of the ninth century the growing power of the Bulgarians clashed violently with the Serb županates. The first Bulgarian empire under Simeon (893–927) was extended over the eastern Serb area which was devastated and depopulated. During the latter part of the tenth century, however, Simeon's successors lost much of the Bulgarian conquests, partly to the Byzantine empire and partly to the Serb župans who were acting in alliance with the emperor. Časlav (931–60), in particular, liberated a large stretch of Serb territory (Fig. 18). Under Samuel the Bulgarian empire, now centred at Ohrid (c. 1015), was only half the size of that of his predecessor, and in 1018 the Bulgarian power was decisively overthrown by the Byzantines (Fig. 16).

The succeeding history of the south Serbs during the eleventh century is a story of civil war and bids for leadership among the various župans, and of complicated relations with the Byzantine empire—sometimes in alliance, sometimes in opposition, according to the exigencies of the moment. Generally speaking, there were two main political groups. The western group (including the modern Hercegovina and Montenegro) was known variously as Dioclea or Zeta, from two of its most important component parts. The eastern group was centred in the inland district around Raš near Novi Pazar and was known as Raška. To the north lay the territory of the more or less independent župans of what is now Bosnia.

The political confusion of the time was particularly marked in Raška, exposed to the Byzantine armies that moved northward along the Morava valley. In the more inaccessible west, a better organized state seems to have emerged by the middle of the eleventh century. The various župans of Trabunja, Hum and Zeta were united under Prince Vojislav (c. 1042). Here, as in Montenegro in later times, a wild independence was maintained at a time when Raška was under Byzantine control. Vojislav's son Michael was able to include Raška, and he received a crown from Pope Gregory VII (1077). Michael's son, Bodin (1081–1101), further enlarged the kingdom (Fig. 18), and we have a glimpse of Bodin from some members of the First Crusade who passed through Scutari. Soon after Bodin's death, however, the kingdom broke up amid civil war, and, in the twelfth century, the main centre of political importance shifted to Raška. In 1169 a certain Stephen Nemanja became grand župan of Raška; and it was from Raška, under the Nemanja family, that the medieval empire of Serbia was built.

A picture of the Serbs at this time has been given by the chronicler William of Tyre who visited Bitolj (Monastir). They were, he says, 'an uncultured and undisciplined people, inhabiting the mountains and forests, and not practising agri-

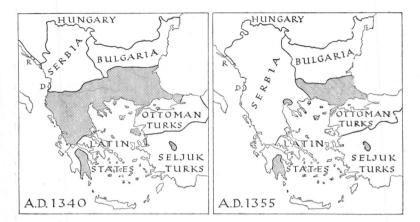

Fig. 17. The Balkan peninsula, A.D. 1340–55. The area included in the Byzantine area is stippled. D, Durazzo; R, Ragusa.

culture, but possessed of much cattle great and small...Sometimes their *župani* obey the Emperor: at other times all the inhabitants quit their mountains and forests... to ravage the surrounding countries.'[1]

THE EARLY NEMANJIDS, 1169–1331

Stephen Nemanja became grand župan of Raška in 1169, and he founded a dynasty that ruled over Serbia for some 200 years. It was the destiny of this royal family to create the great medieval empire of Serbia; and the work of the early Nemanjids made possible the flowering of Serbian greatness under Stephen Dušan in the fourteenth century.

The death of the emperor Manuel in 1180 resulted in a disputed succession at Constantinople, and Stephen Nemanja was able to shake off Byzantine suzerainty and to extend his territory. By 1186 he had united Zeta to Raška, and the cities of Scutari and Kotor, together with a stretch of the Adriatic coastline, were now within his grasp (Fig. 19). 'For the first time a real centre of unity and a real national ruler existed to educate,

[1] Quoted in W. Miller, *Essays on the Latin Orient* (Cambridge, 1921), p. 446.

Fig. 18. Serbia in the tenth and eleventh centuries. Before 1018, much of the area to the south of Serbia formed part of the Bulgarian empire—see Fig. 16. Trab, Trabunja.

to govern, and to discipline the Serbians.'[1] He retired to a monastery in 1196, and from then until the accession of Stephen Dušan in 1331, seven rulers governed Serbia, and their work was marked by three new developments in Serbian history: (1) an attempt to secure internal stability, especially with the aid of the Church; (2) foreign expansion; and (3) considerable economic progress. Each of these must be considered separately.

[1] H. W. V. Temperley, *History of Serbia* (London, 1919), pp. 39–40.

Internal consolidation

The state that Stephen Nemanja handed on to his successors was not easy to unify. The historic županates of this mountainous country were difficult to weld into one coherent whole, and provincial rebellions occurred in almost every reign. Stephen Nemanja's immediate successor, Stephen 'the First-Crowned', was able to strengthen his authority by obtaining the title of 'king' from Pope Honorius III in 1217. But, although at times the Serbian rulers negotiated with the papacy (always anxious to extend its influence in Balkan lands), their destiny lay with the Eastern Church. The influence of that Church was enlisted in the task of organizing and civilizing the Nemanjid realm. The Bogomil heresy which obtained a strong foothold in the country during the twelfth century was vigorously suppressed. Latin influences, too, were put down; and religious dissensions no longer distracted Serbia in the way that they continued to distract Bosnia and Bulgaria.

The youngest son of Stephen Nemanja became a monk at Mt Athos, and then, under the name of Sava, he became the first archbishop of an autocephalous Serbian Church (1219). Its early centre was at Žiča in the north, but, owing to Tartar raids across the Danube, it was later removed to Peć (Ipek). To all later generations the name of St Sava was to stand for education and enlightenment. His ecclesiastical statesmanship had freed the Serbian lands from the jurisdiction of the archbishop of Ohrid, and had given the Serbians a national Church. Though the primacy of the Byzantine patriarch was not always respected, the cultural influence of the Eastern Church was always important in Serbian national life. The Nemanjids, moreover, encouraged the building of churches and monasteries. Other memorials of the medieval Serbian Church are to be found in a considerable number of manuscripts—some are translations from Greek and Latin authors; others, though original, still show strong Byzantine influence. The political centralization of the early Nemanjid state may have been imperfect, but there can be no doubt about the growing vigour of its religious and cultural life.

93

Foreign expansion

The decline of the Byzantine empire towards the end of the twelfth century, gave opportunity not only for the Nemanjid state to throw off its nominal allegiance but for the rise of a second medieval Bulgarian empire which was powerful in Balkan lands during 1186–1258. For a time the Bulgarians were able to extend westwards and to occupy Niš, Prizren, Skoplje and Ohrid, and they allied with Ragusa against Serbia. In the meantime, the Byzantine empire had been all but destroyed by the soldiers of the Fourth Crusade (1204), but the recovery of much territory after 1261 brought the empire into renewed contact with Serbia (Fig. 16). And, despite civil war and internal complications, the Serbians were able to advance at the expense of the empire. Under Stephen Uroš II (1282–1321), they were able to occupy Skoplje, and to make it their capital. Debar (Dibra), too, was occupied, and the Serbian frontier was pushed to the coast near Durazzo. Stephen Uroš II was able to describe himself, not without foundation, as 'king of Serbia, the land of Hum, Dioclea, Albania and the sea-coast'. His successor, Stephen Uroš III (1321–31), succeeded in seizing the strong fortress of Prilep, and won a great victory at Kustendil in 1330 against the combined armies of Bulgaria and the Byzantine empire. After this outstanding defeat the Bulgarians were never again a danger to the medieval Serbian state.

This victory against the Bulgars and Byzantines was not paralleled by similar success in the north. The Serbian attempts to extend their limits to the Sava–Danube line were never successful for long, and the Magyars usually remained in control of a considerable tract to the south of these rivers. Nor were the Nemanjid rulers able to include their kinsmen of Bosnia within their own realm; indeed the principality of Hum and the valley of the lower Neretva were lost to the Bosnians in 1325 (see p. 60).

Economic development

During the thirteenth and fourteenth centuries the economic awakening that was abroad over the whole of Europe began to be felt in Serbian lands. Agriculture was developed; cattle and pigs were important; and there was plenty of cereals, hemp, flax, wine and oil; Serbian flour became famous. Amid the highlands of Raška, the fertile basins or *polja* of Kosovo along the upper Ibar, of Metohija along the upper Drim, of Tetovo along the upper Vardar and of Skoplje–Kumanovo in the region of the Vardar–Morava watershed, were all floored with rich soil, the relic of former lakes. Indeed, it seems likely that the population of some of these basins was greater in the fourteenth century than it is today. It is not surprising therefore that the capital of the growing Serbian state should have been moved from the older centre of Raš to Skoplje in a region at once more fertile and more in touch with the vital south-eastern frontier. The new religious capital, too, was at Peć in the Metohija region. Here, then, around the headwaters of the Ibar, the Vardar, the Drim and the Morava, was the 'metropolitan centre' of medieval Serbia.

An important economic development was that of mining. Copper, tin, silver, and gold, well-known in Roman times, began to be mined again with the help of German colonists from Hungary (known as Saxons), and of immigrants from Ragusa and Italy. The Kopaonik highland, east of the upper Ibar, was particularly important for its mining centres. Gold, silver and copper coins began to be minted by the Serbian rulers, and they provide an index of the economic advance of the state. It was this wealth that enabled the Serbian kings to hire mercenaries to fight against the armies of Bulgaria and the Byzantine empire.

In the midst of this material progress, Archbishop Adam (writing about 1330) tells us that the palaces of the king and his nobles were still of wood surrounded by palisades, and that the only stone houses were in coastal towns such as Kotor, Bar

95

and Ulcinj. There were even no walled and moated castles. The Byzantine envoys, who had come from the luxuries of Constantinople to the court of Stephen Uroš I (1243–76), were shocked to find the 'great king', as he was called, living in so modest a fashion.

But despite their low standard of living, and despite their frequent civil warfare, the early Nemanjid kings had been able to extend and consolidate their frontiers; and, moreover, they were in possession of considerable wealth. It was from these early Nemanjid foundations that Stephen Dušan was able to build the great medieval empire of Serbia.

STEPHEN DUŠAN, 1331–55

Stephen Dušan made a striking impression upon his contemporaries both by his ability and by his commanding presence, and his reign has always been regarded by later Serbians as the most glorious epoch in their history. The work of the early Nemanjids was now to be carried forward to its logical conclusion, for Dušan brought genius both to the development of the internal resources of the Serbian lands and to the execution of a daring foreign policy.

Serbia of course remained fundamentally an agricultural state, but every effort was made to encourage industry and commerce. Foreigners were brought in to work the mines; a colony of Saxon miners, for example, worked the silver mines of Novo Brdo and practised the trade of charcoal burners. Ragusan merchants in particular received trading privileges throughout the entire realm. The east–west Roman roads across the Balkans carried a variety of commodities—oil, wine, manufactures and luxury goods from the coast; metals, cattle, timber, wool, skins and leather from the interior. It was this economic development that made possible the expenses of advance into foreign lands and the creation of the medieval Serbian empire.

Dušan's reign opened inauspiciously enough, for in 1331 he had to suppress serious revolts both in Zeta and in northern Albania. To the south, however, the periodic confusion in the

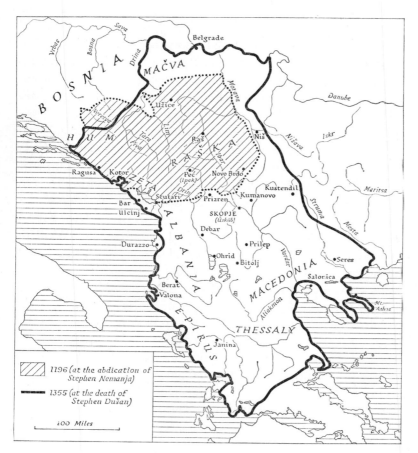

Fig. 19. Serbia under the Nemanjid dynasty.

affairs of the Byzantine empire invited interference, and the main objective of Dušan's policy seems to have been Constantinople. There were, it is true, complicated negotiations with Bosnia, Ragusa, Hungary and Venice, and sometimes even war with Bosnia and Hungary; but all these incidents were so many distractions from the great design that drew Dušan's ambition south-eastwards. With the aid of hired mercenaries, he was able by 1345 to occupy the whole of Macedonia and more; Salonica

97

itself eluded his grasp, but the great fortress of Ohrid and the cities of Valona, Berat and Seres were now in Serbian hands. The new territories were placed under Serbian governors, but their existing customs and privileges were confirmed and respected. In imitation of the Byzantine empire, Dušan gave his officials high-sounding titles like those of 'Despot', 'Caesar' and 'Sebastocrat'. The Serbian archbishop of Peć, despite opposition from the patriarch of Constantinople, was raised in 1346 to the dignity of a patriarchate. Finally, on Easter Day 1346, Stephen was crowned with great pomp at Skoplje as 'Emperor of the Serbs and Greeks', a title which was soon enlarged into 'Emperor and Autocrat of the Serbs and Greeks, the Bulgarians and Albanians'. Since the defeat of 1330, in which Dušan himself had played a part, Bulgaria had remained as a kind of dependency in his family, and the Bulgarian patriarch assisted in the coronation ceremonies of 1346.

Three years after his coronation, Dušan endowed his new empire with the famous 'Zakonik' or Code of Laws (1349) which was a fusion of Byzantine law and Serbian custom. In the same year, too, came a further extension of frontiers, for Dušan was able to occupy the whole of northern Greece up to the Gulf of Corinth; Durazzo alone remained independent (Fig. 19). Stephen's friends at Ragusa and Venice hastened to congratulate the 'Imperator Rasciae et Romaniae' on his new conquests.

The Byzantine emperors in their efforts to deal with the Serbian advance had enlisted the support of the Ottoman Turks from Asia Minor in 1345 and again in 1349. It was to prove a dangerous policy, for when the Turks responded to a similar invitation in 1353 they remained entrenched in the peninsula of Gallipoli. The Turkish danger was now becoming apparent to all Balkan peoples, and the diplomacy of Dušan at the time indicates that he aimed both at conquering Constantinople and at checking the possibility of a Turkish advance into Europe with one and the same blow. He negotiated for help from Venice, and even from the papacy; but, in the midst of great preparations for a march on Constantinople, he died of a fever, in 1355 at the age of forty-six. It was a critical moment in the history of Europe; Dušan died at the very time that the Ottomans were gaining a permanent foothold on the continent.

THE BREAK-UP OF THE SERBIAN EMPIRE, 1355–1459

Stephen Dušan was succeeded by his only son Stephen Uroš V who lived until 1371, but long before this year the Serbian empire had broken into fragments. Disorder and rebellions had immediately followed Dušan's death, and the various districts of the empire were soon able to assert their independence. Thessaly became independent under Simeon Uroš, an uncle of the new emperor; Epirus was disputed and divided by various families—Serb, Albanian and others—and its local history became very confused; Macedonia, too, fell under various chieftains, the most important of whom was a certain Vukašin, despot of Prilep, whose territory at one time seems even to have reached the Danube. To the west, in Zeta, the house of Balša also became independent and founded the state of Montenegro. Finally, a noblemen named Lazar Hrebeljanović ruled the northern portion of Dušan's realm. All central authority disappeared from the lands of Stephen Uroš V.

This disunion came at a most unfortunate moment. After their establishment in Gallipoli in 1354, the Turks immediately began to advance into Europe. Adrianople was captured in 1360, and this was soon followed by the gain of most of Thrace and of Bulgaria south of the Danube; the Turkish capital was moved from Brusa in Asia Minor to Adrianople. Faced with this Turkish threat, the Serb princes for a moment forgot their feuds, and formed a league to resist the Turkish advance, but they were defeated at Tchermen on the Maritsa in 1371; Vukašin was drowned, and many others with him. A few months later Stephen Uroš died, the last of the Nemanjid dynasty and the last emperor of Serbia. During the decade that followed, the Turks gradually took over the whole of Macedonia. Many Serbian princes there still retained a shadowy independence as vassals of the sultan, and the most famous of these was Marko

99

Kraljević, son of Vukašin, and his successor at Prilep. It is somewhat ironical that Marko, a Turkish vassal, should have become the hero of so many Serbian legends and ballads. The chronology of the Turkish advance now becomes confusing, for some localities changed hands several times and there were many shades of vassalage, but, whatever the doubt about this or that point, it is clear that from this time onward the fate of the Balkans lay in Turkish hands.

The hope of Serbia after 1371 rested with Lazar Hrebeljanović, ruler of north Serbia, who did not claim even the title of king, let alone that of emperor, but who was content with that of prince (*knez*). In his principality north of Skoplje, with its capital at Kruševac, Lazar prepared to resist the Turk (Fig. 20). With the aid of Tvrtko of Bosnia, he formed a pan-Serbian league to save the Balkans for the Balkan peoples. At length, the two armies, Christian and Turk, met on 15 June 1389 on the fateful 'Field of Blackbirds' in the plain of Kosovo. The Christian army included Serbs, Albanians, Croats, Bulgarians and Hungarians. Victory, however, lay with the Turks, and the flower of the Serb aristocracy fell in the battle. The Serbian empire, already in ruins, never recovered after this. The disaster left a great impression upon later generations, and the defeat and the exploits of various Serb chieftains inspired some of the most famous ballad poetry in Europe. A great cycle of legends gathered around the name of Kosovo, and village minstrels, on their *gusle*, kept alive the melancholy fate of the Christian captains throughout later centuries; the anniversary of the battle is still celebrated each year in Serbia on Vidovdan (28 June).

Kosovo, however, did not result in the immediate extinction of the state. A diminished Serbian principality continued to exist under its own rulers (now called 'despots') for seventy years. But for most of this time the Serbian despots were tributary to the Turks. Lazar, who had died on the day of the battle, was succeeded by his son Stephen (1389–1427), and the Serbs had a respite for a time when the Turks were involved in a

Fig. 20. Serbia under Prince Lazar (1371–89).

struggle against Tamerlane in Asia (1402). Belgrade, which had
been in Hungarian hands, was recovered and became the capital
(1404). Stephen's successor was his nephew George Branković
(1427–56) who tried, with the help of John Hunyadi of Hungary,
to drive back the Turks. He ceded Belgrade to the Magyars in
return for various advantages, and transferred his capital to
Smederevo (Semendria) lower down the Danube, at its junction
with the Morava (Fig. 22).

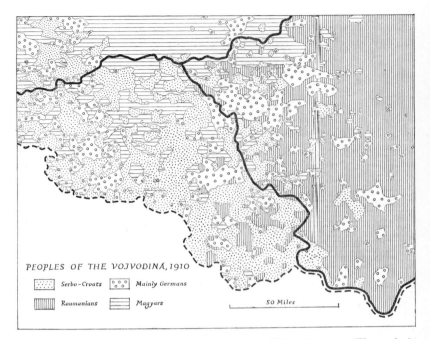

Fig. 21. A Serbian view of the ethnography of the Vojvodina, 1910. The pecked line is the boundary of the old kingdom of Hungary; the solid black lines represent the frontiers of 1941.

The history of Serb-Turkish relations after 1427 becomes even more confusing than before. But amidst the complicated events, and despite the help of John Hunyadi of Hungary, the Turk continued to advance, although there were occasional checks. By 1441 the sultan was master of the greater part of Serbia, and in 1459 he succeeded in capturing the last Serbian stronghold of Smederevo. With it fell the last hope of an independent Serbia. Soon, Bosnia to the west was likewise to fall, and Serb freedom was to disappear completely except from the little refuge of Montenegro.

MIGRATION INTO THE VOJVODINA

After the fall of Smederevo in 1459, the Serbians remained under Turkish rule for some 350 years, but the Turks never succeeded in subduing Serbia as completely as they subdued Bulgaria. The Serbians were more remote than the Bulgarians; they covered a larger area; they always had the example of the Montenegrins to inspire them; and, finally, the mountainous nature of the country made police-work difficult, and there may have been hiding-places and fortresses that were never discovered by the Turk, and that provided homes for brigands or 'hajduks'. Many Serbs, however, chose to leave the country, for one result of the Turkish invasion had been to set in motion a large scale movement of population in the Balkan peninsula. Some Serbs migrated into Bosnia, Dalmatia, and Montenegro, others to Slavonia and particularly to the Vojvodina.

The Vojvodina, consisting of the three districts of Baranja, Bačka, and Banat, had formed an integral part of Hungary from the early days of Magyar settlement. After the battle of Kosovo in 1389, bands of Serb refugees fled before the Turks northward across the Danube. In this northern region, too, the Serbian despots in the fifteenth century held tracts of lands under the Hungarian kings, and they encouraged Serb settlers. With the complete fall of Serbia in 1459, still more Serb immigrants arrived from the south. In 1483 Matthias Corvinus, king of Hungary, wrote to the pope that 200,000 Serbs had settled in the south of his kingdom in four years; and, in 1538 Cardinal Martinuzzi stated that Serbs formed half the population of Hungary. However doubtful these figures may be, it seems fairly clear that by the sixteenth century there was a very considerable Serb population in the area. These Serbs played a great part in the defence of Hungary against the Turks.

After the Turkish conquest of Hungary (c. 1540), the whole Magyar population of South Hungary seems to have disappeared almost completely—some may have migrated, some may have been exterminated. The scanty population that re-

Fig. 22. Serbia under George Branković (1427–56).

mained under Turkish rule was largely Serb, with a Roumanian element in the east. The Slav element was increased during the Turkish occupation by further immigration, although there were occasional Serb revolts against the Turk (e.g. in 1594–5). Among the immigrants were the interesting and obscure groups of the Šokci (in the Baranja) and the Bunjevci (around Subotica). They appear to have originated from the borders of Bosnia and Dalmatia, and, according to some authorities, were led into Hungary by Franciscan friars about the year 1682.

MOSLEM AND CHRISTIAN

The Christians who remained under Turkish rule in Serbia lived under a regime that was oppressive but not intolerable, for it was only after 1683, when the Turkish empire had begun to shrink in Europe, that its worst features made themselves felt in Serbia. Both in local administration and in ecclesiastical affairs the Serbs were allowed a good deal of independence. Few converts to Islam were made, and the people as a whole remained faithful to the Serbian Orthodox Church. The Bogomil heresy had long been stamped out, and consequently there was less fear that the Serbian nobles would become Moslems and retain their lands as did the nobles of Bosnia. In any case, the numerous wars between Turks and Serbians had already destroyed a large number of the great native landowners of Serbia before 1459.

One of the main characteristics of the Turkish regime was toleration in matters of religion, and indeed the Orthodox Serbs probably got better treatment from the Turks than they would have done from their Roman Catholic fellows. A Serbian song tells how George Branković asked John Hunyadi what faith he would impose on the Serbians if they were freed from the Turk, and the answer was 'The Latin.' Branković then put the same question to the sultan who said, 'I will leave the people to bow in the mosque or to cross themselves in the churches as they will'. The story certainly does incorporate a great truth about life in the Balkans during Turkish times. Greek and Latin antagonism was always a factor to be reckoned with in Christian-Turkish relations. Whatever the economic and political condition of the Christian population under Turkish rule, their religious life was their own. Some churches, it is true, were converted into mosques or into public buildings, but still the fact remains that, with few exceptions, the Turkish regime was a tolerant one.

The status of the Serb Orthodox Church was, however, somewhat complicated. The creation of the patriarchate of Peć in 1346 had aroused opposition from the Byzantine patriarch, and in 1352 the Serbian Church had been excommunicated. The ban had been lifted in 1374 at the request of Prince Lazar, and the autocephalous character of the Serbian Church had been recognized. But with the coming of the Turks the position became more complicated, for Turkish policy aimed at managing the Christian populations through the Greek Church at Constantinople. With the fall of Smederevo in the middle of the fifteenth century, therefore, the authority of the Byzantine patriarch was extended over the Church of Peć, which was made subordinate to the archbishop of Ohrid (1459). The details are vague, but the change meant that Greek and Turkish influence were now able to be more important in Serbian national life.

In the next century, however, the ex-Serbian Grand Vizier Sokolović restored the status of the Serbian national Church; Peć once more became the seat of a patriarchate in 1557 (Fig. 23), and so it remained until 1766 as a great focus of national life. It was the Patriarch Jovan II who stimulated the revolt known as 'the Insurrection of St Sava' in 1593. This dragged on with Austrian support until 1609, and it showed how determined was the resistance of the Serbs.

TURKISH ADMINISTRATION

Turkish supremacy did not at first press heavily upon the Serbians, and the lot of the Christian peasantry or *raja* during the earlier portion of the Turkish regime was far from unendurable. While the functions of central government were destroyed or absorbed, those of local government were allowed to continue. The details of government changed from time to time, but generally the area included in pre-1913 Serbia comprised the four pashaliks of Belgrade, Vidin, Niš and Leskovac. The system of taxation was very complicated and included feudal rents to the local spahi or landowner, and payments both to the pasha and to the sultan himself. Christians could appeal to the pasha for protection against the spahi, and were thus often safeguarded against petty tyranny. At first, the taxation does not seem to have been unduly excessive and it was not until later, when the pashas became corrupt and when central

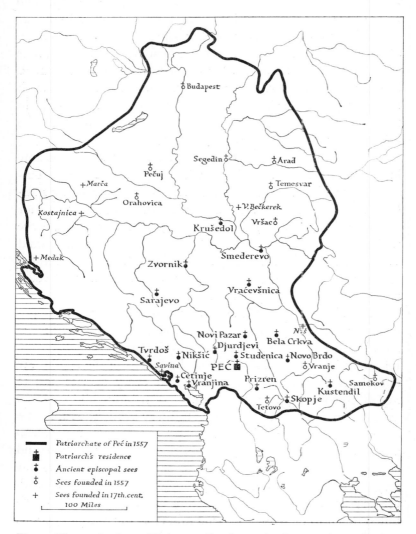

Fig. 23. The patriarchate of Peć, 1557. For the overlap between the patriarchate and the nineteenth-century Bulgarian exarchate, see Fig. 29.

107

8-2

authority became slack, that oppression fully developed. The pashaliks were subdivided into nahies, presided over by kadis, but each nahie had also a native obor-knez elected by the people, and it was he who represented the Christians in their relations with the kadi or the pasha. He was also responsible for much local government (e.g. the assessment of taxation and the work of policing) and for various judicial functions. The nahie, in turn, was composed of villages, each presided over by a knez or headman elected by the village council.

There were, moreover, considerable tracts of Serbia, mainly in the mountainous areas around Novi Pazar, which were outside the jurisdiction of the kadis. They were occupied by Baši-knezes, descendants of Serbian nobles who had managed, for one reason or another, to retain their lands, and who were responsible only to the pasha at Belgrade. As long as they paid their taxes, they were virtually independent. Their number was reduced after the rebellion of 1593; and, after that of 1689, nearly all of them disappeared.

The main grievance of the Serbians, as of all Christian populations in the early days of Turkish rule, was the method of recruiting for the *corps d'élite* of the Turkish army, the janissaries. Its origin is obscure, and many of the details of the system are not clear. But in effect it meant that every district had to supply periodically a certain number of tribute-children to be brought up as Moslems in a sort of military brotherhood. By the sixteenth century the janissaries had grown into a powerful and favoured corps; they became a closed corporation and ceased to be recruited from tribute children; the last regular levy was made in 1676. Ironically enough, during the eighteenth century the exactions and oppression of the janissaries contributed much to increase the social misery of the Serbian people.

THE TURN OF THE TIDE

During the seventeenth century, symptoms of decline were already becoming apparent in the Ottoman empire. The triumph of the Austrian general Montecuculi at St Gothard on the Raab in 1664 was the first decisive land victory won by the Christian powers against the Turks. The repulse from Vienna in 1683 was another indication that the term of Ottoman supremacy in the Balkan lands had passed its zenith, and was a prelude to further disasters. Most of Hungary was reconquered by the Christians in 1686–7. Belgrade was recovered in 1688, and the Austrians, sweeping southwards, stood victorious on the fatal field of Kosovo; they even reached Skoplje. The Serbians rose with enthusiasm against the Turks, but they soon discovered that the Austrians hoped to win them to Roman Catholicism; Jesuit priests followed in the wake of the Austrian army, and many Serbians fell away from the Austrian cause. In any case, the Austrians were obliged to retire beyond the Danube, nor did the decade of fighting that followed bring them further victories in Serbia. By the Treaty of Carlowitz in 1699, Turkey, it is true, lost Hungary and Croatia-Slavonia, but Serbia itself remained under Turkish control (Fig. 8).

The war had been marked by one very interesting episode. The retreat of the Austrians had left the Serbians at the mercy of Turkish reprisals, and, in 1691, the Patriarch Arsenije III organized a great Serbian emigration northward. Estimates vary, but some 30,000–40,000 families crossed the Danube to settle in southern Hungary. Here, the emperor promised them full religious liberty and various privileges; and they, together with those Serbians who had come north in earlier centuries, were to play an important part in the history of the Serbian people. They had left the area around Peć, Prizren and northern Macedonia; and Albanian Moslems spread northward and eastward into the vacant lands which had been Slav since the seventh century. The emperor, Leopold I, promised them complete religious freedom and the right to elect their own *vojvoda* (i.e. civil governor), but the exact terms of the agreement are somewhat obscure. If Serbia were conquered from the Turk, they were to be settled back in their own homes. But the Treaty of Carlowitz (1699) put an end to any hope of their return; by this treaty, the emperor formally acquired Hungary and Croatia-

Slavonia, but Serbia itself remained under Ottoman control. In the years that followed, the imperial attitude to the Serb settlers changed. Their charter, it is true, was confirmed by successive emperors, but no *vojvoda* was granted. Much of their land was detached from the administration of Hungary and formed into additional 'Military Frontier' districts under the direct control of the emperor. Moreover, an attempt was made to wean them from the Orthodox faith by promoting the Uniate creed (i.e. Orthodox in rites but Roman in communion), and some Serbs became Uniates. In the districts that remained under Hungarian administration, the Magyar clergy were able to convert some Serbs completely to the Roman faith.

The year 1715 found Turkey and Austria at war again. The Austrians under Prince Eugene were completely victorious, and at the Treaty of Passarowitz, in 1718, the Turks were forced to cede not only part of Wallachia and the Banat of Temesvar, but also a strip of territory south of the Sava–Danube line (Fig. 8). At last, some portion of Serbian soil was freed from Turkish rule, but the Orthodox Serbians seem to have fared worse under their new Roman Catholic masters than they had done under the Moslems. Indeed a counter-migration started, and large numbers of Serbians migrated southward to the districts still under Turkish control. When war broke out again in 1738, the Serbians did little to help; their Patriarch Arsenije IV persuaded them to rise against the Turk, but they did so half-heartedly, and at the Treaty of Belgrade (1739), the Austrians were forced to withdraw to the north of the Sava–Danube line. Belgrade and the Morava valley were lost permanently to the Habsburgs.

THE CONDITION OF SERBIA IN THE EIGHTEENTH CENTURY

The Serbian lands were at peace from 1739 to 1788, but the condition of the Serbian peasantry greatly deteriorated during this period. As the central authority of Turkey grew weaker, the rapacity of its local officials increased. Serbia, too, had now become a frontier province of the Turkish empire; Belgrade received a garrison of janissaries, and even Turkish law was not enough to protect the Christian peasantry from their exactions and ill-treatment. The social and economic conditions of the Serbian people grew ever worse. Things were bad even as early as 1717. In that year Lady Mary Wortley Montague travelled through the country and she has left us a picture of the land in a letter to the Princess of Wales: 'We crossed the deserts of Serbia,' she wrote, 'almost quite overgrown with wood, through a country naturally fertile. The inhabitants are industrious, but the oppression of the peasants is so great, they are forced to abandon their houses, and neglect their tillage, all they have being a prey to the janissaries, whenever they please to seize upon it. We had a guard of 500 of them, and I was almost in tears every day to see their insolencies in the poor villages through which we passed.'[1]

While Turkish officers and officials were thus increasing the misery of the Serbian people, another foe in the form of the Greek Church was attacking the Serb Church. During the eighteenth century the administrative machine at Constantinople was under the virtual control of Greek officials who lived in the Phanar quarter of Constantinople—hence their name 'Phanariotes'. They, in agreement with the officials of the Greek Church, wished for the hellenization of the whole Orthodox Church, and, in 1737, the nomination to the see of Peć was placed in the hands of the Greek patriarch of Constantinople. In 1766 the patriarchate of Peć was abolished and control of the Serb Church in Turkey passed completely into the hands of the Greek patriarchate. For the rest of the century, the Serb Church was exposed to the full evils of the Phanariot regime. Serb bishops were expelled, and their offices put up to the highest bidder. Many of the lower clergy, too, were deposed. The old Slav liturgies were destroyed and replaced by Greek rites. Fortunately for Serbian religion and education, these conditions were not to last for much more than a generation. One of the

---

[1] *Letters of the Right Honourable Lady M——y W——y M——e*, vol. 1 (London, 1763), p. 152; the spelling has been modernized in this quotation.

first acts of the rebels of 1804 was to expel the Greek clergy and to assert the independence of the Serbian Church.

In striking contrast to the material wretchedness and cultural neglect of the people of Serbia was the growing prosperity and enlightenment of their kinsmen living beyond the Hungarian frontier in the Vojvodina. The Turks had left an uncultivated and depopulated country, and during the rest of the century this area became the scene of a most elaborate scheme of colonization. Low-lying land was drained, roads and bridges were built; and settlers of many nationalities were attracted to the area, mainly Germans from the Rhineland and elsewhere, together with Serbs. The latter had their own churches and schools and gave a Serbian character to towns such as Novi Sad, Sombor, Pančevo and Zemun. A great part of the trade of South Hungary was in Serb hands, and the Serb middle class was relatively large. The Serbs of the Vojvodina, as compared with those of the south, gained, too, from the wider contacts of the Habsburg empire. The first Serbian literary society was founded in Budapest, and the Vojvodina was a far more important centre of Serb culture than Serbia itself. The result was that the new principality of Serbia, after 1817, drew most of its officials, and many of its clergy, from the south Hungarian lands. Dositej Obradović, the founder of Serbia's educational system, was himself a Hungarian Serb (see p. 118); so was Jovanović, the poet. These northern Serbs also supported the cause of free Serbia against the Turks with money, men and arms; and, in the nineteenth century, they played a great part both in the war of liberation and the rehabilitation of the new autonomous Serbia to the south. 'It is no exaggeration to say that the Serbians of Serbia were saved from despair by the Serbians of Montenegro and from ignorance by the Serbians of South Hungary.'[1]

[1] H. W. V. Temperley, *History of Serbia* (London, 1919), p. 122.

RUSSIA, AUSTRIA AND SERBIA IN THE EIGHTEENTH CENTURY

During the eighteenth century a new factor began to affect the destiny of the Serbian people, for a natural corollary to the expansion of the Russian state under Peter the Great (1689–1725) and his successors was Russian interference in the affairs of the Orthodox population of the Balkan lands. Austria thus found a new ally in forcing back the Ottoman frontier, and the two powers, Austria and Russia, acted more or less together during the eighteenth century. Their alliance, however, was always tinged with rivalry, for both aimed at the hegemony of the Balkans.

After the middle of the century, both Austrian and Russian propagandists were preparing the Balkan Christians for the day of liberation, and Joseph II and Catherine came to a secret understanding in 1782 for partitioning the peninsula between them. Austria was to have Bosnia, Hercegovina, part of Serbia, Dalmatia and Montenegro, while Russian influence was to be dominant in the rest of the area—partly in the form of direct sovereignty and partly in the form of a restored Byzantine empire for Catherine's grandson, with Constantinople as its capital. Venice was to be given the Morea, Cyprus and Crete in compensation for Dalmatia.

War broke out between Turkey, on the one hand, and Russia and Austria on the other, in 1787. Joseph II invited the Serbs to join his forces, and the response was great. A rising was organized in northern Serbia, in the district of Šumadija, and many Serbians now served their first military apprenticeship. National feeling rose high as the campaign progressed favourably. But Serbian hopes were doomed to disappointment. Under pressure from England and France, Austria concluded the Treaty of Sistova (August 1791), and Russia concluded the Treaty of Jassy (June 1792). The Serbians had to remain content with an amnesty, and some gain of civil rights. The Christian attack had been unsuccessful—but only for the moment. What the great powers had failed to do, Serbia was shortly to do largely for herself.

The following decade opened with a period of mild Turkish rule, and the janissaries were expelled from the pashalik of Belgrade. Soon, however, the janissaries returned, and there was some confused fighting in which the Turkish pasha had to rely on Christian help to put down their forces (1798). But their recovery was quick, and they instituted a reign of terror which the sultan was powerless to suppress, and before which both Turkish kadis and Serbian knezes were helpless. The Serbians began to fear a general massacre, and in 1804 they rose, not against the sultan, but against the virtually independent forces of the janissaries.

THE FIRST RISING, 1804–13 (KARA GEORGE)

'The story of the Serbian revolt is an epic, with folk tales for its history and Kara George for its hero. The deeds of the Serbians and of their leader are so remarkable that even legend can hardly exaggerate them. A handful of peasantry or *rajas* arises suddenly, routs great Turkish armies, besieges citadels, alternately defends and defeats pashas, and finally wins its independence by its own bravery.'[1] But despite these heroic beginnings the rise of modern Serbia presents in many ways a sorry tale. Amidst the many complications, and against the background of rising national self-consciousness, two *motifs* can be discerned. On the one hand, there was the internal rivalry of two native dynasties—that of Karageorgević and that of Obrenović—and, of the ten modern rulers of Serbia, four were deposed and three were murdered. On the other hand, there was the external rivalry of Austria and Russia for hegemony in the Balkans. And so it was that upon the smaller wheels of Balkan politics the greater wheels of European diplomacy turned, and, in due course, Serbian affairs were to form a pre-text for the great conflagration of 1914–18.

The Serbian ring-leader in 1804 was a dealer in pigs called

[1] H. W. V. Temperley, *History of Serbia* (London, 1919), p. 174.

George Petrović, better known as 'Black' George, or Kara George, from his black hair. He had been born in 1760, and had already served in the revolt of 1787–88. 'His was one of those wild elemental natures so often found among the savage peasants of the Balkans, cruel yet heroic, wild yet generous.'[1] The centre of the revolt was in the Šumadija district between the Morava and the Drina rivers. Village knezes, hajduk chiefs and warlike priests led the peasantry in local actions against the janissaries, and Kara George co-ordinated their efforts. Attempts were made to obtain the support of Austria and Russia, and the latter gave financial and diplomatic aid. It was a strange situation. The Serbian Christians were in effect fighting to maintain the sultan's authority over the rebellious janissaries, yet they were distrusted by the local officials of the sultan and were appealing for outside help. With their successes, Serbian ideas had grown, and, in April 1805, a *Skupština* or Assembly summoned by Kara George submitted to Constantinople proposals which amounted to local autonomy. The sultan, however, rejected these, and the struggle against the janissaries was converted into a war for independence.

Turkish forces were now sent into the Morava valley, but during the autumn of 1805 and in the following year the Serbians, aided by the character of the country, were able to maintain themselves against vastly superior numbers. The towns of Belgrade, Požarevac, Smederevo and Šabac were now in Serbian hands, and, by June 1807, Užice, the last fortress of any size in northern Serbia, had fallen. The arrival of Russian troops, and a change of government in Constantinople, helped the Serbian cause, but the Turkish armies were still greatly superior in number and there were some Serbian defeats. Events became confused during the years 1808–11. There were dissensions among the Serbian leaders, many of whom resisted the authority of Kara George. Russian policy, too, was bound up with the wider politics of the European scene. Threatened with the Napoleonic invasion, Russia concluded the Treaty of Bucharest

[1] H. W. V. Temperley, *op. cit.* (London, 1919), p. 183.

with Turkey in May 1812. Article VIII of this treaty promised internal autonomy for Serbia, but the wording was vague and open to misinterpretation. The rest of the year passed in negotiations between the Serbians and the sultan. While Russia was busy with Napoleon, the Turks hoped to deal with the rebellious Serbians and assembled their armies for renewed attack. By October 1813 they were masters of Belgrade once more. Kara George, faced with intrigues among his followers and with the overwhelming forces of the enemy, escaped with a few followers across the Danube into Hungarian territory. The first revolt was over.

THE SECOND RISING, 1815–17 (MILOŠ OBRENOVIĆ)

Among the leaders that remained was Miloš Obrenović, a man some twenty years younger than Kara George. He had not, it is true, played one of the most prominent parts in the late rebellion, and he was far from friendly to Kara George, who was said to have murdered his half-brother. For a time, Miloš used his influence in helping the Turkish authorities to pacify the country, and he was appointed obor-knez of the three nahies of Rudnik, Požega and Kragujevac, i.e. of practically the whole Šumadija district. But the Turkish reoccupation was marked by plunderings, executions and unspeakable cruelties. Garrisons of janissaries and Albanians were scattered through the country. The Congress of Vienna paid little attention to the woes of the Serbians, and all Russia could do was to threaten. A general massacre was expected, and once more the Serbians were ready to rise in revolt. Faced with this situation, Miloš started the rebellion on Palm Sunday in April 1815, outside the church of Takovo, his native village. Like Kara George, he was of peasant stock, but he was a much more shrewd, adroit and complicated character, better fitted to deal with the inscrutable character of Turkish diplomacy.

The rising that followed was marked by astonishing success. By July the towns of Rudnik, Čačak, Požarevac and Kraljevo had been captured, and the north had been freed. The final

Fig. 24. The growth of Serbia, 1817–1913.

defeat of Napoleon, too, left Russia in a stronger position, and the Serbians began negotiations with the Turks. An arrangement was made which gave considerable autonomy to the Serbians who lived immediately south of the Danube (Fig. 24); they were allowed to retain their arms, to collect their own taxes, to participate more fully in the administration of justice, and to hold a national assembly or *Skupština* at Belgrade. On the other hand, the area was still under Turkish sovereignty; Turkish garrisons still remained; and a Turkish pasha still resided at Belgrade.

While these negotiations were proceeding, Miloš was harassed by a series of revolts from his compatriots, who were dealt with in no tender fashion. Thus, in June 1817, Kara George himself returned to Serbia—an embarrassment both to Miloš and to the Turkish authorities. He was soon murdered under suspicious circumstances; and this started a blood-feud between the two families, which was to disturb the political life of Serbia throughout the nineteenth century. In November the *Skupština* elected Miloš as hereditary prince (*knez*) of the country. The second revolt was over, and Serbia, if not free, was at any rate an autonomous principality. It was only a small province, including not much more than Šumadija, but at any rate it was a beginning.

SERBIAN NATIONAL FEELING

The struggle for political independence was not only a revolt against Turkish misrule, but an expression of Serbian national feeling that was to become more and more vigorous as the nineteenth century progressed. The feeling manifested itself in a variety of forms, but one of its most important symptoms lay not on the battlefield nor in the political arena, but in the linguistic studies of a number of scholars. By the early nineteenth century the literary language of Serbia did not correspond with the popular speech of the Serbian people. It was an artificial language with an Old Slavonic foundation upon which Russian forms had been grafted. Thus there were eighteen letters in the Old Slavonic alphabet for which the Serbo-Croat language had no use, and, on the other hand, there were six sounds in Serbo-Croat without symbols. The Hungarian Serb scholar Dositiej Obradović (1739–1811) was the pioneer who championed the idea that the literary Serbian tongue should correspond with the vernacular speech, and it is interesting to note that he was the first Minister of Instruction in Kara George's administration.

His work was carried on by Vuk Karadžić (1787–1864), who completely reformed the Serbian literary language (see p. 19).

Karadžić's work had two aspects, both closely connected. In the first place, he collected all available Serbian folk songs and folk-lore, and in 1814 published his first book at Vienna—'A small collection of Slavonic-Serbian songs of the common people'. This was a time when the Romantic Movement in Europe led many groups of people on the continent to the study of their own customs, legends and dialects. The Serbian ballads presented a rich field for the investigator, and the fame of Serbian folk-poetry soon spread; Goethe and Grimm were loud in their praise. To the Serbian people itself it brought a more intense self-consciousness about their past glory and traditions.

On the other hand, there were more purely linguistic reforms, for Karadžić aimed at making the literary language correspond to popular speech. In 1814, at Vienna also, he published his first grammatical essay, 'The grammar of the Serbian language as spoken by the common people'. He published a larger grammar later, together with a great Serbian dictionary. His work reformed the Cyrillic alphabet according to strict phonetic principles, and the result was one of the most simple and logical systems of spelling in the world. At first the reform was opposed by the Church and by the more conservative elements, and the Serbian authorities were even induced to prohibit the printing of books with the new letters. But the prohibition was withdrawn in 1859, and before Karadžić died in 1864 the success of his work was assured.

Military activity and political complication fill much of the Serbian scene in the nineteenth century; but, behind it all, the importance of this linguistic work must not be forgotten. The work of Karadžić and his associates was important not only in shaping the literary language of the future, important as that was, but in the wider spheres of national feeling and political self-consciousness. In reminding the Serbs of their past glory and traditions, Karadžić was also providing a political programme for the future. It was a phenomenon that was common all over Europe—among the Czechs, the Poles, the Greeks and many other peoples. It was particularly common among the Slavs of the Balkan peninsula, in Slovenia, Croatia and elsewhere; and the work of Karadžić was to become not Serbian but Yugoslav in its scope.

MILOŠ OBRENOVIĆ, 1817–39

The revolt was over, but much still remained to be settled, and it was a long time before the election of Miloš as hereditary prince was recognized by the sultan. The delays of Turkish negotiation were interminable, for it was a policy well suited to the Turkish interests. A contemporary British ambassador at Constantinople summed up Turkish diplomacy as 'coffee, pipes and preliminary deliberations'. In this case, the preliminary deliberations stretched from 1815 to 1833. Russian influence helped to clarify the position of Miloš. The Convention of Akerman between Russia and Turkey in 1826 contained a clause promising to implement the eighth article of the Treaty of Bucharest (see p. 115). But there were delays, and not until the Russo-Turkish war of 1828–9 had ended in the Treaty of Adrianople was any real attempt made to meet the Serbian demand. At last, in November 1830, under the terms of the treaty, Miloš was acknowledged as hereditary prince of Serbia. The Russian right to protect the Serbians was recognized, and complete internal autonomy was granted. The independence of the Serbian Church was also acknowledged, and all Turks were to withdraw from the country except for the garrisons of eight towns.

Even now, the question of boundaries remained open. Serbia still did not include all the territory that had risen for Kara George, for there were six nahies in the south that were excluded. Finally, at a time when the Turks were embroiled in Egypt, Miloš fomented disturbances in these southern areas, and then invaded them to restore order. On 25 May 1833 he received formal acknowledgement of his jurisdiction in the district (Fig. 24). The 'preliminary deliberations' were at last over.

But the difficulties of Miloš were not only external. Within the state itself, he did much. Trade was encouraged; the army was reorganized; schools were founded; roads were built. He refused to grant out the crown-lands that now became available, thus preventing the creation of big estates and preserving Serbia as a peasant state of smallholders. But his methods were autocratic, and more than once he had recourse to assassination. There were dissensions among his followers; there was disillusion when the expenses of the new state had to be met. The wild chiefs and hajduks, moreover, 'found the time hanging heavy with no Turks to plunder'. Several revolts broke out, and Miloš was forced to grant a constitution in 1835, but this remained only a statement on paper. Under Russian influence, another attempt at a constitution was made in 1838; and, faced with increasing difficulties, Miloš abdicated in favour of his son, Milan, and retired to his estates in Roumania. His career was not ended for, after twenty years, he returned again to rule his country.

Milan Obrenović was mortally ill at the time of his father's abdication and he died within a month, not even knowing that he had become Prince of Serbia.

MICHAEL OBRENOVIĆ, 1839–42

Milan was succeeded by his brother Michael, who was only sixteen years old. The sultan, however, refused to acknowledge Michael's position as hereditary, and insisted on appointing two advisers. Difficulties were further increased by general discontent at increased taxation and by the supporters of the Karageorgević family. At length, one of the advisers, Vučić, carried out a *coup d'état*; and Prince Michael, despite the support of Russia, was forced to resign. He left Serbia, but after eighteen years he was called back to rule once more over his stormy principality.

ALEXANDER KARAGEORGEVIĆ, 1842–59

The *Skupština* now deposed the Obrenović dynasty, and elected Alexander, son of the great Kara George. There were difficulties with Turkey, who again refused to acknowledge the hereditary character of the office, and also with Russia who insisted on the exile of the advisers to whom Alexander owed his throne. There was, moreover, the continued hostility and intrigue of the Obrenović party, and this unrest broke out into rebellion in

1845. Yet despite these difficulties the period saw considerable improvement in the material condition of the province, and considerable public works were undertaken.

But Alexander proved incapable of steering his way through the complicated foreign politics of the time. In 1848 the Magyars revolted against the emperor, and the Serbs of South Hungary took the opportunity to rise against the Magyars. The latter, impelled by the rising tide of national feeling in Europe during the nineteenth century, had been striving to impose a Magyar character on the Vojvodina. When therefore, in the 'year of revolutions', the Magyars rose in revolt against the Austrian emperor, the Serbs of southern Hungary, like the Croats to the west rallied to the emperor. They received little reward. The *Ausgleich* between Austria and Hungary in 1867 meant the complete abandonment of the Hungarian Serbs to the Magyars and the end of their hopes for an autonomous Vojvodina. An intensive programme of colonization was introduced, making of the Vojvodina the most intricate linguistic mosaic in Europe (Fig. 21).[1] Faced with the prospects of losing their national identity, the Serbs of Hungary turned more and more in sympathy to the Serbian state which was beginning to free itself from Turkish sovereignty south of the Danube.

[1] The following comparative table shows the estimated ethnic composition of the Vojvodina. Based on (i) the Hungarian Census of 1910; (ii) the Yugoslav Census of 1921 in which Serbs, Croats, Bunjevci and Šokci are collectively classified as Serbo-Croat; (iii) an estimate for 1931, based partly on ecclesiastical figures. as no linguistic statistics were given in the Yugoslav Census of 1931; (iv) the Hungarian Census of 1942 for Baranja and Bačka together with an English estimate for the Banat.)

	1910	1921	1931	1942
Serbs	381,872		461,864	404,600
Croats	6,559	502,415	16,000	9,000
Bunjevci and Šokci	62,904		68,000	61,000
Slovenes	—	7,105	7,700	3,000
Magyars	421,567	376,107	385,500	472,000
Germans	301,035	316,579	317,300	315,500
Roumanians	75,806	69,530	71,950	76,000
Slovaks, Ruthenes and other Slavs	58,003	65,434	71,200	74,400
Others	12,152	9,357	16,292	12,500
	1,319,898	1,346,527	1,415,806	1,428,000

Alexander had to steer a course shaped by complex international factors. Russia, whilst herself helping Austria to deal with the recalcitrant Magyars, was not anxious to see Serbia involved lest the interference might result in the union of the Serbs of South Hungary and of Serbia under Austrian protection. Austria, on the other hand, although glad of assistance, did not wish that the idea of Serbian freedom should extend to her own Serbs. Alexander therefore followed a policy of neutrality with regard to the events of 1848, which cost him much popularity at home, for there were many Serbians who felt he should have gone to the rescue of their kinsmen across the Danube; nor was the situation helped by the fact that the Obrenović family in exile had openly championed the cause of the Hungarian Serbs.

In the years that followed, Austria did all she could to bring Serbia under her influence and so check the power of Russia in the Balkans. Alexander proved susceptible, and during the Crimean War, Serbia remained neutral despite the pro-Russian feeling of the Serbian people. By the Treaty of Paris in 1856 the status of Serbia was guaranteed, but the exclusive 'protection' of Russia was replaced by that of all the powers; the sultan retained the right of garrisoning certain towns, but was to make no armed intervention without the consent of the powers. These external complications produced a reaction within the state. The combination of anti-Austrian feeling and of pro-Obrenović sympathy led to plots and disorders, and in 1859, Alexander was deposed by the *Skupština*.

MILOŠ OBRENOVIĆ, 1859–60

Prince Miloš, now an old man of seventy-nine, was recalled from exile amidst much enthusiasm. He quickly showed his independence of Austria, and he took a strong line against Turkey. He wished the sultan to acknowledge the hereditary character of his office, and to withdraw the Turkish garrisons from the eight towns they occupied. But in the midst of these plans he died, and was succeeded by his son.

MICHAEL OBRENOVIĆ, 1860–68

Michael, like his father, ascended the throne for the second time. He had travelled a great deal and had spent some time in the capitals of the west. With this wide experience he was to do much for his country and was one of the ablest rulers it ever had. He at once set about reorganizing the army, and established a regular force that ultimately reached 100,000; the arsenal at Kragujevac was kept busy. He also succeeded in making constitutional reforms; an electoral law based the franchise on the payment of taxes; a regular judicial system was established; many reforms in administration were carried out. He also managed in 1862 to secure the withdrawal of the Turkish garrisons from two fortresses in Serbia; and it was again stated that all Turks not in the remaining garrisons were to be deported from Serbia, and their property sold. Finally, in 1867, all the Turkish garrisons were withdrawn. But these very successes only served to feed the enmity of his political opponents, including the supporters of the Karageorgević dynasty. On 10 June 1868, while walking in a park outside Belgrade, he was assassinated, and the mystery of the crime was never solved.

MILAN OBRENOVIĆ, 1868–89

Whoever had done the deed, the assassination brought no advantage to the Karageorgević family, for the *Skupština* elected the fourteen-year-old cousin of the late prince as ruler. He came of age four years later, and soon showed more interest in the pleasures of Vienna and Paris than in the politics of Belgrade. In 1876 public opinion forced him to declare war on Turkey in support of the Bosnian insurrection, but he was only saved from disaster through the diplomatic intervention of Russia. The Turks, however, refused to carry out their promises, and Russia declared war in April 1877. Russia, supported by Roumania, Serbia, Montenegro and Bulgarian rebels, was victorious, and the result was the Treaty of San Stefano (March 1878). Serbia gained much, including an acknowledgement of her

Fig. 25. The Balkans in 1878. M, Montenegro.

complete independence, but Bulgaria gained more (Fig. 25). It was the high-water mark of Russian influence in the Balkans.

The great powers, however, put a restriction upon Russian aspirations at the Treaty of Berlin in June 1878. The problem was to remedy Turkish misrule without increasing Russian influence. 'Greater Bulgaria', which, it was feared, would be subservient to Russia, was diminished; but Serbia still received a considerable slice of territory and an acknowledgement of her independence. All the new districts were Serbian-speaking with the exception of Pirot. Her demand for 'Old Serbia', including Skoplje, was refused owing to the influence of Austria-Hungary, already alarmed at the growth of Serbia and at the influence of the Serbians over the Serbs of South Hungary. By the Treaty of San Stefano Serbia had almost touched Montenegro, but now the two states were kept apart by the Austrian administration of Bosnia and by the sanjak of Novi Pazar, under Turkish sovereignty but containing Austrian garrisons. The sanjak appeared as a gateway leading down to Salonica and its commerce and making possible the Teutonic dream of *Drang nach Osten* in the next generation. The Austrian statesman Andrássy had made the best of a bad bargain. Serbian independence had been achieved, it is true, but she had been left without a seaport, without contact with Montenegro, and at the mercy of Austria. Moreover, any designs the Serbians might have had on Bosnia seemed to be completely checked.

To seal its new independence, Serbia was declared a kingdom in 1882, but this new dignity brought no wisdom to Milan. The scandals of his private life were public property. There was one party in the state which would have preferred to see a Karageorgević on the throne; another party would have liked Prince Nicholas of Montenegro whose resistance to the Turk had won golden praise. The whole country was full of unrest. Milan had turned for support to the very power that aimed at holding Serbia in subjection. In 1880 commercial agreements put the Serbian export trade at the mercy of Austria-Hungary; and in 1881 Milan concluded a secret agreement by which he promised to negotiate with no other government without first consulting Austria. By this treaty Milan also promised to discourage Serbian agitation in Bosnia in return for Austro-Hungarian support for Serbian claims southward, i.e. towards Macedonia (see p. 145). Milan has been described as one who subordinated everything to Vienna. Serbia had ceased to be a tributary of Turkey only to become a vassal of Austria.

In 1885 Milan, encouraged by Austria, and eager for a spirited foreign policy to make up for his internal difficulties, declared war on Bulgaria, which in that year had enlarged itself by the addition of eastern Rumelia. The campaign was a failure; Milan was saved only by Austrian diplomacy; the treaty that followed maintained the *status quo*. By now, the position of Milan was impossible. His quarrels with his wife were not only scandalous but assumed political importance, for Queen Natalie was a Russian with anti-Austrian sympathies. He attempted to regain popularity by a new constitution in January 1889, but, within a few months, he abdicated in favour of his son aged thirteen.

ALEXANDER OBRENOVIĆ, 1889–1903

Milan and Natalie, now divorced, continued to live in Serbia for four years, causing trouble and scandal, until at last they left the country—Milan to Vienna and Natalie to Biarritz. The country was now ruled over by a regency, but in 1893 the young king declared himself of age, arrested the regents, and dissolved the constitution of 1889. The country as a whole was in a state of unrest, and its energies were absorbed in bitter party strife. Milan himself returned in 1897 to become Commander-in-Chief of the army. In the meantime, Austrian influence continued to be important.

In the summer of 1900, despite the wishes of his ministers, his army and his people, Alexander married his mistress, whose past was very doubtful and who was publicly believed to be incapable of childbirth. Crisis followed crisis. Constitutional government was becoming a farce. There were disorders and plots. The finances of the country were disorganized, and there was a general feeling of failure in the country. At last, on 10 June 1903, the king and his wife were brutally murdered. The circumstances were particularly revolting and brought discredit upon the country, but the Serbian people as a whole could only feel relief when they heard that the last Obrenović was no more. Bands played and Belgrade was decorated with flags.

PETER KARAGEORGEVIĆ, 1903–14

The *Skupština* now offered the throne to Peter Karageorgević, then in exile at Geneva; he was the son of Prince Alexander who had been deposed in 1859. The tact of the new king coupled with his strictly constitutional rule brought about a great change in the life of the state, and the court of Belgrade escaped from the unpleasant limelight of recent years. The constitution of

Fig. 26. The 'contested zone', 1913.

1889 was revived and made more liberal. The finances were organized, and trade began to improve despite tariff disputes with Austria-Hungary. It was this solid progress at home that made possible the brilliant foreign policy of Serbia in later years.

With the progress of education, and the improvement in communications, closer relations were developed with the Slavs of Croatia-Slavonia and of South Hungary, but this *rapprochement* was viewed with great distrust by Austria, no longer in favour at the court. The economic servitude of Serbia to Austria-Hungary, led moreover to a search for an outlet to the sea. 'Serbia must expand or die' became the watchword. Some looked towards Macedonia, and propaganda was spread among the Slav-speaking populations of that province; but more people looked towards Bosnia and Hercegovina, now under Austrian administration. Unfortunately, personal relations between Peter and Prince Nicholas of Montenegro were not good, and many Montenegrin students who came to Belgrade complained of the autocratic nature of their ruler. But despite these factors, the foreign policies of the Balkans drew both countries together, and a series of crises precipitated an Austrian-Serbian 'question' that was also of vital interest to the fellow-Serbs of Montenegro.

The pig war of 1906

Nine-tenths of Serbian exports and three-fifths of her imports passed through or from Austria-Hungary, and in 1905 the Serbians started tariff negotiations with Bulgaria. Austria, wishing to keep the Balkan states apart, at once objected, and demanded, moreover, that all Serbian orders for munitions should be placed only in the Dual Monarchy. When Serbia refused, a prohibitive duty was placed on all Serbian livestock. The so-called 'pig war' threatened disaster to Serbia, for pigs formed her main export; but, despite the difficulties, the Serbians refused to give in, and sought new markets in western Europe. By arrangement with Turkey, the Serbian export trade left via Salonica. The blow turned out to be far less severe than was expected, and Serbia gained politically as well as economically from her new contacts. The situation, however, only convinced the Serbians of the need for an outlet to the sea, and increased their bitterness against Austria. Within two years that bitterness had almost reached breaking-point.

The Bosnian crisis of 1908

The final annexation of Bosnia and Hercegovina by Austria-Hungary on 7 October 1908 aroused fierce resentment in both Serbia and Montenegro. Russia, too, was loud in condemnation, but was not prepared to go to war against Austria-Hungary supported by Germany. The Serbian press clamoured for war, and there was unrest among all the Slavs of the Balkan peninsula; the international crisis was not over until the following year. In response to German pressure at St Petersburg, Serbia was forced to acquiesce. It is true that in February 1909 Austria withdrew her garrisons from the sanjak of Novi Pazar, in return for formal recognition of her sovereignty over Bosnia and Hercegovina by Turkey. But even this withdrawal was ominous. In 1878 the Austrian General Staff had thought the road to Salonica lay through the sanjak; but by 1909 it was clear that the way lay not through that difficult mountain country, but along the old route of the Morava–Vardar, i.e. through Serbia itself.

Austria, moreover, fearful for her own Slav populations, was loud in complaints about subversive pan-Serb propaganda. The Agram (Zagreb) trials and the Friedjung forgeries that aimed at bringing discredit upon Serbia only recoiled, however, on the Austrian Foreign Office (see p. 41). The Serbian Foreign Office, in turn, whatever the activities of Serbian unofficial organizations may have been, maintained a strictly correct attitude.

The Balkan wars, 1912–13

The hopes of Serbia, deprived of Bosnia and of access to the Adriatic, were now centring more and more on Macedonia. The memory of Dušan's empire led them here, and unrest and crises within the Turkish empire made the time ripe for intervention. The Turks were weakened by war with Italy, and the sufferings of the Christian populations of Turkey, despite repeated proposals for reform, were reaching boiling point. In the course of 1911–12, various alliances were formed between Bulgaria, Greece, Serbia and Montenegro. They marked a triumph over centuries of disunion and distrust. The Serbian-Bulgarian treaty of 13 March 1912 made provision for the partition of Macedonia along the following lines: 'all the territory north of the Šar range' was to go to Serbia; 'all the region east of the Rhodope range and the Struma valley' was to go to Bulgaria. Bulgaria hoped the intervening country should form an 'autonomous Macedonia', but, if this should prove im-

possible, a new line was to be drawn leaving Kumanovo, Skoplje
and Debar to Serbia, and giving Kratovo, Veles, Bitolj and
Ohrid to Bulgaria (Fig. 26). Serbia undertook to make no
claim south of the line; Bulgaria reserved the right to claim
territory to the north, in which case Russia was to act as arbi-
trator. The area of overlapping claims was known as the 'Contested Zone'.

War began with the declaration of Montenegro on 8 October,
and, within a few months, to the amazement of Europe, the
Turkish forces had collapsed. The Serbian victory at Kumanovo
wiped out the stain of Kosovo, and King Peter occupied Skoplje,
the ancient capital of Stephen Dušan (Fig. 19). The Treaty of
London (30 May 1913) ceded to the Balkan allies all territories
'west of a line drawn from Enos on the Aegean Sea to Midia
on the Black Sea, with the exception of Albania'. It was not
only a defeat of the military forces of the Turkish empire,
but a defeat of the Austrian dream of *Drang nach Osten*. There
was only one compensation: Austria-Hungary and Italy, rather
than see Albania partitioned between Slav states on the north
and Greece on the south, had succeeded in blocking Serbian
access to the Adriatic by proposing the creation of an autonomous Albania.

But the division of the spoil from Turkey caused difficulties
among the Balkan allies. Bitolj and Ohrid, now occupied by
Serbian troops, were claimed by Bulgaria according to the letter
of the agreement of March 1912. The Serbians, however, were
not disposed to yield. Their reasons were two. In the first place,
during the course of the war, Bulgaria had not fulfilled all her
obligations according to the military agreement between the
two states. In the second place, the creation of an independent
Albanian state by the great powers had not been foreseen, and
this now cut Serbia off from an outlet to the sea. The Serbians
therefore had no desire to see themselves separated from the
Aegean by a belt of Bulgarian as well as of Greek territory.
Russian intervention proved ineffective, and the result was the
Second Balkan War of June–July 1913. The Bulgarian army

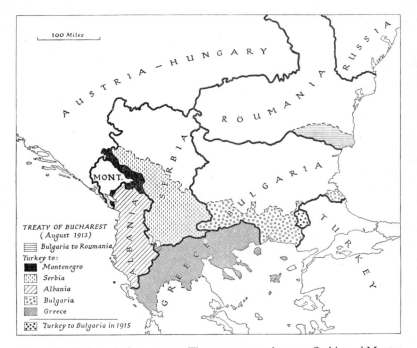

Fig. 27. The Balkans in August 1913. The arrangement between Serbia and Monte-negro respecting the partition of the Sanjak of Novi Pazar was not made until 4 November.

attacked both the Serbs and the Greeks; but Serbia and Greece, supported by Montenegro and Roumania, were victorious. The subsequent adjustment of frontiers gave the whole of northern and central Macedonia to Serbia, and also divided the sanjak of Novi Pazar between Serbia and Montenegro (Fig. 27).

In Serbia and Montenegro the result was great rejoicing and a return of national self-confidence. After so many internal and external difficulties throughout the nineteenth century, triumph was at last in Serbian hands, and the old capital of Skoplje had been redeemed. Amongst the Slavs of Austria-Hungary—in Bosnia, Hercegovina, Dalmatia, Croatia-Slavonia and South Hungary—the result of the Serbian victories can only be described as electrifying. Weary of the Habsburg regime, many now felt that the future of all Yugoslavs lay with Belgrade.

To Austria-Hungary, the victory brought bitter disappointment. Not only was the road to the east blocked, but the Serbian triumph had intensified the whole Slav question in the Habsburg monarchy. It now became the avowed policy of the governments at Vienna and Budapest, supported by that of Berlin, to liquidate once and for all the people who have been aptly described as the 'Guardians of the Gate' to the east.

Austrian designs, 1913–14

A pretext for war was not long in coming. On 28 June 1914 the Archduke Francis Ferdinand, heir to the Austrian and Hungarian crowns, and his wife were assassinated in the streets of Sarajevo by a Bosnian revolutionary (see p. 72). It is true that the archduke was not on friendly terms with the Emperor Francis Joseph, that he was known to have Slav sympathies, and that he was disliked in pan-German circles in Vienna. Adequate precautions for his visit to Sarajevo had not been taken. But, at any rate, his death provided an excuse, and in the following month the Austro-Hungarian government accused the Serbian government of tolerating terrorist organizations directed against Austria-Hungary. Much has been written about the Sarajevo murder and much will probably always remain in doubt. It seems that the assassin and his accomplices were the agents of Serbian officers and revolutionaries. The Serbian government, though aware of what was being plotted, does not appear to have been directly responsible for the crime. In any case, exhausted as she was after the Balkan wars, it was hardly to the advantage of Serbia to be embroiled in warfare at that moment.

It was on 23 July that the Austro-Hungarian government presented its ultimatum, with ten demands, to Serbia. This stated that the crime had been planned in Belgrade, and that it was part of a 'subversive movement with the object of detaching a part of Austria-Hungary from the Monarchy'. Only forty-eight hours were allowed for a reply to the ultimatum which is now known to have been shown to the German government some twelve hours before it was sent to Belgrade. The Serbians accepted most of the demands, but demurred at two—the dismissal of unspecified officials and officers, and the participation of Austro-Hungarian officials in suppressing anti-Austrian activities in Serbia. The Serbians, however, suggested that the whole question should be submitted to the Hague Tribunal or to the great powers. On 28 July Austria-Hungary declared war. But a war which brought in Russia and involved Germany's dream of *Drang nach Osten*, could not be isolated. Within little more than a week, the great struggle of 1914–18 had started.

CHAPTER 8

MACEDONIA

THE MACEDONIAN PROBLEM

The area included under the term 'Macedonia' has varied from time to time and has never corresponded with any single administrative or political unit. It is usually used to describe the central part of Turkey in Europe before the changes of 1912–13 —that is an area lying between the river Mesta on the east and Lake Ohrid on the west, and between the Aegean Sea to the south and the mountains of the Šar Planina and the Kara Dagh to the north. This area included the Turkish vilayets of Salonica together with the greater part of those of Kosovo and Monastir. The population of the area in 1910 was estimated at something over two million made up approximately as follows:

Slavs	1,100,000
Turks	500,000
Greeks	250,000
Albanians	120,000
Vlachs	100,000
Jews	75,000
Gipsies	10,000

But all figures must be taken with the greatest reserve.[1] How intermixed the different elements were in some places may be seen from the fact that the area has given rise to the culinary term 'macédoine'.

The ethnographic complexity is further increased by the indeterminate character of the Slavs who form the greater part of the population. Much controversy has raged over the question as to whether the Macedonians speak Serbian or Bulgarian. They can, without difficulty, be understood both by Serbians or Bulgarians, but there are differences. On the one hand, the

[1] The table on p. 136 gives a comparative view of Serb, Bulgar, Greek and German estimates.

135

Macedonians, like the Bulgarians, use the suffix article, and, also, words which in Bulgarian have an 'l', have it too in Macedo-Slav, while it is omitted in Serbo-Croat—e.g. Macedonian *belo* (white), Bulgarian *belo* and Serbo-Croat *beo*. On the other hand, it has been argued that they are Serbo-Croat by the laws of phonetics and morphology. The truth seems rather that Macedo-Slav is not one dialect but a group of similar dialects, and that the Macedo-Slavs pass by scarcely perceptible grades from the Bulgars of eastern Macedonia to the Serbs north of Skoplje.

There are likewise other contradictory arguments based on popular social and domestic customs. Thus marriage, burial and saint's day customs have been shown to be very much like those of Serbia, while peasant costumes and embroidery designs have been shown to have Bulgarian affinities. Yet other people have again pointed out that this is a transitional area in such matters.

The bitter struggle of rival nationalities dates from the middle of the nineteenth century when the growing self-conscious feelings of the Balkan peoples were asserting themselves not only

	Serbian view, 1889	Bulgarian view, 1900	Greek view, 1889	German view, 1905
Turks	231,400	489,664	576,600	250,000
Bulgars	57,600	1,184,036	—	—
Serbs	2,048,320	700	—	—
Macedo-Slavs	—	—	454,700	2,000,000
Greeks	201,140	225,152	656,300	200,000
Albanians	165,620	124,211	—	300,000
Vlachs	74,465	77,267	41,200	100,000
Other	101,875	147,244	91,700	—
Total	2,880,420	2,248,274	1,820,500	2,850,000

From J. Cvijić, *Questions Balkaniques*. The sources are as follows:

(1) *Serbian view*—S. Gopčević, *Bevölkerungsstatistik von Altserbien und Makedonien* (Wien, 1899).

(2) *Bulgarian view*—V.Kančev, *Macedonia: Ethnography and Statistics*—in Bulgarian (Sofia, 1900).

(3) *Greek view*—C. Nicolaides, *Makedonien* (Berlin, 1899).

(4) *German view*—K.Oestreich, 'Die Bevölkerung von Makedonien', *Geographische Zeitschrift*, vol. XI, p. 292 (Leipzig, 1905); these figures are only an estimate.

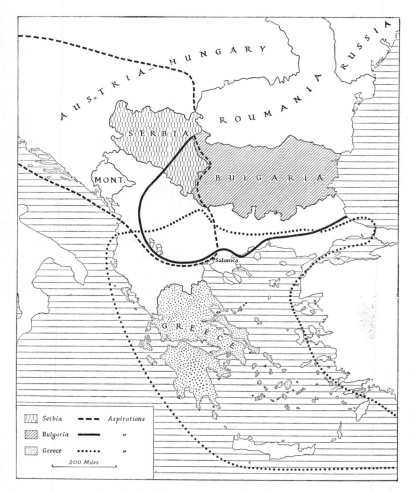

Fig. 28. Conflicting claims in Macedonia, 1912.

against their Turkish overlords but also against one another. Thus the Bulgars emancipated themselves from Greek ecclesiastical control only to dispute the issue with the Serbs, while the presence of Moslem Albanians and Turks, Greeks, and Roumanian-speaking Vlachs, together with Jews and gipsies, only served to increase confusion. The local ingredients among the Macedonian peoples constituted so many *irredenta* that tempted and stirred the surrounding states to action. Thus Macedonia was a common factor in all the pre-1914 dreams of a 'Greater Bulgaria', a 'Greater Serbia' and a 'Greater Greece' (see Fig. 28). There were Roumanian interests, too, and even if Roumania could not, owing to her position, advance any territorial claims in Macedonia, the existence of a Roumanian Vlach population was always a possible factor that might achieve compensation elsewhere in any final Balkan settlement.

But the Macedonian Problem was much more complicated even than these considerations would indicate. Macedonia was not only a medley of peoples and an arena for competing Balkan nationalities; it was also, for many years, the meeting place for the international rivalries of the great European powers—particularly of Austria-Hungary and Russia, the former anxiously seeking to control the growth of Slav political sentiment in the Balkans, the latter interested in pan-Slavism and the control of the 'Straits'. Thus the decline of the Turkish empire in the nineteenth and twentieth centuries not only gave scope for the rising nationalities of the Balkans but also provided an opportunity for the interference of the greater powers intent on maintaining a balance of power in Europe. As Tzar Nicholas I, speaking of Turkey to the British ambassador at St Petersburg in 1853, said: 'We have on our hands a sick man—a very sick man; it will be, I tell you frankly, a great misfortune if one of these days he should slip away from us, especially before all necessary arrangements are made.' Composed thus of rival peoples and subjected to conflicting interests, Macedonia has been described as the quintessence of the Balkan problem, for here most of the different elements that made up the 'Eastern Question' came together.

THE MEDIEVAL EMPIRES TO 1430

The medieval history of Macedonia is of importance in any study of the later Macedonian Problem because memories of Byzantine, Bulgarian and Serbian control of the area survived, to be caught up in the modern policies of the Balkan states. The coming of the Turk in the fifteenth century, it is true, stifled the rivalries of the Christian powers; but, with the decline of the Turkish empire in the nineteenth century, overlapping claims in Macedonia once more leaped into prominence. The Byzantine empire had left a tradition of Greek civilization and culture; while the medieval Bulgarian and Serbian empires also bequeathed historic claims that helped to inflame the rivalries of the nineteenth and twentieth centuries.

The arrival of the Slavs

With the final partition of the Roman empire in A.D. 395, Macedonia passed under the control of the East Roman or Byzantine empire. But during the sixth century the Danube frontier of the empire broke down, and Slavs began to raid southwards into Balkan lands. In 597, and again in 609, Salonica was besieged by surrounding Slav tribes in Macedonia. Raiding soon passed into settlement. It was convenient for Byzantine diplomats to speak of the lands occupied by Slavs in Thrace, Macedonia and Greece as grants made through the generosity of the emperor; and the frontier might be placed either at the Danube or at no great distance from the Aegean Sea according to the imperial or the Slav point of view. Despite the recovery of control made by the empire, the arrival of the Slavs had wrought a great ethnographical change in the Balkans. So widespread were their settlements that much of the Balkan lands, including mainland Greece, became known by the eighth century as 'Sclavinia' (Fig. 3); there is also reference to 'Macedonian Slavonia'.

The first Bulgarian empire

To the north, the Bulgars, coming from the steppe-lands, had established themselves about 679 in the area south of the Danube. Here they found a land already peopled by Slavs, and the new state that came into being was the result of fusion between Bulgars and Slavs. The two centuries following 679 were marked by intermittent warfare with the Byzantine emperors. Under

Simeon the Great (893–927), the Bulgar state extended its frontiers far to the west—over Macedonia to within sight of the Adriatic Sea. The Byzantine emperor was able to keep only the coastlands in Macedonia and Epirus (Fig. 16). But the Bulgarian realm soon broke into two owing to revolt in the western provinces. In 922 eastern Bulgaria came to an end; and by 1018 the western half, after a revival under Samuel (976–1014), was also recovered by the Byzantine empire. The Bulgarian patriarchate, set up in Ohrid, now fell, and Macedonia once again became a Greek province.

Byzantine control, 1018–1186

Byzantine authority in Macedonia remained unimpaired for over a century and a half after 1018. The emperors tried to strengthen their position by introducing Asiatic colonists. Some Turks, later known as Vardariotes, had been settled in the neighbourhood of Salonica in the ninth century; and, from the eleventh to the thirteenth century, colonies of Uzes, Patzinaks and Cumans were introduced.

The second Bulgarian empire

From 1018 to 1186 Bulgaria had no existence as a separate state, but in the latter year a revolt headed by Vlachs and Bulgars, coupled with the growing weakness of the Byzantine empire, led to the establishment of a second Bulgarian empire. The new state spread over an area almost as wide as that of its predecessor, and it included northern and central Macedonia. Only the southern coastlands were left to the Byzantine Greeks. But the second empire was short-lived. By 1258 Bulgaria had shrunk to a small state, and the Byzantine rulers were once more in control of the whole of Macedonia.

The confusion after the Fourth Crusade

To the south of Bulgaria, however, the Byzantine power had undergone a great setback before 1258. After the conquest of Constantinople by the Fourth Crusade in 1204, southern Macedonia became, for a few years, part of the Latin kingdom of

Salonica which stretched into Thessaly. Then after 1223 it was part of a Greek despotat of Epirus until, in 1246, it was back again under Byzantine control. And so it remained until the rise of Serbia under the Nemanjid dynasty.

The Serbian empire

With the expansion of the Serbs in the fourteenth century, almost the whole of Macedonia passed under the control of Stephen Dušan. In 1346 he was crowned at Skoplje and soon took the title of 'Emperor and Autocrat of the Serbs and Greeks, the Bulgarians and Albanians'. Although the Serb empire fell apart so quickly after the death of Dušan in 1355, its glory was kept alive through later centuries by the ballads and folk traditions of the Serbs. For a time after 1355 various Serb chieftains held large tracts of Macedonia, but already the destiny of the Balkan lands was passing into other hands. After the battle of Kosovo in 1389, the greater part of Macedonia was secured in Turkish possession. Salonica, it is true, was an exception, but in 1423 its Greek rulers sold it to Venice. After some vicissitudes, it was finally taken by the Turks in 1430, and held by them until 1912.

THE TURKISH REGIME

The Turks who now came into the country in the fourteenth and fifteenth centuries fell mainly into two categories—landowners and peasants. Large tracts of land were distributed among the Ottoman chiefs, and these feudal landowners or *begs*, with their large farms (*čifliki*) were to be found everywhere. The Turkish peasantry was concentrated in fairly well-marked areas, and they included the descendants of shepherds from the district of Konia in Asia Minor who were settled here even before 1360, and who became known as Konariotes. In addition to these main groups, there were also Turkish officials and military colonists established at strategic points. Finally, the Moslem element included the Albanians of western Macedonia who adopted the faith of the conquerors.

141

The general conditions of life were similar to those of the Turkish regime in Serbia. The circumstances of the Christian population deteriorated with the decline of the central power in the seventeenth and eighteenth centuries. Towards the end of the eighteenth century many of the local governors became practically independent; thus western Macedonia fell under the control of Ali Pasha of Janina while Ismail Bey at Seres established a benevolent despotism of his own. With the nineteenth century came attempts at reform by the central government. In 1839 came the Hatt-i-Sherif, a decree which even went so far as to proclaim the equality of races and religions within the empire. But these proposals, and those of 1856 and 1864, brought no relief to the local populations of the empire. The Macedonians—Christian and Moslem alike—continued to suffer from the lack of an effective central administration and from the rapacity of local officials. The impact of rising national feeling among the Balkan peoples upon this inefficiency was to develop with dramatic consequences before the century was over.

THE BULGARIAN EXARCHATE, 1870–72

In the early decades of the nineteenth century, the dormant nationality of the Bulgarians began to awake and manifest itself in the form of a literary and educational revival. The first printed work in the vernacular appeared in 1824, and the first school in which the Bulgarian language was taught was founded at Gabrovo in 1835. During the next ten years some fifty Bulgarian schools came into existence, and five Bulgarian printing presses were set up. This increasing Bulgarian self-consciousness led inevitably to a reaction against Greek influence. The privileged position of the Greek clergy under the Ottoman regime was tending as much as the temporal power of the Turks to destroy Bulgarian nationality, especially after the abolition of the patriarchates of Peć and Ohrid in the eighteenth century. The supporters of the new literary movement recognized that their real enemy was the ecclesiastical ascendancy of the Greek patriarchate at Constantinople.

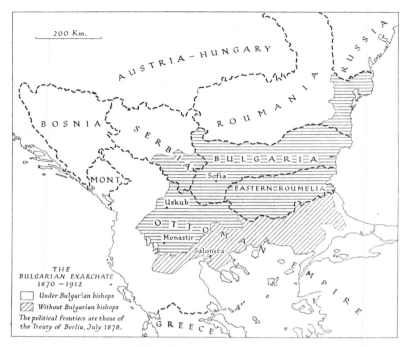

Fig. 29. The Bulgarian exarchate, 1870–1912.

Some of the Bulgarian leaders even went so far, about the year 1860, as to negotiate with Rome for the establishment of a Bulgarian Uniate Church (i.e. Orthodox in rites but Roman in allegiance). Every effort was made to reduce the influence of the Greek clergy appointed to Bulgarian sees, and there was a series of insurrectionary movements. After much controversy, the Turkish government granted ecclesiastical autonomy to the Bulgarians by creating a separate Bulgarian Church under an exarch resident, like the patriarch, at Constantinople. Its jurisdiction extended over the greater part of the vilayet of the Danube, and included the towns of Niš and Pirot, afterwards transferred to Serbia by the Treaty of Berlin in 1878. Moreover, it was arranged that other areas might pass under the authority of the exarch if two-thirds of their inhabitants so wished (Fig. 29).

The election of the first exarch was delayed until February 1872 owing to the opposition of the patriarch who immediately excommunicated the new ecclesiastical authority and his followers.

This ecclesiastical liberation was followed by great educational activity, and Macedonia became the battleground for rival patriarchist and exarchist propaganda. These literary and ecclesiastical aspirations in turn were but a prelude to wider political ambitions as the Bulgarian movement gained ground.

THE TREATIES OF SAN STEFANO AND BERLIN, 1878

The insurrection in Bosnia and Hercegovina in 1875 aroused excitement throughout the Balkans. There were widespread fears of Turkish reprisals against all the Christians, and the Bulgarians attempted to anticipate Turkish action by rising in revolt themselves (May 1876). The rebels were suppressed with great severity by irregular troops. The Pomaks (Bulgarian Moslems) in particular massacred men, women and children without discrimination, and the report of these 'Bulgarian atrocities' aroused horror throughout Europe. The Treaty of San Stefano which concluded the ensuing war, proposed the creation of a very large autonomous Bulgarian state under Turkish suzerainty (Fig. 25) extending over almost the whole of Macedonia and part of Thrace, and corresponding roughly with the wide extent of the Bulgarian exarchate. It is interesting to note that the treaty-makers had before them an ethnographic map of the Balkans by the German geographer Kiepert (May 1876). This showed a great westward extension of Bulgars, and the new frontiers appeared to be in agreement with the known ethnographic facts. Many maps, both before and after that of Kiepert, show a similar westward extension of Bulgarian-speaking peoples but, on the other hand, this has been disputed again and again.

Whatever the ethnographic facts, San Stefano was speedily replaced by the Treaty of Berlin which provided that Macedonia should remain Turkish (Fig. 25). But despite these new changes, the Treaty of San Stefano was of great importance. It came to constitute a charter for the Bulgarian claim to

Macedonia. What is more, the Bulgarian exarchate was left unimpaired, and Bulgarian schools and churches now set out to redeem the outlying territory that had seemed to become, even if only for a few months, an integral part of the Bulgarian state.

PROPAGANDA AND TERRORISM, 1878–1908

Churches and schools

The creation of a Bulgarian principality in 1878, and the union of this with eastern Rumelia in 1885, greatly increased the importance of the Bulgarian exarchate. In 1891, under the Bulgarian prime minister, Stambuloff, the Macedonian sees of Ohrid and Skoplje received Bulgarian bishops; in 1894, those of Veles and Nevrokop; and in 1898, those of Bitolj (Monastir), Strumica and Debar (Dibra). Bulgarian propaganda also made progress in Macedonia during these years through the establishment of Bulgarian schools. The Serbs and Vlachs were under the double disadvantage of being late in the field, and of lacking a separate ecclesiastical organization covering Macedonia.

At the Treaty of Berlin, the Serbs had claimed 'Old' Serbia (including Skoplje), but this had been opposed by Austria-Hungary. In 1881, however, the secret treaty between King Milan of Serbia and Austria-Hungary promised that Serbia would discourage Serbian agitation in Bosnia in return for Austro-Hungarian support of Serbian claims southward, i.e. towards Macedonia. Despite the difficulties of the Obrenović regime, Serb influence advanced rapidly in Macedonia after 1890, and the Serbian government went to considerable expense to open and maintain schools. A great step forward was made in 1902, when the Turks allowed the appointment of a Serb as bishop of Skoplje. Nor were the Roumanians inactive in their support of the Vlachs. In 1886 a Roumanian school was founded at Bitolj, and others soon followed, being supported by funds from Bucharest. In 1905, too, the Vlachs were recognized by the creation of a Vlach bishopric at Bitolj. Statistics are notoriously dubious in Macedonia, but by 1900 there seem to have been upwards of 800 Bulgarian schools and about 180 Serb schools in the three vilayets of Kosovo, Bitolj and Salonica; while Greek figures for 1901 claimed over 900 schools in the two latter vilayets.

These rival educational activities sometimes resulted in anomalous situations. 'The passion for education is strong', wrote H. N. Brailsford in 1906, 'and the various propagandas pander eagerly to it. If a father cannot contrive to place all his sons in a secondary school belonging to the race which he himself affects, the prospect of a bursary will often induce him to plant them out in rival establishments. It is, of course, a point of honour that a boy who is educated at the expense of one or other of these peoples must himself adopt its language and nationality. The same process is at work among the villages. I remember vividly my amazement when I encountered this phenomenon during my first visit to Macedonia.'[1] Thus it sometimes happened that a 'Greek' father had 'Bulgarian', 'Serbian', and 'Roumanian' children.

Terrorist activities

Educational competition was not the only feature of Macedonian life during these years. In the eighteen-nineties there appeared a number of secret societies aiming at revolution against the Turk. The relation between the different societies is not always clear, for their activities were disturbed by rivalries and disputes among themselves. One body of opinion aimed at securing Macedonian autonomy, and attempted to gain support for a policy of 'Macedonia for the Macedonians'. This seems to have been the object of the 'Internal Organization' (VMRO) founded in 1893 at Resana between Bitolj and Ohrid. Its influence grew rapidly, and it soon divided Macedonia into districts, each with its own officials. It attempted unsuccessfully to gain the support of all the Christian population, but the idea of autonomy was, of course, held in suspicion by Greeks and Serbs who felt that such autonomy might only end in Bulgarian predominance; the union of eastern Rumelia with Bulgaria in 1885 was too recent to be forgotten.

[1] H. N. Brailsford, *Macedonia: Its Races and their Future* (London, 1906), p. 102.

Other groups had more definite Bulgarian aspirations, and the 'Supreme Macedo-Adrianopolitan Committee' formed at Sofia in 1895 found many supporters, for there were large numbers of people of Macedonian origin living in Bulgaria; indeed it has been estimated that one-half of the population of Sofia was of Macedonian extraction. This Committee had its own newspapers and its own deputies in the Bulgarian parliament; and it made the Macedonian question one of the chief political issues in Bulgaria. It armed its supporters, and accumulated stores of ammunition in the mountainous country along the Macedonian frontier. These activities frequently embarrassed Bulgarian foreign policy, but popular sentiment was usually too strong for any Bulgarian government to take effective action against the irregular warlike preparations within its realm. Within a short time, 'incidents' began to multiply as different bands of raiders (*comitadjis*) crossed the frontier into Macedonia to wage guerrilla warfare against the Turks.

The progress of the Bulgarian cause in Macedonia was viewed with great alarm by the other Christians of the Balkans. The Greeks in particular were fearful lest Macedonia be lost for Hellenism, and in 1894 the secret patriotic society of the *Ethniké Hetaerea* was founded. One of its principal aims was the promotion of Greek influence in Macedonia and the preparation of an insurrectionary movement; and in 1896 it sent numerous armed bands into the southern part of the area. The outbreak of the Greco-Turkish war over the question of Crete in 1897 seemed a favourable opportunity for rallying the Christian cause against the Turk, but concerted action was prevented by mutual jealousy and by the interference of Russia and Austria who aimed at preserving the *status quo*.

In the years following 1897, the condition of Macedonia went from bad to worse; in that year the Turks had accidentally come across a Bulgarian store of arms at Vinica in the vilayet of Kosovo, and, after this, repressive methods became more severe. On the other hand, Bulgarian and Greek irregular troops disturbed the life of the countryside. They raided not only the

Turk but also one another, and each raid produced reprisals. 'A word from a Greek bishop would often condemn a whole Bulgarian hamlet to the flames. A Bulgarian band, descending by night upon a hostile village to murder a spy-priest and to burn his house, was not always careful to save his widow and her children from the conflagration.'[1] The Serbs, too, complained of villages depopulated or destroyed. The Albanian area was the scene of feuds and disorders. In short, each group had its own heroes and its own victims. The Turks meanwhile attempted to play one group against another. None of the reforms stipulated in Article 23 of the Treaty of Berlin, pledging reform and reorganization in European Turkey, was carried out. In the autumn of 1901, conditions in Macedonia gained world-wide notoriety when an American missionary, Miss Stone, was captured by a Bulgarian band, and ransomed for £T16,000.

In the autumn of 1902 there occurred a rising stimulated by incursions of Bulgarian bands over the border; but it came to nothing, and was followed by ruthless Turkish reprisals. The Porte attempted to anticipate foreign interference by a scheme for reform, and Hilmi Pasha was appointed Inspector-General of the three vilayets of Kosovo, Bitolj and Salonica (December 1902). But Russia and Austria were now prepared to interfere and, in February 1903, they proposed a series of administrative, financial and police reforms that included the employment of foreign officers to reorganize the gendarmerie. All these proposals did but little to improve the condition of the area. It is true that the Bulgarian government, under pressure from Russia, dissolved the Macedonian Committee in Bulgaria, but the Internal Organization continued its preparations for deliverance. In April, a series of bomb outrages took place, culminating in the blowing up of the Ottoman Bank at Salonica. There were raids and skirmishes elsewhere, and on 2 August the general unrest broke out into revolt in the vilayet of Bitolj and into sporadic risings elsewhere. The rebels achieved some brief success; but by the end of September they had been overcome.

[1] H. N. Brailsford, op. cit., p. 130.

As winter drew upon them, some 60,000 peasants remained homeless refugees in the mountains. The confusion of the year was increased by disturbances among the Albanians of 'Old Serbia', who had been steadily gaining ground in the region since 1878 (Fig. 35). They now rose in revolt in March, fearing interference with their freedom, and had to be pacified partly by force and partly by concessions.

The Mürzsteg programme

The great powers had in the meantime been considering ways and means of forcing reform upon the sultan, and, in October 1903, Austria and Russia issued a second set of proposals known as the 'Mürzsteg Programme' from the place, near Vienna, where they were signed. This was accepted by the sultan, and, as a result, two 'civil agents'—Austrian and Russian—were attached to the Inspector-General, Hilmi Pasha. Moreover, the greater part of the area was divided up for police purposes into five sectors, each under the control of a different power; the British took Dráma; the French, Seres; the Italians, Bitolj; the Austrians, Skoplje; and the Russians, Salonica. In 1905, on the proposal of the British government, some further changes were made, and a Financial Commission was established to help the civil agents put the finances of the area upon a satisfactory basis.

But all these attempts at reform proved a failure, partly owing to the lack of effective co-operation from the Turkish authorities, and partly because of the rivalries ablaze within the area. 'Exarchists' and 'Patriarchists' still continued to murder one another. Greek bands (composed largely of Cretans) raided in the south; the Serbs renewed activity in the north; while the Bulgarians resisted all newcomers, and chaos reigned complete. European intervention was proving a complete failure.

In January 1908 Austria announced a project for building a new railway through the sanjak of Novi Pazar to connect up with the Turkish terminus at Mitrovica, thus uniting Vienna and Salonica. As a result of Russian counter-proposals, the scheme was dropped, but the whole incident was indicative of the conflict of interests between the two powers. At this time, too, the Anglo-Russian *rapprochement* led to the 'Reval Programme' issued when Edward VII visited Nicholas II at the Baltic port in June 1908. It aimed at more effective European supervision in Macedonia; but, before any action could be taken, affairs in the Turkish empire had taken a completely new turn.

THE 'YOUNG TURKS', 1908–12

Meanwhile, the Turkish regime had enemies within its ranks. A secret 'Committee of Union and Progress', the so-called 'Young Turks', had long been planning a revolt among the officers of the Turkish army. The committee was originally formed at Geneva in 1891. It had then moved to Paris, and finally to Salonica. The revolt against the despotism of Sultan Abdul Hamid started at Resana in July 1908; and, by the following April, the sultan had been deposed. There were great scenes of enthusiasm in Macedonia. One of the Young Turk leaders, Enver Bey, declared, 'Henceforth we are all brothers. There are no longer Bulgars, Greeks, Rumans, Jews, Moslems; under the same blue sky we are all equal, we glory in being Ottomans'. For a short time there was fraternization among the peoples of Macedonia. Serbs and Bulgars walked together in processions with Turks. The great powers decided to abolish the international control; the officers of the gendarmerie left the country; the Finance Commission was withdrawn; and the Reval Programme was not put into operation.

But this promise of peace in Macedonia did not last long. The Greeks, in particular, had always been suspicious. The Young Turks proved to be violently nationalistic, and the so-called equality of races was found to mean nothing other than centralization and the merging of all differences into one Ottoman regime. By the summer of 1910 the old hatred between Moslems and Christians was as fierce as ever. Macedonia was once more the scene of pillaging and murder, as the Christian population recoiled before the 'Ottomanization' of the empire.

It was under these conditions that signs of better relations among the Balkan states became evident. Soon came a series of alliances that marked a triumph over long years of distrust. On 13 March 1912 Serbia and Bulgaria concluded a treaty of alliance in which they defined their respective claims in Macedonia (see p. 130); a military convention followed on 12 May. A month or so later, a treaty was signed between Greece and Bulgaria (29 May 1912), and this was also followed by a military agreement on 22 September. Montenegro was likewise in negotiation with Bulgaria and Greece, and in September she signed a treaty with Serbia. The whole group of these arrangements is sometimes collectively described as the 'Balkan League'. The Turks at this time were weakened by their war with Italy, and the moment seemed ripe for intervention.

The immediate outbreak of war between the Balkan states and Turkey was forced by the condition of Macedonia, and in particular by a revolt of Albanians. In 1909 they had risen in Kosovo, Metohija, and adjoining regions, against the threat of increased taxation, disarmament and a census. The rebellion was suppressed by the Turkish army, only to break out again in 1911. In August 1912 the rebels captured Skoplje and demanded autonomy and the cession of large areas including the vilayets of Bitolj and Kosovo. These disturbances weakened the Turkish government and also greatly alarmed the neighbouring states, who viewed a possible 'Greater Albania' as a threat to their own interests in Macedonia. In September the states of the 'Balkan League' appealed to the great powers for immediate reforms in Macedonia, but the result was only a declaration urging peace and promising reform. By this time, tension had increased to breaking-point, and Montenegro declared war on 8 October. The other three states, on the 14th, presented an ultimatum to the sultan demanding radical changes and the enforcement of Article 23 of the Treaty of Berlin. Faced with this, the sultan declared war on Bulgaria and Serbia on 17 October, and on the following day Greece declared war on Turkey.

THE BALKAN WARS, 1912–13

The amazing success of the Balkan allies astounded Europe. Within a few months, the Turkish forces had collapsed, and the Treaty of London (30 May 1913) ceded to the Balkan allies the greater part of the Turkish domain in Europe. But success brought its own seeds of disaster. Bulgaria and Serbia could not agree upon the division of the spoil (see p. 131), and the result was the Second Balkan War of June–July. Serbia and Greece, supported by Montenegro and Roumania, were victorious. The Treaty of Bucharest partitioned Macedonia to the great advantage of Serbia and Greece, while Bulgaria was excluded from her 'promised land' (Fig. 27).

Two groups of problems then faced the Serbians in their occupation of their part of Macedonia—economic and political; those facing Greeks were very similar. The economic problem was the revival of production in a land long neglected by its Turkish governors, and then disturbed by irregular raiding, and devastated by warfare. Rivers were unembanked; marshes were undrained; great stretches of cultivable land lay waste or were tilled only by the most primitive methods; large numbers of refugees were homeless. On the other hand, the new territories were potentially rich. The fertile plains of Kosovo and Bitolj and the basin of the middle Vardar were ready for the plough. Moreover, the mineral wealth of the new Serbian lands was considerable, and had lain almost unworked since the Turkish conquest. Silver, lead, iron and manganese were only some of the metals awaiting exploitation. Finally, an outlet for the produce of the area through Salonica was promised by an agreement with Greece.

The other group of problems was political. The new territories included large numbers of Albanians and Macedo-Slavs. The former had a long tradition of restlessness behind them. Many of the latter had, since 1870, looked to Bulgaria as their spiritual guardian; their schools and churches were Bulgarian. Now, in 1913, the task that faced the Serbian government was that of conciliating this heterogeneous population among which racial hatreds ran high; while across the frontier lay Bulgaria brooding over what she regarded as her unjust treatment. But before these problems—economic and political—could be tackled, the war of August 1914 broke upon Europe. In 1915 Macedonia, for the third time in four years, became the scene of Balkan conflict.

CHAPTER 9

THE FORMATION OF THE
YUGOSLAV STATE

ASPIRATIONS TOWARDS YUGOSLAV UNITY

Though the 'Illyrian Provinces' had so quickly passed away
with the defeat of Napoleon, the possibility of some union
among the various Southern Slav groups was never lost sight of
during the nineteenth century. South Slav consciousness was
fostered by the linguistic and literary work of Vuk Karadžić
(1787–1864) among the Serbs, and by that of Ljudevit Gaj
(1809–72) and Bishop Strossmayer (1815–1905) among the
Croats. Moreover, the disciples of Jernej Kopitar (1780–1844)
among the Slovenes were making closer contacts with the Croats
and with the Yugoslav movement in general. But this growing
feeling of common nationality had many difficulties to contend
with, and the ultimate union of all the Southern Slavs was far
from being a foregone conclusion. They were scattered among
so many different political and administrative units which made
concerted action difficult.[1] The various units, too, had different

[1] The following is an estimate of Yugoslav population in 1914, based on the
Austrian and Hungarian censuses of 1910.

Attached to Austria

Dalmatia	Serbo-Croats, 611,000
Carniola	Slovenes, 491,000
Styria	Slovenes, 410,000
Carinthia	Slovenes, 82,000
Küstenland	{Slovenes, 267,000 {Serbo-Croats, 171,000
Made up as:	
Trieste	{Slovenes, 57,000 {Serbo-Croats, 2,000
Görz and Gradisca	Slovenes, 155,000
Istria	{Slovenes, 55,000 {Serbo-Croats, 168,000

[continued opposite]

historical backgrounds, and, not least, there was the antagonism between the Roman Catholic and the Orthodox sections of the population. But, with the twentieth century, the Yugoslav ideal advanced by leaps and bounds. A variety of circumstances drew the Southern Slavs together, and affected both those within and those outside the Austro-Hungarian monarchy (Fig. 30).

Within the monarchy, the unconstitutional regime in Croatia, and the attempts to suppress the Croat language and nationality were rapidly destroying any pro-Hungarian feeling among the Croat population. Some of the older generation, it is true, were still doubtful about an alliance with the Orthodox Serbs, but the leaders of the younger generation were avowedly in favour of breaking away from Hungary. Croat feeling was reflected in Dalmatia, and the Resolutions of Fiume and Zara in 1905 were signs that Roman Catholic-Orthodox antagonism was breaking down, or, at any rate, was being submerged in other issues. Even so, it must be remembered that both resolutions professed allegiance to Hungary provided that an autonomous Croatia-Dalmatia could be secured. The Catholic Slovenes and the Orthodox Serb peoples of south Hungary were not such im-

Attached to Hungary	
Croatia-Slavonia	Serbs, 654,000
	Croats, 1,638,000
Vojvodina	Serbs, 382,000
	Croats, 7,000
	Bunjevci and Šokci, 63,000
Fiume	Slovenes, 2,000
	Serbo-Croats, 13,000
Rest of Hungary	Serbs, 79,000
	Croats, 186,000
	Slovenes, 70,000
Attached to Austria-Hungary	
Bosnia and Hercegovina	Serbs, 825,000
	Croats, 400,000
	Moslem Serbo-Croats, 610,000
Serbia	
Serbs	3,000,000
Macedo-Slavs	550,000
Montenegro	
Serbs	250,000
Total	10,789,000

Fig. 30. Yugoslavia in relation to Austria-Hungary.
C, Carniola; K, Küstenland; S, Salzburg.

portant groups, but here, too, the Austro-Hungarian regime was producing dissatisfaction and unrest that increased as the twentieth century went forward. Finally, in Bosnia the whole situation was unstable, and all sections of the population supported the demand for a greater measure of autonomy.

Among the Southern Slavs outside the monarchy, the most important feature of the twentieth century was the change of regime in Serbia when the Karageorgević dynasty came once more to the throne (1903). The contrast between Serbian democracy and the alien rule of Austria and Hungary became

156

all the more glaring. An increasing number of Southern Slavs now felt that any hope of liberation lay with Serbia, and the triumph of the Serbian armies in the Balkan wars of 1912–13 aroused great excitement throughout the South Slav world. The favourable Concordat made by Serbia with the Vatican in June 1914 helped, moreover, to allay Roman Catholic suspicions of Orthodox intolerance. The other independent state was Montenegro, and this, despite the dynastic rivalry of Nicholas and Peter, was, early in 1914, about to enter into the closest fiscal and diplomatic union with Serbia. Yugoslav ideas were in the air, and Serbia was accused of pan-Serb aspirations in the Balkans.

But the factors affecting the fate of the Southern Slavs inside the Austro-Hungarian monarchy could not be separated from those affecting the Slavs without. There was an inevitable interaction between the domestic policy of Austria-Hungary towards the South Slavs within the monarchy, and the foreign policy of Austria-Hungary towards the Southern Slavs outside. Serbia was not only the 'Guardian of the Gate' blocking expansion to the south-east, but she was also a 'Piedmont' that might do for the South Slavs what Savoy had done for Italy; this indeed had been the aspiration of some Serbian statesmen, such as the able Foreign Minister Ilija Garašanin, since the middle of the eighteenth century. Thus it was that the German-Austrian dream of economic penetration towards Turkey and beyond became interlocked with the racial problem of the Dual Monarchy. The 'Eastern Question' or the 'Macedonian Problem' or the 'Germanic Threat' in Europe could not be separated from the 'South Slav Question' or the 'Croat Problem' in Austria-Hungary. With the outbreak of war in 1914, all the problems were put into a melting pot. Of the many possible solutions, four stood out, and they must be considered separately.

One possibility was the maintenance of the *status quo*, or of something very near to it. This was unlikely because the unrest among the Southern Slavs of the monarchy was too general to be dealt with by repression; it is difficult to exterminate a whole nationality. Moreover, to the south, the destruction of Serbian independence, even if it could have been achieved, would only have added to the intransigent elements already within the monarchy.

A second possibility was the so-called Trialist solution. This, in various forms, envisaged the conversion of the Dual Monarchy into a Triple Monarchy by the grant of some autonomous status to the Southern Slavs, comparable with that of the Magyars. The Magyars, however, were bitterly opposed to an arrangement that would rob them of direct access to the sea through Croatia, and that might serve only to strengthen the position of the Austrian emperor at the expense of Magyar nationalist aspirations. It is true that many Austrian aristocratic and Catholic circles in Vienna were in favour of some kind of federalism along these lines, but, on the other hand, the German nationalists of Austria had no wish to see their own access to the Adriatic cut off by an autonomous Slovenia, or by the inclusion of Slovenia within an autonomous South Slav unit. The Serbs of the monarchy, too, were afraid that this proposal might only end in Catholic Croat dominance. And the Serbians of the kingdom to the south could only be suspicious of any attempt to organize Southern Slavs within the monarchy lest it might ultimately involve themselves or at any rate outbid the suggestion of union with Serbia.

A third possibility was that of 'Greater Serbia'. This pan-Serb solution, dear to the heart of the conservative 'Old Radical' party of Serbia, would have meant the inclusion of all the Orthodox elements among the Southern Slavs under one rule. To Serbia would be added Montenegro, southern Dalmatia, much of Bosnia and Hercegovina, eastern Croatia (Srem) and southern Hungary. Roman Catholics would thus have been excluded, and it was a scheme that was thought to have had the approval of Russia, which was anxious to identify the Slav cause with the Orthodox Church.

A fourth solution was the union of Serbs, Croats and Slovenes in a Yugoslav state. This would have meant the realization of the dream of the nineteenth-century idealists; and it would have carried forward to a logical conclusion the increasing *rapproche-ment* of Serb and Croat and Slovene during the twentieth century. But so many historic prejudices were against such a union; sheer inertia alone made it difficult to bring about. When war broke out in 1914, it still seemed an unlikely possibility to many people. Still, the seeds had been sown, and, as Baron Burian said, the war proved to be a 'hot-house for forcing plants'.

MAIN FEATURES OF THE WAR
OF 1914–18

The story of the Yugoslav contribution to the war of 1914–18 is too complicated to tell in detail, but certain trends of opinion and certain outstanding incidents in the war must be mentioned, however briefly, as essential clues to a right understanding of later developments. The first and most decisive factor was the heroic Serbian army, which thrice drove the Austrians back across the frontier in 1914, and, after succumbing to superior Austrian, German and Bulgarian forces, made a great retreat over the Albanian snows. After an interval of recuperation at Corfu, it played an important part in holding the Salonica front and, supplemented by volunteer Yugoslav Legions, shared in the final Allied victory over Bulgaria. Without this heavy sacrifice of life (and Serbia and Montenegro probably lost not less than one out of five million souls), all political efforts would have been in vain.

The second tendency was entirely opportunist; the Serbo-Croat coalition in Zagreb continued to attend the joint parliament in Budapest and to profess loyalty to the Hungarian crown, and indeed attended the coronation of Charles IV, who succeeded his uncle, Francis Joseph, in 1916. It thus was able to husband Croatian resources and to maintain its autonomous institutions unimpaired till the end of the war, but it steadily declined to make any public disavowal of its colleagues abroad and maintained secret contacts with them, in the same way as did the Czech 'Mafia' with the Czech National Committee of Masaryk and Beneš.

Thirdly, there was parallel action among the Croats and Slovenes in Austria, and when the Austrian parliament was again allowed to meet in May 1917, their leaders in it, Monsignors Krek and Korošec, put forward an open claim for the union of the Yugoslav lands of the monarchy in a single free state under the Habsburg sceptre, of course suppressing any reference to the completion of that union by the addition of Serbia and Montenegro.

Finally, the Yugoslav committee, consisting of over twenty fairly representative exiles from all the different provinces of the monarchy (the most notable being Franjo Supilo, Ante Trumbić, the sculptor Meštrović and the advocate Hinković), made London its headquarters and put forward manifestos claiming unity and independence and repudiating the Habsburgs.

THE TREATY OF LONDON, 26 APRIL 1915

A serious complication was introduced by the Treaty of London of 26 April 1915, by which the Entente (Britain, France and Russia), in return for Italy's entry on their side, assigned to her wide territories in Gorizia, Carniola, Istria and Dalmatia, inhabited by an overwhelmingly Slovene and Croat population of not less than 700,000 (Fig. 31). A special clause reserved Fiume as the port of Croatia. The provisions of the Treaty, though a strictly guarded secret, were discovered by the Croat leader Supilo in conversation with the Russian Foreign Minister Sazonov in St Petersburg: and it became known that both Russia and the Serbian Premier Pašić—a man of narrowly Serb nationalist outlook—were inclined to leave the Catholic Croats and Slovenes to their fate, if the territory where the Serb and Orthodox population predominated could be secured for Serbia and, with it, ample access to the Adriatic. This caused a temporary revulsion of feeling in favour of Austria-Hungary; and the Yugoslavs in the Austrian army fought manfully against Italy, knowing that they were defending Slav soil against

Fig. 31. The Treaty of London, 26 April 1915.

Italian aggression. The supreme command on the Isonzo was given to Marshal Borojević, an Orthodox Serb belonging to one of the *Graničar* (Frontiersman) families long in Habsburg service.

THE SERBIAN GOVERNMENT AND THE
YUGOSLAV COMMITTEE

By the winter of 1915 the conquest of Serbia, by Austrian, German and Bulgarian forces once more closed the ranks of the Yugoslavs, whose sole hope lay in unity; but for the next eighteen months a deadlock ensued. The Russian Revolution and the entry of America weakened the position of the reactionary and pan-Serb Pašić, and his party split into Old Radicals and Young Radicals, the latter demanding democratic institutions no less than national unity and equality. On 20 July 1917 the Declaration of Corfu was signed between Pašić as Serbian Premier, and Trumbić as President of the Yugoslav committee in exile, and this may be called the birth certificate of the future Yugoslavia. It declared in favour of the union of all Serbs, Croats and Slovenes as a single nation, under the Karageorgević dynasty: the new state was to be 'a constitutional, democratic and parliamentary monarchy', with equality for the two alphabets, the three national names and flags and the three religions, with manhood suffrage in parliament and in the municipalities. The details were left to a future constituent assembly, and, in particular, the Declaration of Corfu left open the question whether the state should be centralized or federal.

During the following winter, after the disaster of Caporetto, Italian statesmen were in a more chastened frame of mind, and long negotiations, at first of an entirely informal and non-committal kind, were conducted in London between representative Italians and the Yugoslav committee. On the basis of an agreement between them, subsequently known as the 'Pact of Rome', a 'Congress of the Oppressed Nationalities of Austria-Hungary' was held on 8 April 1918 at the Roman Capitol. Active propaganda was now started on the Austrian front, and this had a direct effect in blunting the point of the Austrian offensive on the Piave. The success of the congress influenced President Wilson, who, during the summer, revised that one of the Fourteen Points which recommended 'autonomy' for the subject races, and now insisted upon Yugoslav and Czecho-slovak unity as essential parts of his programme. Unhappily, increasing readiness of the allied governments to recognize the Yugoslav idea was counterbalanced by the jealous, narrowly pan-Serb attitude of the Serbian Premier Pašić, in the teeth of strong opposition from the Young Radicals, and when the war ended, agreement had still not been reached—with the result that the Italian government went back upon the Pact of Rome and demanded of the embarrassed allies the fulfilment of the Treaty of London.

THE BREAK-UP OF AUSTRIA-HUNGARY

Meanwhile, there were signs of the impending break-up of Austria-Hungary from within. A mutiny, staged by the strong Yugoslav element in the Austro-Hungarian fleet, occurred at Kotor in February 1918, and the following autumn there were plans for a rising along the whole coast. On land, 'Green Bands' of armed deserters were forming everywhere, and when Bulgaria surrendered on 29 September, the authority of Vienna and Budapest rapidly crumbled throughout the Southern Slav pro-vinces. When the news came that President Wilson made recognition of Yugoslav and Czechoslovak unity a condition of further negotiation with Austria-Hungary, there were extra-ordinary scenes in every town, soldiers tearing off their badges and the crowd pulling down Austrian inscriptions and flags. The National Council (*Narodno Vijeće*) under Mgr Korošec, strengthened itself by including representatives of all parties, and within a few days virtually became a provisional govern-ment for all the Southern Slav provinces of the monarchy. The emperor's twelfth-hour proclamation of federalism fell on deaf ears. On 29 October 1918 the Croatian Diet met, declared the Union with Hungary to be at an end, assumed control of Fiume, and handed over supreme authority in the new state to the National Council, which in its turn proclaimed the desire for union with Serbia and Montenegro without specifying further conditions. The proposal was carried with one dissentient vote,

163

but this unhappily was that of Stephen Radić, the peasant leader, who declared the masses of his people to be opposed to centralism and militarism, and 'for a Republic no less than for a national agreement with the Serbs'. On 1 December 1918 a delegation of Croats from Zagreb was received by the Prince Regent Alexander who proclaimed the establishment of 'The Kingdom of the Serbs, the Croats and the Slovenes'. In the meantime the Montenegrins had risen against the Austrian occupation, deposed King Nicholas and his dynasty, and declared for Montenegro's incorporation in Serbia.

The confusion of this initial period was increased by the fact that the delegates of the National Council in Zagreb reached Paris only to find a virtual rupture between Pašić and the Old Radicals on the one hand and the Yugoslav Committee, supported by the Young Radicals opposition (which had a paper majority in the *Skupština*) on the other hand. The leaders of the latter were actually threatening to start a Republican campaign, in the erroneous belief that the Crown Prince was a mere tool in the hands of Pašić. Under strong French pressure a conference was held at Geneva between the three groups, and on 9 November 1918 a declaration was signed, constituting the new Yugoslavia 'from today as an indivisible state-unit', the cabinet being composed of representatives of the two rival Serbian parties (Old and Young Radicals), of the Yugoslav Committee and of the Zagreb National Council. The governments of Belgrade and Zagreb were to retain their respective functions until a constituent assembly could meet and draft a new constitution for the whole country. But the Geneva decisions remained operative only on paper, centralizing tendencies rapidly asserted themselves, in view of the dangers threatening from all sides; for the Entente governments, under pressure from Italy, withheld their recognition from the newly united state. Thus did the various sections of the Yugoslav people rush into union, without any very clear idea of the lines on which it was to be worked out, and without any generally recognized bargain or contract.

COMPOSITION OF THE NEW STATE

The new Yugoslav state comprised a population of some 12 million people,[1] four-fifths of whom were supported by agriculture. There were only three towns—Belgrade, Zagreb, and Subotica—with populations of more than 100,000, and much of the national territory had been depopulated by the warfare which had afflicted the area almost continuously since 1912. The component parts of the new state were as follows:

1. The independent kingdom of Serbia.
2. The independent kingdom of Montenegro.
3. Croatia-Slavonia, hitherto possessing some measure of 'Home Rule' under Hungary.
4. Dalmatia, an Austrian province.
5. Carniola, part of Styria, a small corner of Carinthia and two small fragments of Istria—all these were former Austrian provinces.

[1] According to the census of 31 January 1921, the linguistic composition was as follows:

Serbo-Croats	8,911,509
Slovenes	1,019,997
Germans	505,790
Magyars	467,658
Albanians	439,657
Roumanians	231,068
Turks	150,322
Czechs and Slovaks	115,532
Ruthenes	25,615
Russians	20,568
Poles	14,764
Italians	12,553
Others	69,878
Total	11,984,911

The composition by religion was:

Orthodox	5,593,057
Roman Catholic	4,708,657
Greek Catholic (Uniate)	40,338
Moslem	1,345,271
Protestant	229,517
Jewish	64,746
Other religions	1,944
Without religion and unknown	1,381
Total	11,984,911

165

Fig. 32. The territorial formation of Yugoslavia. P, Prekomurje, and M, Medjumurje. C, Caribrod; B, Bosiljgrad; S, Strumica.

6. Baranja, Bačka, and the western portion of the Banat,
together with the districts of Prekomurje and Medjumurje—
all formerly integral parts of Hungary.

7. Bosnia and Hercegovina, formerly administered jointly by
Austria and Hungary.

The consolidation of the new kingdom was impeded by the
fact that the greater part of its frontiers remained unregulated
and involved disputes with neighbouring states. In each area,
one claim—ethnic, historic, economic, or strategic—had to be
balanced against another, and the result inevitably left dis-
satisfied minorities. The most serious disagreement arose over
the Italo-Yugoslav frontier, where the problem was complicated
by the promises made by the allies under the Treaty of London

166

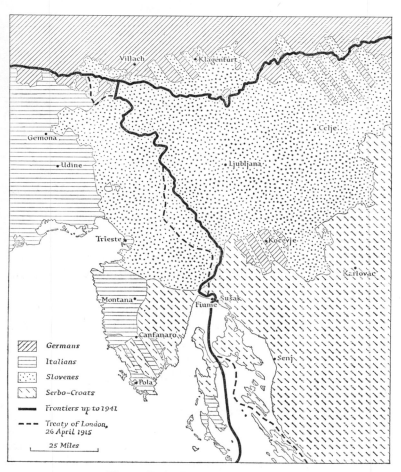

Fig. 33. Istria: languages and frontiers.

which were in contradiction to President Wilson's principle of national self-determination and the practice of open diplomacy. Matters were not made easier by d'Annunzio's seizure of Fiume, in which the allies tamely acquiesced. By the Treaty of Rapallo (12 November 1920) Italy finally received the whole of Istria, the watershed of the Julian Alps, together with Zara and the island of Lagosta. With the coming of Fascism, the

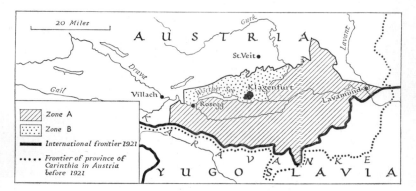

Fig. 34. The Klagenfurt plebiscite, 10 October 1920.

cultural, economic, and national life of the large Slovene and Croat minority left within the frontiers of Italy was ruthlessly suppressed.

In Austria, the Slovene German linguistic frontier lay across the provinces of Styria and Carinthia. In the latter, the political boundary was settled by a plebiscite in charge of an inter-allied commission at Klagenfurt. Voting took place on 10 October 1920, and resulted in a victory for Austria in Zone A (the most southerly zone). While 22,025 people voted in favour of Austria, only 15,279 voted for the new Slav kingdom; and some 10,000 Slovenes must have voted for Austria. In view of this fact, no voting was held in Zone B to the north, and the whole area passed to Austria (Fig. 34). The line of the Karawanke range remained the southern frontier of Austria. To the east, in Styria, the frontier drawn by the Peace Conference ran roughly along the linguistic line.

In the Vojvodina, the complexity of the racial groupings inevitably led to the inclusion of considerable numbers of Germans and Magyars within the Yugoslav state. A settlement with Albania also raised many difficulties and was not concluded until 1926, when nearly half a million Albanians, whose colonization of Kosovo, Metohija, and Novi Pazar had

168

Fig. 35. Albania and the Albanian minority in Yugoslavia, 1913–43.

been steadily encouraged under Turkey, were left on the Yugoslav side of the frontier. A few strategic rectifications of Yugoslavia's frontiers at the expense of Bulgaria were also approved.

CHAPTER 10

YUGOSLAVIA BETWEEN THE WARS

CENTRALISM VERSUS FEDERALISM

The Constituent Assembly, which was to draft a constitution for the new state, met at Belgrade in March 1919. From the first the crucial political issue was between Centralism and Federalism, the former being more in consonance with the dominant practice in the small pre-war Serbia, the latter with the diversified practice of the Habsburg monarchy. Unfortunately these two views tended to coincide with the narrowly pan-Serb and the Yugoslav outlook respectively.

The two chief parties were the Radicals (under Pašić and Protić), who had been really radical and even revolutionary in the eighties, but who were now essentially conservative, and the Democrats, a new party formed out of the union of the Serbian dissident Radicals, the old Serbo-Croat Coalition of Zagreb, and the Slovene Liberals. Both groups, however, were as yet too bourgeois in outlook for large sections of the peasantry, not only in Croatia and Bosnia, but also in Serbia itself; and there was keen competition between them over the vexed question of land reform and compensation for expropriated landlords. As no one party could obtain an absolute majority, a coalition government had to be formed, and it was under the auspices of that government that elections for a constituent assembly took place in November 1920. These, however, did not result in a majority for any party, and the unnatural alliance of Radicals and Democrats continued. It was at this stage that Radić, who had swept the boards in Croatia with a republican and federalist programme, adopted the fatal policy of abstention from Parliament. He thus not only facilitated Pašić's cynical tactics of buying the support of a number of weak and scattered groups (such as the Moslem landowners), but also enabled

Pašić to draft the new constitution on far more centralist lines than would have been possible if its critics had taken part in the debates.

In its final form the constitution of 1921—known as the Vidovdan constitution because the Prince Regent took the oath to it on St Vitus' Day, 28 June 1921—was not merely unacceptable to the great majority of Croats and Slovenes, but was also disapproved of by Trumbić and some Radicals, in particular by Protić.

The ceremony of Vidovdan was marred by an attempt on the life of the Prince Regent in Belgrade: and the Minister of the Interior was murdered a month later by a young Bosnian Communist. This provided the government with an excellent excuse for reprisals, and the *Skupština* (Parliament), by 190 to 54 votes, passed decrees for the defence of the state, which authorized the most drastic and elastic measures against terrorists. The fifty-eight Communist members were then removed, and henceforth the Communist party was forced to lead a clandestine existence.

PARTY RIVALRIES, 1919-29

Having thus rid himself of serious opposition, Pašić proceeded to strengthen his political position on a centralist and narrowly Serbian basis; and Radić played straight into his hands by refusing to form a coalition with the Democrats. This attitude on the part of the Croats produced a complete deadlock, and there was dangerous talk in many quarters of either resorting to dictatorship or treating the Croat Peasants as a subversive party and annulling their fifty mandates, on the analogy of the Communists. Neither the king nor Pašić was prepared to go so far, and indeed the latter's parliamentary majority depended on Radić's abstention. Radić on his part was mercurial and unreliable, trying to square the circle by erecting a 'pacific and humanitarian Croat Peasant Republic' inside the unitary monarchical Yugoslav state, and preaching political tenets which roused the masses but which were repugnant equally to the Radicals and Democrats. He also had ill-digested ideas of a Peasant 'Green International', but they suffered a serious blow from the overthrow and assassination of the Bulgarian Peasant leader Stambuliski in June 1923. That summer Radić escaped abroad and spent some months in London and Vienna denouncing the Pašić regime, but rendering it unassailable by his own abstentionist tactics.

During his voluntary exile the progressive forces began to form an opposition bloc of Democrats, Agrarians, Slovenes and Moslems, and in July 1924 Davidović became premier; the Croats showed less intransigence, but still boycotted the *Skupština*. But the new government's attempt to probe the question of political corruption and even indict guilty ministers, led to an ominous concentration of vested and conservative interests; Davidović was dismissed, and Pašić was again allowed to monopolize power, though when it came to fresh elections he obtained 300,000 votes less then the united Opposition. Pašić went so far as to dissolve the Croat Republican Peasant Party and to imprison Radić; but Radić, apparently realizing that he had the prospect of considerable Serb support if he abandoned his utter intransigence, yielded to the more moderate wing of his supporters and changed the name of the party to 'Croat Peasant Club'. This made possible the formation of a 'Bloc of National Agreement' with Democrats, Croat bourgeois, Slovenes and Moslems. Pavle Radić, Stephen's nephew, appeared in the *Skupština* to announce his party's acceptance of the existing constitution, its recognition of the dynasty, its 'desire to follow a positive policy, in the sense of working for the Croat nation', and its appreciation of the Serbian Army.

This obviously created a new situation, and ought to have made things easier. In reality, it made confusion worse confounded, for Pašić immediately released Radić from prison and made his own bargain with him, as a result of which the Croat Peasants seceded from the opposition bloc and formed a rival coalition with their Radical enemies. This involved Pašić throwing over his temporary ally, Svetozar Pribičević, the leader of the Independent Democrats (Serbs of Croatia), and Radić, on his side, leaving Trumbić and the Croat bourgeoisie in the air. The bitterness engendered by this unnatural alliance between the two strongest parties in the state was kept alive by Radić's constant turns and twists. Even the death of Pašić in December 1926 did not ease the situation. In 1927 Radić reverted to opposition, and when the Radical government secured a working majority at the elections of that year, Radić performed the last of his endless *volte-faces* by allying himself with his boyhood friend and his political enemy, Pribičević. This had very great importance for the future, as it meant a recognition on the latter's part that his centralist policy had been mistaken and that the *prečani*—people from the 'other side', beyond the river, i.e. from the former provinces of Austria-Hungary—must combine and hold together against the oppressive and often corrupt centralized regime in Belgrade. Much was at this time heard of the 'corruptionists'—but it is essential to point out that the keenest protests came from the liberal-minded Serbs, who were handicapped, not helped, by the Croat-Radical alliance—and again of the *Čaršija* clique (a Turkish nickname roughly equivalent to the 'Deux Cent Familles' of France) which pulled political strings in the background. This confused and kaleidoscopic period is the least edifying in Yugoslav history, and in itself utterly barren; yet the sequel can hardly be understood without some reference to it.

ECONOMIC PROGRESS, 1919–29

Economic progress had not been impaired by political strife within Yugoslavia. For example, a new railway line connecting Zagreb with Split had been completed in 1925, thus providing the Adriatic coast with direct communication to the hinterland. Agriculture, too, had shown a remarkable recovery from the effects of the war of 1914–18; harvests had been good, production had increased and the area under cultivation had been extended. In 1924, for the first time, exports exceeded imports and there was a favourable trade balance during the following two years.

The Yugoslav mercantile marine also showed signs of development; the Peace Treaties had restricted its number to 138 vessels, mostly small, but in 1926 this number was increased by one half. Again, the tourist industry prospered, and there was an increasing flow of visitors to the Dalmatian and Croatian coasts. There had been a financial crisis in 1922, with inflationary dangers, but the cautious policy of the government led to the stabilization of the dinar at about 275 to the pound sterling, and by the end of 1926 the repayment of the Yugoslav war debt, first to the U.S.A. and then to Great Britain, had given the state a more advantageous position to attract capital to her industries.

THE SKUPŠTINA MURDERS

During 1928 it was obvious to all students of the Yugoslav situation that the seething pot was about to boil over. On 20 June Puniša Račić, a Montenegrin deputy belonging to the Radical majority, fired his revolver in the *Skupština*, killed Pavle Radić and another Croat deputy, and mortally wounded Stephen Radić. The assassin was notoriously pan-Serb in outlook and was in touch with a 'revolver journal' named *Jedinstvo*, which was openly inciting to bloodshed and was known to have been subsidized by the premier, Vukičević. The king saved the situation for the moment by hastening to Radić's bedside; but nothing was done to conciliate the Croats, and Račić was treated with an ominous leniency.

Radić's successor as the Peasant leader, Dr Maček, declared that 'there is no longer a constitution, but only king and people'. This ambiguous phrase was interpreted to mean that the Crown should dissolve Parliament and deal direct with the Croats; and there were growing signs that King Alexander was tired of the scandals of the post-war regime, and was contemplating drastic measures. The crisis was no mere cabinet crisis, such as the country had experienced about twice a year for ten years. It was a crisis of the state. The country was divided into two camps, respectively centred at Belgrade and Zagreb. The division may be roughly described as one between Serbians and *prečani*; and the fundamental cause of the rift was the public administration by the more primitive Serbians, who were unequal to the task of running a state which had suddenly swollen to three times the size of the Serbia of 1914. But this simple antithesis was complicated by several minor factors. In the camp of Belgrade were to be found elements devoted to Serbia, such as most of the Bosnian Serbs and some of the Serbs of Croatia and the Vojvodina, and also more opportunist elements which saw advantages in adherence to the centre of power, such as the Slovenes and some of the Bosnian Moslems. On the other hand, the camp of Zagreb had its sympathizers in the barely articulate Macedonians and Albanians of southern Serbia and some of the Montenegrins. The motto of Belgrade was unity: one king, one state, one people; that of Zagreb was harmony: federalism, one king, but several states embodying distinct, but associated, peoples.

For six months, government was carried on by a coalition of the Belgrade parties under the premiership of Mgr Korošec, the Slovene leader, while at Zagreb the *prečani* opposition began to organize a counter-government of Croatia. In December the withdrawal of the Democratic party from the government put an end to this unsatisfactory state of affairs and Mgr Korošec's cabinet resigned. The parliamentary system had broken down. As the king said in an interview to the *Matin* (15 January 1929), 'The machine no longer works'. It was time for the Crown to step in. King Alexander was encouraged to do so by the attitude of Zagreb. *Obzor*, the intellectualist Zagreb newspaper declared that 'only the crown can end the crisis. We adopt the motto, "The People and the King".'

For what desperate remedies the situation called, in the king's estimation, is shown by his action in summoning Dr Maček and Dr Pribičević, and asking their views on the 'amputation' of Croatia and Slovenia from the state. He suggested the possibility of a friendly agreement to separate, as in the case of Norway and Sweden in 1905. His government might then withdraw its troops and officials to the east of a line which would leave to

Belgrade southern Dalmatia, Bosnia-Hercegovina and the Vojvodina. But the *prečani* leaders did not represent an alien minority only anxious to join another state; nor yet a population capable of forming a sovereign state. Left to themselves, the *prečani* would not only have had the problem of the Slovenes on their hands, but would have had to expect partition at the hands of Italy and Hungary. They had no desire to be excluded from Yugoslavia, a proposal which Dr Pribičević described to the king as 'high treason'. The king then asked for their programme, which they gave as federalism. This the king submitted to the leaders of the Serbian parties. Their unqualified refusal to amend the constitution brought the king's efforts at mediation to an end. On 6 January 1929 he declared the *Skupština* dissolved and the constitution of 1921 abolished. All authority was vested in the Crown.

THE ROYAL DICTATORSHIP

The dictatorship of King Alexander was unlike most of those established in Europe of recent years. It was supported by no organized party and it was announced to be merely a temporary expedient. The king was to be the trustee of the nation until such time as passions had subsided. In the meantime the worst abuses of the parliamentary regime were to be removed. 'Is not that dictatorship,' said King Alexander, 'when a party leader, who has not even a programme, decides of his sovereign power that this or that one of his friends shall be elected in a constituency, of whose first needs he is utterly ignorant? Or when that party leader gets a crowd of his followers nominated as officials, although they have no aptitude to recommend them except their support of that politician, who in return enables them to live at the expense of the country?' By the purification of public life, by directing the minds of his people away from party or regional or religious differences to a common patriotism, by the reform of the civil service and by its decentralization, King Alexander proposed to provide the conditions for true democracy. His proclamation of 6 January said, 'We shall have to seek new methods of work and tread new paths. I am sure that all, Serbs,

Croats and Slovenes, will loyally support my efforts, whose sole aim will be to establish as rapidly as possible such administration and organization of the state as will best conform with the general needs of the people and the interests of the state.'

The king's bold assumption of responsibility was on the whole well received at first. It was generally hoped that he would raise the standard of administrative efficiency, attack corruption and press forward with the unification of the six still surviving systems of law; while the *prečani* hoped at least for equal treatment with the Serbians as well as an equal share in the service of the state, and at most for a federal constitution which would ensure home rule to the clearly distinguishable portions of the country. Dr Maček himself expressed his relief that 'the waistcoat (the centralist constitution of 1921) was unbuttoned', and his hope that 'by the wisdom of the king the Croats would become free in their free Croatia'.

Further, the new regime enjoyed the advantage of national prosperity. While more industrialized countries were staggering under the onslaught of the financial crisis, Yugoslavia appeared to be an island of the blessed, still enjoying the material welfare of the nineteen-twenties. The years 1929 and 1930 were marked by excellent harvests; and, behind a stiff tariff wall and with machinery supplied by Germany on account of reparations, the young Yugoslav textile industry developed rapidly. People were not sorry to have a rest from politics.

The proclamation of the royal dictatorship was accompanied and succeeded by several decrees which made clear the character of the new regime. A law for the defence of the realm announced the penalties of death or twenty years imprisonment for those convicted of terrorism, sedition or the propagation of communism. All political parties of a regional or religious character were declared dissolved; and no associations were permitted unless approved by the government. All the elected municipal and departmental councils were dissolved. The law of the press was stiffened to provide in fact for the suppression of all liberty of the press. A law on the organization of the judiciary gave the

177

crown the power to remove judges, thus placing them at the mercy of the government. A 'Supreme Legislative Council', established on 18 February, had no powers of control, and was only used to give legal coherence to the government's decrees. At the head of the political system were the king and the Council of Ministers, who were responsible solely to him.

If these political laws established a strong, centralized auto-cracy, the composition of the ministry, with General Živković as premier, showed that the dictatorship was not really depart-ing from the policy of Serbian hegemony. The king had doubt-less made sincere efforts to form a ministry drawn from all his peoples. But the only Croats whom he could get were isolated intellectuals who could neither affect the policy of the govern-ment nor recommend it to their fellow-Croats. To the king, intent on the benefits of a unified patriotism, the Croats must have appeared unjustifiably obstinate and suspicious. To the Croats, intent on their national existence, the king was already showing signs of merely infusing a new efficiency into the Serbian hegemony which they hated.

Of the government's strenuous pursuit of efficiency there could be no doubt. In its first year it poured out a flood of legislation dealing with religious, legal and administrative affairs. Ordinary crime diminished considerably, and brigandage ap-pears to have virtually ceased. To deliver the peasantry from their dependence on usurious creditors, the Privileged Agrarian Bank was established in August with the duty of lending to farmers at 10 per cent or less, with easy terms of repayment and with a dividend of 6 per cent guaranteed by the state to the shareholders. Measures were also introduced for the inspection and standardizing of various crops, and for a permanent cam-paign against destructive pests. Finally, on 3 October, came the law reorganizing the administration. The 33 departments were swept away and the country was divided into nine large *banovine* and the prefecture of Belgrade. At the same time the official name of the state was changed from that 'of the Serbs, Croats and Slovenes', to Yugoslavia.

THE CROAT PROBLEM, 1929–31

One result of this determined effort at centralization was that early in 1929 some Croatian leaders fled the country. They were of two clearly distinguishable kinds. Pavelić and Perčec, who fled to Vienna and then to Bulgaria to establish contact with the Macedonian revolutionaries, were frankly separatists and terrorists, refusing all connexion with Serbia and prepared to accept money and assistance from Italy and Hungary in the years to come. Their supporters were few and drawn chiefly from the Croatian students and bourgeoisie. On the other hand, Ing. Košutić and Dr Krnjević were prominent officials of the Peasant Party. They set themselves to conduct a journalistic campaign from Geneva, and in the press of Britain, France and America, for Croatian autonomy, but countenanced no terrorism or co-operation with states hostile to Yugoslavia.

What chance of success the king's project of unification had it is difficult to estimate. His government certainly dealt severely with all expressions of particularism. The summer of 1929 saw the police prisons filled with alleged 'communists' or agents of foreign powers, and stories circulated about statements extracted by means of atrocious torture. But strenuous efforts were made to rally Croatian opinion to the support of the regime. These efforts, however, received a severe setback with the promulgation of the Sokol Law, on 4 December. This dissolved the Croatian, the Slovene and the specifically Catholic *sokols*, or physical training societies, which had been built up before 1914 by popular subscriptions, as well as the more official Serbian *sokol*, and established a single Yugoslav *sokol* under government control. This artificial imposition of unity was carried a step further, on 6 September 1930, when at a military parade Serbian regiments gave up their Serbian flags, so rich in military traditions, and received Yugoslav flags in exchange. There followed a royal order of 26 November providing that in future the military displays always held on Vidovdan, 28 June, the Serbian national day, should be transferred to 6 September.

The king thus showed his intention of merging Serbian, no less than Croatian, feeling in Yugoslav loyalty. But his doctrinaire insistence on a little-shared idea irritated far more than it gratified.

The year 1930, however, passed quietly, despite the trial of Dr Maček and twenty-three Croats, from 24 April to 14 June, for terrorism or its encouragement. The trial brought to light more police brutality, but the courts could still be trusted to administer the law, draconian as it was, and not to pronounce an arbitrary condemnation. Dr Maček and nearly half of the accused were acquitted, the remainder getting varying terms of imprisonment.

In the autumn, the city council of Zagreb offered the king a castle in the neighbourhood of Zagreb; and finally in January 1931 the king and queen paid a visit of ten days to Zagreb. The visit appears to have been a real personal success for King Alexander, whose courage, manliness and sincerity aroused the appreciation of all. He walked unattended in the streets and spoke with enthusiasm to the Croatian crowds of the solidity of their common fatherland. Circumstances that specially aroused the Yugoslav sympathies of the Croats and Slovenes at this time were the Italian government's execution of four Slovenes and the imprisonment of eleven others in connection with a bomb outrage at Trieste, and the stern repression of the Yugoslavs in Venezia Giulia.

By the winter of 1930–1, however, the regime was beginning to get into difficulties, and the Croat problem was still far from being solved. In May 1931, exiles at Geneva submitted to the League of Nations a memorandum on conditions in Croatia, which penetrated to Western public opinion. It contained a long list of persons imprisoned without trial, of the use of torture and of *agents provocateurs* by the police, and of alternative offers of office or prison made to prominent Croats.

THE CONSTITUTION OF 1931 AND THE
GROWTH OF OPPOSITION

Discontent was not confined to Croatia. Now too, the smoulder-
ing resentment of the Serbians at the disappearance of all the
liberties to which they were accustomed began to gather force,
and police action was directed against them also. Political discontent, however, might possibly have been overcome but for
the beginnings of the economic crisis which was soon to over-
whelm the whole state. To these difficulties, the rising irritation
amongst the Serbians, the necessity to increase foreign, especially French, confidence in Yugoslavia, the need of support for
the government's economic battle and the alarming example
of the Spanish revolution in April, may be attributed the king's
decision to revive parliament. This was done by the constitution
promulgated on 3 September 1931.

The constitution of 1931 left the power of the government
undiminished in fact, if not wholly so in law. It proclaimed an
impressive array of civil liberties, freedom from arrest, freedom
of expression, of assembly, of association; but in each case, the
liberty was 'within the limits of the law' and the law, as established under the dictatorship, remained in force, while all associations for political purposes or physical training on a religious,
regional or particularist basis, were expressly forbidden. Parliament was to consist of two houses, but ministers were to remain
solely responsible to the Crown. Security of tenure was promised
to judges, but postponed for five years.

The arguments for this constitution were that it provided the
first step towards democracy, while still ensuring national unity
by keeping the royal power intact and only permitting the
existence of nation-wide parties. Its Serbian critics rejected it
as a mere disguise for autocracy, and the *prečani* because they
saw in it only a continuation of the Serbianization of the
previous twelve years. With minor alterations, and subject to the
establishment of Croatian autonomy in 1939, the constitution of
1931 remained the public law of Yugoslavia until April 1941.

181

The elections held under the new constitution were widely boycotted, and the *skupština* returned consisted exclusively of government supporters. In April 1932 General Živković resigned and was succeeded as premier by Dr Marinković, who announced the formation of a new 'Yugoslav Peasant Radical Democratic Party', a fantastic title designed to borrow the mottoes of all the greater parties, and urged deputies diligently to organize the new party throughout the kingdom. But the venture met with little response, and the old Serbian parties began to re-emerge and to play the part of an opposition. They were at one with the *prečani* in demanding a neutral government of officials, truly free elections followed by parliamentary government, and decentralization; they differed only on the issue of federalism. In Belgrade, opposition manifested itself in student riots where cries of 'Down with the King; Cheers for the Republic' were heard. In Croatia, violent incidents involving Croat nationalists occurred. Even Slovenia was agitated, and in Maribor a 'Communist plot' was unearthed amongst the officers of the garrison, and the accused received sentences of death or of long imprisonment. Amidst these discontents, Dr Marinković was succeeded by Dr Srškić, a Bosnian Serb detestable to the Croats as a centralist and unpopular with the Serbians as a monarchist. A period followed during which the antagonism between rulers and ruled reached its height. Although the new premier promised a gradual return to democratic methods, he declared that the old parties would not be allowed to revive, and the censorship was once more strictly applied, though the inspired press was permitted to publish sinister threats against the Croat and other opposition leaders. In September there occurred a desperate rebellion of starving peasants in the Lika district of southern Croatia and in the Dalmatian hills. The rebels were armed with rifles smuggled in from the coast and, after it had taken the gendarmerie and troops some weeks to restore authority, the survivors fled to Zara (Zadar). The Italian hand in the matter was manifest, even if the resentment of destitute men against harsh government was the cause.

The winter of 1932–3 saw an intensification of opposition to the regime marked by the publication of a document known as the Zagreb Manifesto, which bore the signatures of ten of the best-known leaders of organized opinion not only in Croatia, but of the Serbs and Croats of Bosnia and the Vojvodina. In its five points, the manifesto outlined the essential conditions for political settlement within the kingdom: the application of the principle of popular sovereignty, the safeguarding of the peasantry, the removal of Serbian hegemony, a return to the *status quo* of 1918 and the reorganization of the state on the basis of an association of interests to safeguard the 'Serbian nation, the Croat nation and the Slovene nation'. There were many expressions of at least partial sympathy with the manifesto. Mgr Korošec claimed autonomy for the Slovenes. Likewise, twenty-eight leaders of all parties in the Vojvodina issued a statement demanding autonomy for their district, and the Moslem Organization claimed the same for Bosnia-Hercegovina, underlining the Zagreb assertion of popular sovereignty. The regime responded vigorously by interning Dr Maček and Mgr Korošec and imprisoning Dr Spaho, the Moslem leader, and others for a short period. But the regime was finding the basis of its support growing ever narrower. Even the Radical party protested against the imprisonments and demanded a general settlement by democratic methods.

Thus, after four years of existence, the dictatorship had succeeded in alienating all the organized parties in the country, while its own supporters were becoming increasingly divided into mutually hostile groups. At the same time, Yugoslavia's neighbours were giving assistance to the terrorist exiles, and waiting to make use of an expected Croat rebellion. Incidents were occurring on the Macedonian border, which were followed by the exchange of sharp notes between Belgrade and Sofia, while the escapade of the defacement of two Lions of St Mark, carved on the walls of Trogir, in Dalmatia, provoked a savage attack from Mussolini himself in the Italian Senate on 14 December 1932. Nevertheless, the king and his ministers persevered on their chosen path of repression. Trials of Croat leaders culminated on 24 April 1933 in that of Dr Maček, who was prosecuted for the Zagreb Manifesto of November and for seditious statements to foreign journalists. His condemnation to three years' imprisonment not only enraged Croatia but drew a united protest from all the Serbian parties against the 'persecution perpetrated by this un-national regime imposed on the people'. By this time probably nothing but the fear of Italian aggression prevented a rebellion in Croatia.

Except for the efforts of ministers to popularize the official party led by former Radicals and in July rechristened the 'Yugoslav National Party' (YNS), the summer of 1933 saw no change in the situation. All criticism was stifled by internments and imprisonments. Assassination became an everyday affair. King Alexander, however, could not be brought to realize that the many failures of the past decade were above all a consequence of the refusal to disentangle three entirely distinct problems: the trial of strength between Serb and Croat, which was also a struggle between centralist and regional ideas; the need for a return to constitutional government; and economic and social problems which had their roots in the national and constitutional issues and which were now being aggravated by the world depression. By 1933 it was already fairly obvious that the king had not solved any of the three; all that he had done was to establish a police regime, to entrench himself in the support of the High Command and to govern by rigorously excluding men of independent character. He had made a double miscalculation: he had hoped to break the passive resistance of the Croats and ended by making them more united than ever before; he had also hoped to strengthen the Serb element in the state and to ensure its predominance, yet in actual fact he hastened the real disintegration of Serbian party life to an extent for which there was no precedent.

THE ECONOMIC CRISIS, 1931–3

Economic conditions in Yugoslavia began to deteriorate in 1931. During the first six months of that year, exports and imports fell by 25 per cent. The trade balance for the same period showed a deficit of over 265 million dinars. A loan arranged in May at Paris of 1,025 million francs at 7 per cent was used to stabilize the dinar. But matters became rapidly worse. The National Bank's foreign credits became exhausted and a series of temporary expedients was adopted. In August came the cessation of German reparation payments, which meant a loss of 700 million dinars a year, entailing the necessity of severe cuts in administrative salaries and pensions and an increase in taxation. The collapse of the prices of agricultural products now hit the country severely, and in June the government in desperation undertook to buy up the whole wheat harvest at about 60 per cent above the world price, an arrangement that greatly added to the country's financial embarrassments.

The full force of the economic catastrophe came in 1932, at a time when political unrest was at its stormiest stage. The first serious blow had been a run on the banks in September 1931, which followed the British government's repudiation of the Gold Standard. Just when the banks most needed credit, the National Bank found it necessary to deny them such facilities, and the banks were only given moratoria on condition that they came under government control. Then the government's grain monopoly, intended to protect the peasants against the collapse of cereal prices, worked disastrously. The government agents were unable to store all the quantities of wheat received, much of which was consequently ruined. On the other hand, many of the peasants were paid in bonds, which were not available for the payment of taxes. The whole scheme was dropped early in 1932, at a loss of over 400 million dinars to the taxpayers. Other disasters took place. The winter was exceptionally severe and was followed by extensive floods. Some 30,000 persons were homeless. The scarcity of fodder resulted in the slaughtering of a quarter of the country's cattle, which made the export of stock impossible. Something had to be done for the peasants, bewildered by the collapse of their whole economy, exasperated against the urban *gospoda* (gentry) who ruled and exploited them, and unable to repay the debts which, especially in the Serbian districts, they had contracted in the carefree years of prosperity.

In March the government announced a moratorium of six months for peasant debts. This expedient was also followed by unhappy consequences. The peasants found themselves unable to obtain any credit at the time of year when they most needed it and were accustomed to having it. Their creditors had less prospect than ever of recovering their debts. The peasants were unable to buy anything. Retailers were unable to pay wholesalers, who, in turn, could not pay manufacturers and importers. The number of bankruptcies and compulsory settlements in 1932 was more than three times as great as that in 1930. There was even an outcry for a general moratorium on all debts. Nevertheless in October the government continued the suspension of peasant debts indefinitely, and it lasted till 23 November 1933.

Meanwhile export trade had been falling heavily; the National Bank's supply of foreign exchange ran short; exchange control was introduced with increasing severity, till in March it was made illegal for money to leave the country. Foreign trade was in consequence almost paralysed. To meet the desperate situation the government began to negotiate for clearing agreements with most of the European countries. In June the Commercial Secretary at the British Legation reported, 'it seems likely that when any form of trade revival appears there will be a great re-orientation, due not only to changes in international relationships but to the fact that old business connexions have been severed and old sources of credit cut off during this period of currency control'. His prediction was indeed fulfilled.

FOREIGN AFFAIRS, 1933–4

Amid these disasters the country experienced a relaxation of interest in public affairs, the problem of the next meal being uppermost in most men's minds, though bitterness against the government was prevalent in all districts. At the same time Yugoslavia's international position was deteriorating. The victory of the Left in the French elections of May 1932 meant that France would withdraw from her position of paymaster to Yugoslavia. As *La Volonté* interpreted the situation, 'France has voted against the policy of the European status quo which inevitably entails conflict. She has realized that the policy of alliances with a view to encircling Germany is no longer practicable, and that the burden of armaments, incompatible with a minimum of prosperity, does not even assure security.' The Yugoslav government soon felt the truth of these words, for in July Yugoslavia failed to obtain the fresh loan of which the regime was in pressing need and only secured a moratorium of one year for the payments due on previous loans. On the worst of terms with her neighbours, Italy, Hungary and Bulgaria, and with her French patron alienated and preoccupied, Yugoslavia was in a position that justified anxiety.

In this period of political violence and economic depression at home, the importance of foreign affairs became more urgent. Here the king inaugurated policies which rapidly produced satisfactory results. In September 1933 King Boris of Bulgaria was passing through Yugoslavia on his way home. At King Alexander's suggestion, the two monarchs met informally in Belgrade station and the foundation was laid for a mutual friendship, which in 1934 led to a Yugoslav-Bulgarian *rapprochement*, a more conciliatory regime in Serbian Macedonia, the suppression of the Internal Revolutionary Organization in Bulgaria, and finally, in 1937, to the pact of eternal friendship between the two states. Immediately after that interview, the king made a tour of Roumania, Bulgaria, Turkey and Greece, which was a prelude to the inauguration, on 9 February 1934, of the Balkan Entente, in which it was not his fault that Bulgaria was not included. The king was doing his best to find security by linking the Little Entente (Yugoslavia, Roumania and Czechoslovakia) and the Balkan States. Danger was apprehended from Italy and from a revived union, whether Habsburg or Italian, of Austria and Hungary.

The challenge of Germany to the established order was veiled by the friendly attitude of the Nazi government towards Yugoslavia, as shown by General Göring's visits to Belgrade and by the German-Yugoslav treaty of commerce in May 1934, which facilitated the diversion of German tourists from Austria to the holiday resorts of the Yugoslav coast. Nevertheless, the visit of M. Barthou to the Little Entente Conference and to Belgrade in June gave the government an opportunity of making the most emphatic declarations that they would resist the slightest revision of the *status quo*. Strained relations with Hungary developed into an open dispute before the Council of the League of Nations in June 1934, when the Hungarian representative complained of the difficulties caused by the severity of the Yugoslav frontier control, and the Yugoslav reply, with a wealth of corroborative evidence, accused Hungary of training terrorists and assisting them in their attacks on the Yugoslav government.

Early in October 1934 King Alexander left by sea for an official visit to Paris; after landing at Marseilles, on 9 October, he was assassinated by agents of Pavelić, the exiled leader of the Croat separatists, while driving through the streets; M. Barthou was at the same time mortally wounded. It is no secret that the king intended to carry a stage further the discussions and plans for Balkan consolidation in view of the disturbing developments in Central Europe. But it is less known that he had latterly reached the conclusion that the dictatorship was a failure, and was firmly resolved on his return to revert to constitutional government. The outburst of grief and rage throughout Yugoslavia was a sure sign that his people, an overwhelming majority of whom disapproved of the dictatorship and desired a return to democracy, none the less recognized that in the eyes of the enemy he was a symbol of unity and independence and had been removed for that reason. Popular legend at once constructed the tale that with his last breath he gasped, 'Protect Yugoslavia for me'. Convinced that federalism would mean disruption, he had believed that only the use of force could serve the unity of the state. At his death Alexander left the country torn by dissension and distrust, with more party differences even than under the parliamentary system, the ills of which he had set out to cure.

ESTABLISHMENT OF THE REGENCY, 1934

It was to a country overshadowed by economic distress as well as by political bitterness that the young King Peter II was brought from his preparatory school in Surrey. King Alexander had left a will appointing a triple Regency consisting of his cousin Prince Paul, Dr Stanković (a distinguished Serbian specialist and Professor of Medicine at Belgrade University), and Dr Perović (a Serb official, for a time Ban of the Coastal *banovina*). Since the latter two were little known as public figures it was upon Prince Paul that the mantle of authority had been conferred; and hopes were aroused that he would inaugurate a return to constitutional government. Early in November he received a memorandum from 250 leading Croatian ecclesiastics, ex-ministers, bankers, writers and artists, urging a general amnesty, especially for Dr Maček, free elections and the appointment to high office of men respected for their characters and abilities. This appeal was strikingly supported by a similar memorandum from fifty of the most eminent Serbian intellectuals. But Prince Paul walked warily, knowing that he was distrusted by many Serbians as a 'foreigner' educated in Russia and at Oxford. He interviewed leaders of parties likely to accept the existing constitution, especially the Radicals, who had already applied for registration as a party. But he retained the Uzunović cabinet appointed by King Alexander in January 1934. Meanwhile the foreign minister, M. Jevtić, was engaged at Geneva on the difficult task of branding Hungary with complicity in the murder of the late king, without recourse to war, without loss of national dignity and without stimulating the anger which was felt in the country and the government. The memorandum which the Yugoslav government presented to the League and then published to the world at large was a formidable indictment of Hungary, the more so as it was now known that for many months past Belgrade had made representations to Budapest regarding the terrorist activities conducted from Janka Puszta, and that among the persons of whom it had complained by name were some of those now implicated in the Marseilles crime. Yet nothing had been done to fulfil the undertakings of Budapest to suppress terrorism on Hungarian soil.

The discussions of the League of Nations, however, ended in only a qualified condemnation of Hungary. Nevertheless, M. Jevtić was made prime minister, with a cabinet containing no prominent politicians except General Živković and one of the younger Radicals, M. Stojadinović, a financial expert.

THE ELECTIONS OF MAY 1935

The new government made the conciliatory gesture of releasing Dr Maček and Professor D. Jovanović, the Serbian Peasant Party leader, from prison, and the censorship was relaxed, but the premier announced that the existing constitution, which was designed to prohibit opposition parties, would be upheld. In February 1935 the *Skupština* was dissolved and elections announced for 5 May. It was the first electoral contest to be held for eight years, and it was anything but free. The opposition was prevented from holding meetings or publishing appeals, the press only permitted to print official announcements and speeches. Several of the opposition leaders were temporarily interned. The voters were subjected to the most open intimidation and violence, and state employees received instructions such as those issued by the Ban of the Coastal *banovina* (*Primorska*) to his subordinates on 20 March: 'This (the official) list must have a majority, and every official who does not vote for it will be held responsible and punished without mercy.'

The first published results of the elections—Government 1,738,000, Opposition 983,000—were so vigorously challenged that they were revised to show Government 1,746,982, Opposition 1,076,346. When allowance was made for all the voters whose livelihood depended on their support of the government, as well as for the abstention of the Radicals (the 'grand old

Serbian party') and the Slovenes, and for the official tampering with the figures which was assumed as a matter of course, the elections amounted to a moral victory for the opposition. The electoral method, however, attributed 301 seats to the government and only 67 to its opponents.

These scandalous elections were quickly followed by dramatic consequences. The deputies of the opposition bloc boycotted the *Skupština* and met in a counter-parliament at Zagreb. The aged Catholic Archbishop of Zagreb requested an audience of Prince Paul, and laid before him a statement of the grosser outrages committed during the elections in his diocese. The three Croat ministers resigned and were quickly followed by General Živković and M. Stojadinović. The prince regent then took the bold step of inviting the Croat leader to visit him. Dr Maček drove in a royal car from Belgrade station to the palace, cheered by the Belgrade crowd. After his interview with Prince Paul, he spent the evening with the Serbian Democratic and Agrarian leaders and reached agreement about their common aims. He accepted the Dynasty, the common Army and Foreign Office, but insisted on a democratic basis for both the state and its federation, and suggested the formation of a neutral ministry to govern till the autumn during the negotiations for the revision of the constitution.

The result of these promising events was that on 23 June the regents invited Dr Milan Stojadinović to form a cabinet. The new government was accepted as one of appeasement and reconstruction, and it included Dr Spaho, the Moslem leader, and the Slovene leader, Mgr Korošec. On the other hand, except for the war minister, General Živković, who was believed to favour conciliation of the Croats, there was a clean sweep of the figures connected with the dictatorship. The rest of the cabinet consisted of new men, either Radicals or Croatian non-political experts. Most of Dr Jevtić's three hundred deputies submissively transferred their support overnight to the new premier.

PROBLEMS OF FEDERALISM

Dr Stojadinović proceeded cautiously. He relaxed the censorship and spoke approvingly of the American two-party system, a change from the totalitarian attitude of his predecessors. But he was in no hurry to reach a settlement with Zagreb. His immediate aims seem to have been to give the regime that organized popular support which it had hitherto lacked, and to prevent the consolidation of a united *prečani* front. In August 1935 he announced the formation of a new government party, the JRZ (Yugoslav Radical Union) composed of Radicals, Slovenes and Moslems. He thus proposed to unite the strongest Serbian party with two special interests from the new provinces. The party's policy was described as including democratic government and a wide measure of autonomy. The promises seemed fair, and were welcomed by the opposition in Belgrade and Zagreb with the proviso that the government would be judged by its deeds rather than by its words. In July a Concordat with the Holy See, which the late king had ardently desired, had been signed and it was hoped that relations with the Catholic Church would now be untroubled. Much satisfaction was caused on 1 December by a generous amnesty for political offences, which affected some 10,000 persons.

The government, however, gave no sign of an early return to true parliamentarism. Whether on that account (as was stated) or on account of personal jealousy at the promotion of a young colleague to the highest office, the committee of the Radical party announced on 31 March 1936 that they had decided to join the opposition. The Serbian foundation was thus removed from Dr Stojadinović's JRZ, which was left consisting only of the Slovenes, the Moslems and the premier's official adherents. It was not clear whether the government was gradually liquidating the dictatorship by comparatively mild administration of the law or merely camouflaging, with phrases and gestures, the re-entrenchment of the army and a sprinkling of ex-Radicals in absolute power.

All shades of opinion were agreed that a solution of the Croat question must be found, and that quickly, before an explosion could take place in Europe, when the Croats might rebel and Yugoslavia be dismembered. Prince Paul had a long and cordial conversation with Dr Maček in December 1936, and they appear to have agreed on the necessity of federalism, though differing on methods of procedure.

The outlines of a possible federal solution were beginning to take shape. The Dynasty, the common Army and Foreign Office were already accepted by Dr Maček. He was now prepared to leave to the central government at least state finance, commerce, posts and telegraphs, and customs. The number and extent of the proposed federalized units were thornier problems. There were eight possible units which could claim autonomy on historic, linguistic or racial grounds—Serbia, Montenegro, Macedonia, Croatia-Slavonia, Dalmatia, Bosnia-Hercegovina, Vojvodina and Slovenia. About Slovenia, there was no dispute. The existing *banovina* of the Drava contained hardly any Yugoslavs except the Slovenes, and their title to autonomy was accepted by all who would discuss federalism at all. But the Serbians were vigorous in declaring that Macedonia and Montenegro must be included in the Serbian unit. To which the reply of the *prečani* was that in that case the former Habsburg provinces, except Slovenia, must be theirs. That Dalmatia should be joined to Croatia-Slavonia was agreed, the only doubtful area being the extreme east of Slavonia, Srem, which was rather to be reckoned as a part of the Vojvodina.

This left the two difficult problems of Bosnia-Hercegovina and the Vojvodina. In the former, the Croat minority would prefer attribution to Croatia, the much larger Serb element would vote for union with Serbia, and the Moslems would desire autonomy. The Croats, if faced with the alternative of Serbia or autonomy, would choose the latter and so give the Moslems a majority, while the Moslems, if refused autonomy, would prefer Croatia to Serbia. Any scheme of partition by which only the solidly Serb eastern border of Bosnia-Hercegovina would be merged in Serbia was resented by the Serbians, who pointed out that the number of Serbs then left in Croatia would be vastly greater than that of the Croats in Serbia. This difficulty applied with equal force to the Vojvodina, which the Serbians claimed on the grounds that the Serbs were the largest single element in the population, that in the past the Vojvodina had been the cultural centre of Serbism and that it was geographically and economically tied to Belgrade.

THE CONCORDAT, 1937

The summer of 1937 had been marked by a curious outburst of popular feeling in Belgrade and Serbia. In July a bill, embodying the terms of the Concordat, negotiated by the Jevtić government in 1935 and largely the work of King Alexander himself, was laid before the *Skupština*. The bill was carried, amid an uproar inside and outside the *Skupština*, on 23 July by 167 votes to 127. The Synod of the Orthodox Church duly excommunicated all the Orthodox ministers (except General Marić, since that might have alienated the army) and the deputies who had voted for the bill. The JRZ ejected those of its members who had not voted for the bill. Eventually in October Dr Stojadinović capitulated and announced that the bill would not be sent on to the Senate (where he was not sure of a majority). The excommunications were lifted in February 1938, and the assembly for the election of the new patriarch, in which Orthodox ministers had a legal right to vote, was summoned for 24 February. Thus the project of a Concordat was indefinitely shelved and the Roman Catholic Church remained the only considerable religious body whose relations with the state were unregulated.

The whole episode was a remarkable illustration of the character of Serb Orthodoxy. The cry of 'No Popery' was perhaps the one expedient by means of which Serbian chauvinists could arouse serious opposition to the government in Serbia. The Orthodox Church in Yugoslavia is revered by the Serb peasants as the beloved and historic expression of their nationality. The Serbian bourgeoisie, accustomed to ignore their own nominal religion, were irritated to find their government coming to terms with their bugbear, the Catholic Church, which insisted on spiritual independence and ecclesiastical discipline and whose head was not amenable to secular control. Dr Maček and the Croats ignored the whole affair, whether from a desire not to see Serbo-Croat relations embittered by a religious issue or from a suspicion that the Concordat was a bribe to detach the Catholic hierarchy from support of Croatian claims.

FOREIGN RELATIONS, 1934–8

The most striking feature of Yugoslav trade in the period after the disastrous year of 1932 had been the rapid development of commercial relations with Germany. The German economic penetration had begun, after 1919, with the deliveries of machinery and technical equipment on account of reparations. German firms followed up these deliveries by supplying the demand for renewals and adapting their goods to suit Yugoslav requirements. German manufacturers thus became well established in the Yugoslav market. After the commercial treaty of 1934 Yugoslav raw materials began to be exported to Germany in rapidly increasing quantities, a process accelerated by the cessation of Yugoslav trade with Italy in 1935–6. In March 1936 Germany granted new preferential rates and quotas, to the value of 450 million dinars, in respect of Yugoslav exports of cattle, pigs and wheat; while the Yugoslav government placed considerable contracts for rolling stock, machinery and bridging material in Germany. In June 1936 Dr Schacht visited Belgrade to propose a great increase in trade by barter, and as Germany offered to take Yugoslav raw materials at prices well above world parity it was not surprising that she obtained them. At last the unfortunate Yugoslav peasant was finding a sure market for his produce, although a large part of the price failed to reach the actual producer.

The bonds of goodwill between Germany and Yugoslavia thus became proportionately stronger and the resistance of the Yugoslav government to a possible German annexation of

Austria correspondingly weaker. In the autumn came a further sign of Yugoslavia's changing international position. In his speech at Milan in November, Mussolini referred to 'the extraordinary improvement of atmosphere' between Italy and Yugoslavia and stated that there 'now exist the necessary moral, political and economic bases' for friendship. The Yugoslav premier alluded several times in speeches, early in 1937, to the continued improvement of relations with Italy, and finally Count Ciano visited Belgrade and signed a treaty of friendship on 25 March 1937. Moreover, in the meanwhile, on 24 January, a pact of 'eternal and indissoluble' friendship between Yugoslavia and Bulgaria had been signed. In itself this was all to the good. It was a further step on the path of Yugoslav-Bulgarian amity and was enthusiastically received in the country. But there were those who felt alarm at the successive departures from the policy of reliance on France and the Little Entente (Yugoslavia, Roumania and Czechoslovakia); and in April 1937 the leaders of the Serbian parties united to protest in that sense. Dr Stojadinović was able to reply that the links with Yugoslavia's old friends were as strong as ever, but that he had succeeded in converting old enemies also into friends. In other words, and in view of the heightened tension in Europe, the premier was ensuring his country's safety by conciliating all parties who might affect her position.

Behind these arguments were the growing strength of the anti-democratic powers of the Axis and the good relations of the premier with them, as well as the prosperity brought by German trade. In due course, therefore, the German conquest of Austria was taken calmly by official circles and the Belgrade press; and this attitude was defended by Dr Stojadinović in the Senate on 16 March 1938, on the grounds of German official declarations that the new German-Yugoslav frontier was henceforth inviolable and of his information that the Czechoslovak government were satisfied with the similar German declarations concerning their frontiers.

TOWARDS A SERBO-CROAT AGREEMENT

By the end of 1938, a common dissatisfaction with the Government's pro-Axis and dictatorial policies had drawn the Croatian Peasant Party and the opposition parties in Serbia closer together. But the surrender of the western powers at Munich in September 1938 confirmed Stojadinvović in his conviction that he was backing the right horse, and that the time was ripe for him to seek a renewal of his mandate from the electorate. But the official results of the elections which were held the following December showed only 1,643,783 votes cast for his party against 1,364,524 for the Opposition, compared with 1,746,982 for the government and 1,076,346 for the opposition in 1935. The complex electoral law gave the Government 306 seats and the opposition 67; but the facts remained that the opposition had considerably increased its votes and come within a reasonable distance of defeating the official lists.

As Dr Stojadinović seemed determined to continue his regime of the 'strong hand', five ministers—M. Cvetković (a Serbian), two Moslems and two Slovenes—seized the opportunity to resign when a fellow-minister, on 3 February 1939, made a Serbian chauvinist speech with derogatory references to the *prečani*. Thereupon Dr Stojadinović presented the resignation of his cabinet, which was promptly accepted. Thus the supposedly indispensable strong man disappeared from the scene. It subsequently transpired that immediately after the elections in December Prince Paul had conducted confidential negotiations with Dr Maček and had been assured that the Croats utterly distrusted Dr Stojadinović. The prince now installed M. Cvetković in power with a mandate to achieve a settlement with the Croats.

The new government, like its predecessor, was drawn from the official JRZ and contained no outstanding political figures except the premier and the Moslem leader, Dr Spaho. This time determination to reach a settlement of the Croat question was sincere. Hitler's seizure of Prague in March 1939—which

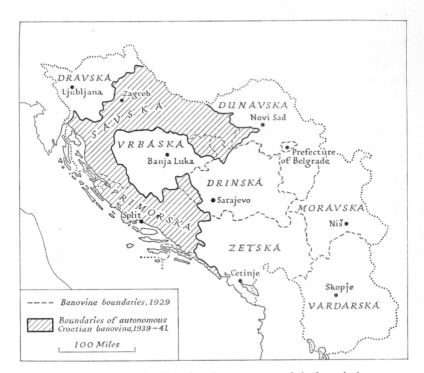

Fig. 36. The boundaries of the *banovine*, 1929–41, and the boundaries of the autonomous *banovina* of Croatia, 1939–41.

evoked such consternation and rage as to show beyond all doubt the sentiments of the whole nation towards both Germans and Czechs—was like the writing on the wall, warning Prince Paul and his rather colourless team of politicians to agree with the Croats while there was yet time, for the extreme nationalists were becoming more and more aggressive and made little secret of their connection with Pavelić and the other separatists in exile.

For over six months, highly confidential negotiations were conducted between Prince Paul and Dr Maček, and it was not till late in August that all difficulties were overcome. Maček had originally demanded that all the lands of the former monarchy should form a single autonomous unit, that the constitution of

198

1931 should be abolished forthwith, and that a coalition government should then steer a new constitution through a constituent assembly. He eventually agreed to the creation of three *banovine* in the first instance—a Serbian, a Croatian and a Slovene respectively—subject to two modifications, that the southernmost tip of Dalmatia around Kotor, and the easternmost district of Slavonia, known as Srem (Syrmia), should be assigned to Serbia, and portions of Bosnia and Western Hercegovina added to Croatia. These three provinces would be run on federal lines, and Maček, who would have preferred to add two more federal units—the Vojvodina and Bosnia-Hercegovina—insisted on leaving open the possibility of some particular district later voting itself into, or out of, one or other federal unit. All of these proposals, however, came to nothing.

By this time it was abundantly clear that Prince Paul, who all along had tried to keep the two questions, national and constitutional, strictly apart, and to solve the former without yielding on the latter, was now bent upon separating the Croats from their allies of the Serbian opposition. The regent undoubtedly feared that Hitler and Mussolini might make trouble if Yugoslavia adopted a frankly democratic settlement of her internal problems, though the endless demonstrations in favour of the Czechs were unmistakable signs of what the country was feeling, and how utterly out of sympathy it was with the hedging policy of the Regent.

The *Sporazum* (Agreement) of 26 August 1939 was in the end concluded in such a way as to give no little offence to the Serbian opposition and to postpone the constitutional issue, as Prince Paul had wished. Dr Maček was reproached in many quarters for not having insisted on the inclusion of his allies of the three parties in any joint action. In actual fact he only yielded to the direct appeal of the first regent, recognizing that a European war was imminent and that to leave the Croat question still unregulated would have been to play into the hands of the separatists.

The *Sporazum* provided for the creation of a new *banovina* which was to be known as 'Croatia'. It comprised a population of 4,400,000 out of a total of 14,000,000: of these 164,000 were Moslems and 866,000 Serbs, the Croats forming 74 per cent of those inside the new boundaries. The office of Ban was restored to its historic importance, and the *Sabor* or Diet of Zagreb was revived for specific purposes—foreign affairs, defence, commerce, transport and public security being reserved for the central government. The legislative power was to be shared by *Sabor* and Crown, and the Ban was to be appointed and dismissed by the latter. At the same time the existing artificial *Skupština* was dissolved, and the government was authorized to prepare a new electoral law, and laws on the press, and rights of association and assembly.

The new government formed on this basis was a coalition, under Cvetković as premier, with Maček as vice-premier and Cincar-Marković as foreign minister. Maček, and his nominee for the Banship, Dr Šubašić, who enjoyed the prince's confidence, lost no time in setting the new autonomy in motion, with its centre at Zagreb. There was a political amnesty, and the Zagreb press became so out-spoken, not to say indiscreet, as to become the envy of the still much-censored press of Belgrade. The dominant note of the new regime in Croatia was that 'the peasant wants to be, and will be, the chief factor in his fatherland'. But there was much unrest below the surface, and a crop of outrages in Zagreb itself prompted Maček to issue a manifesto denouncing these anarchic tendencies as unchristian and as endangering the national future. This was an unmistakable hit at the separatists, who now looked to Hitler for the achievement of a mock-independent status for Croatia. The *Sporazum* undoubtedly produced some measure of agreement, but the opportunity for a real political settlement had been missed.

PRINCE PAUL AND THE AXIS, 1940

In February 1940 the four foreign ministers of the Balkan Entente (Yugoslavia, Greece, Turkey and Roumania) conferred in Belgrade and issued grandiloquent pronouncements calculated to cover up the painful fact that the Balkan Entente had come to an abrupt end. Cincar-Marković quite gratuitously argued that the Balkans were not threatened from any side, and paid compliments varying in warmth to Italy, Bulgaria and Hungary—to the first especially for 'her wise attitude of non-belligerency'. Though this Balkan window-dressing deceived no one, there can be no doubt that Yugoslav-Bulgarian relations showed a steady upward tendency. Another sign of the times was the restoration of trade relations between Belgrade and Moscow, after an interruption of twenty years (Yugoslavia having been the most intransigent of all European states towards Soviet Russia), and the marked satisfaction publicly displayed by the Bulgarian foreign minister at this step on the part of the neighbouring state. The intense alarm at the long series of Germany's aggressive acts and the sense of insecurity generated by the loss of the Skoda armament works as a source of military supply and by the inability of the Western Powers to make good even one per cent of the deficiency, help to explain the current of Russophil opinion which now spread through Serbia and Croatia, and led to the dispatch of first a trade, then a military, delegation to Moscow. The restoration of diplomatic relations followed logically. On the other hand, M. Stojadinović was interned by the government in the remote mountain village of Rudnik.

The fall of France in June 1940 and the September *Blitzkrieg* against Britain caused almost universal dismay in Yugoslavia; and though the way in which Britain rallied round Mr Churchill caused corresponding jubilation in all sections of the Yugoslav nation, it was realized that Britain would not in the near future be in a position to send practical help to her friends in the Balkans, and there were therefore a few opportunists in high quarters who favoured a 'realist acceptance of hard facts'—a euphemism for coming to terms with the Axis. While the first German troops began to arrive in Roumania, ostensibly as 'instructors', and while Berlin scarcely deigned to conceal its plans, Belgrade made a great show of neutrality, but talked very categorically of resistance to aggression from whatever quarter, and of the impossibility of permitting the transit of foreign troops across Yugoslav soil. Italy's treacherous attack upon Greece still further incensed Yugoslav opinion against the Axis, and the Yugoslav General Staff, encouraged by the success of Greek resistance, was inclined to join hands for the defence of Salonica against Italy. Berlin privately encouraged Belgrade to take possession of Salonica while the Greeks were occupied elsewhere, but the trap was altogether too obvious.

On 6 November General Milan Nedić was replaced as war minister by General Pešić, a distinguished officer of the previous war, who had latterly made several doubtful incursions into politics and diplomacy, but who seemed best qualified for a Pétainist role. This occurred only a few days after Italian planes had twice dropped bombs on Bitolj—as a sort of reprisal, it was alleged, for the Yugoslav refusal to allow Italy to outflank the Greek right wing by crossing Yugoslav territory. This gave rise to two entirely contradictory versions of Nedić's departure— on the one hand that he was dismissed as anti-German, and on the other that he had submitted a memorandum urging agreement with the Axis and had resented its rejection. The latter is now known to have been nearer the facts. Already those in authority in Yugoslavia were reduced to a policy of anxious negotiation, clinging to neutrality and playing for time, but utterly at a loss where to rearm or to find allies.

At this early stage of the Balkan tragedy the Turks were specially alarmed and annoyed at King Boris's visit to Berchtesgaden, and warned Sofia that they would not remain inactive in the event of a Bulgarian attack on Greece. They saw the Balkan Entente dissolving before their very eyes, and proposed to Belgrade an immediate Turco-Yugoslav military convention. This was not merely refused by Prince Paul, but carefully concealed from all Yugoslav statesmen, save the pliable Cvetković and Cincar-Marković. Another feature of Prince Paul's balancing policy in these final months of crisis was his cordial response to overtures from Budapest, almost certainly made under prompting from Berlin and Rome. The 'pact of lasting peace and eternal friendship' signed by Hungary at Belgrade on 12 December was received without enthusiasm by a public which had in no way forgotten the fate of Czechoslovakia.

GERMAN INTIMIDATION

It was early in 1941 that Yugoslavia showed the first open leanings towards the Axis. On 15 February Cvetković and Cincar-Marković were summoned to meet Ribbentrop at Salzburg, and to the Führer's mountain eyrie at Berchtesgaden. At this meeting Cincar-Marković appears to have assured Hitler that Yugoslavia had done all in her power to prevent Greece from accepting British help, and was now ready to give him a guarantee that she would not become an instrument of British policy against the Reich. Hitler thereupon suggested as a fitting achievement of Yugoslav policy the adhesion of the three still neutral Balkan powers—Yugoslavia, Bulgaria and Turkey—to the tripartite pact between Germany, Italy and Japan; otherwise he made no specific demands and was full of soft phrases, stressing his eagerness to see Yugoslavia take her rightful place among the powers of south-eastern Europe.

Prince Paul was now in the toils. At the very moment when Cincar-Marković was absent on a brief return visit to Budapest for the purpose of ratifying the new Hungaro-Yugoslav pact, Bulgaria took the final plunge; and on 1 March her premier, Filov, flew to Vienna to sign Bulgaria's adherence—a step which was at once followed by the entry of German troops into Bulgaria. Prince Paul, too, visited Berchtesgaden in dire secrecy on 3 March. On his return he argued that it was specially difficult for him to make concessions to Germany, owing to his close contacts with Greece and Britain, yet he felt impelled to save the country from war at all costs. In the end it was decided to resume negotiations with Germany. At this stage Prince Paul still hugged the illusion that in return for signing the tripartite pact, he would be dispensed from giving the Axis military help or even from opening his territory to German troops in transit. On 13 March the cabinet resumed its discussions, and by this time it was doubtful whether even adherence to the tripartite pact would avert warlike complications. As there were already grounds for fearing that Germany was looking round for puppets capable of replacing those actually in power, it was considered wiser to remove M. Stojadinović out of harm's way; on 19 March, in agreement with the British and Greek governments, he was sent from his place of internment to Athens and thence to the island of Mauritius. That Prince Paul consented to the banishment of Stojadinović is generally ascribed to fear lest the latter would overthrow the weak Cvetković and assume control of the situation.

When the cabinet met again on 20 March, Prince Paul was already resigned to what he regarded as the inevitable, and held that the patriarch and the chiefs of the opposition should be informed of the position. In the diplomatic corps it was already feared that Paul's intense unpopularity might provoke an upheaval and that his overthrow, if it took place, might involve the Serbo-Croat *Sporazum*, upon which national unity precariously rested. The first public sign of trouble came on 21 March with the resignation of four ministers. During the crucial discussion the war minister, General Pešić, absented himself. Maček's attitude was extremely reserved, but he did not vote against compliance with the German proposals, though by doing so he would probably have tipped the scales against Prince Paul.

The final proposals, which Cvetković and Cincar-Marković were instructed by the prince regent and cabinet to take with them to Vienna, were that Yugoslavia should adhere to the tripartite pact, but with a special protocol suspending certain clauses; in return for this, she would be given a guarantee of her existing frontiers and not compelled to join in the impending military action of the Axis. It is, however, scarcely credible that any of the ministers can have seriously supposed that they would be let off with an agreement which gave Germany nothing save a paper pledge, and those who resigned were therefore convinced that secret clauses were held in reserve. In any case, the premier and foreign minister left Belgrade on 24 March for

Vienna, despite the parting warning that under no circumstances would Britain 'condone' such action. They signed the pact next day and returned to Belgrade on 26 March to be confronted with a situation that was completely out of hand.

PRINCE PAUL'S MOTIVES

Three main motives had determined Prince Paul's action. In the first place, he was obsessed—and with good reason—by the military unpreparedness into which his regime had allowed the country to drift during the previous seven years, and which had become acute since the fall of Czechoslovakia and the acquisition of the Škoda armament plants by Germany. He knew that the democracies were unable to supply Yugoslavia or Turkey with war material. He and his generals knew, too, that, quite apart from deficiencies of arms and training, the northern frontier was indefensible, that the railway system was entirely inadequate for purposes of war, that the defence of Belgrade could be outflanked both from Temesvar and from the Fruška Gora, and that the sole hope of a successful defence lay in abandoning the four principal cities—Belgrade, Zagreb, Ljubljana and Subotica —to enemy occupation, with unforeseeable consequences.

His second obsession was Bolshevism, which, he was uncomfortably aware, might make its appeal to a people thoroughly tired of dictatorship and now enraged at the discovery of its military incompetence.

There was a third and probably decisive motive to Prince Paul's action. In 1939 he had genuinely desired a solution of the Serbo-Croat dispute, but had held out stubbornly until Maček consented to base that solution on a direct agreement between himself and the Prince, instead of basing it on a concentration of all parties, and above all, of the three parties which really represented something in Serbia proper. But this would infallibly have meant the end of the dictatorship and the reestablishment of a democratic regime, and to that he was firmly opposed—using the flimsy pretext that there could be no change of regime until the young king came of age in September 1941.

In exactly the same way, in March 1941, to have yielded to the popular demand would have involved replacing the Cvetković government (which was entirely unrepresentative of Serbia, and could only exist by the complaisance of the Croat and Slovene parties which really stood for their respective peoples) by a coalition or concentration in the face of which the dictatorship would have shrivelled and collapsed. The signing of the pact was not only a vital act of foreign policy; it was the prince's last bid for retention of power at home.

THE COUP D'ETAT

The journey of the two ministers to Vienna had been concealed from the general public, but was widely suspected, and on 26 March, when they returned to Belgrade, the news spread like wildfire. That night a bloodless *coup d'état* was effected; Cvetković and Cincar-Marković, the regents Stanković and Perović, and other high officials, were placed under arrest; King Peter's majority was proclaimed (though he would not be 18 till September 1941); and Prince Paul (who after hearing the report of his two dutiful ministers had quickly left Belgrade for his castle of Brdo near the Slovene frontier) was stopped at Zagreb by telephonic order of the new government and sent back to Belgrade, whence, after a short interval, he and his family were sent into exile. Finding no support from any direction, he submitted unconditionally, and thus deprived the wilder spirits of any temptation to more drastic action.

The suddenness and complete success of the *coup d'état* were due to the coalescing of a number of different elements; first and foremost, the younger officers, regular and reservist, in marked contrast to 'the Generals'; then all the old Serbian parties; then the students, and a considerable number of the staff, of Belgrade University; and, not least of all, the Orthodox clergy and hierarchy, led by the Patriarch Gavrilo.

A new cabinet was now formed under General Simović, with Dr Maček and Professor Slobodan Jovanović, as vice-premiers and it can be said without exaggeration that, since the creation of Yugoslavia, no government so representative of all sections of opinion from Left to Right had ever held office.

The tremendous ovations and demonstrations throughout the country which greeted the change of government left Hitler in no doubt as to popular sentiment. The rebuff came at a specially awkward moment, when the Japanese foreign minister was visiting Berlin. It was rubbed in further by public statements from Mr Churchill and Mr Sumner Welles; and the official Moscow journal, *Pravda*, while denying the story that the Soviet government had congratulated Belgrade, took care to add that the Yugoslav people was worthy of its glorious past and deserved congratulations. On the other hand the Nazi propaganda machine launched a violent campaign against Yugoslavia, publishing a mass of entirely imaginary atrocities. The procedure was the same as that against Czechoslovakia in 1938, when elaborate details were woven round places where no incident of any kind had occurred. Chaos, it was claimed, now reigned in Yugoslavia, promoted by 'agents of Britain'.

General Simović issued an order of the day, urging calm and bidding people remain at their posts and avoid demonstrations or spreading of rumours. The proclamation of Belgrade, Zagreb and Ljubljana as open cities showed that the government was under no illusions. In Zagreb, Maček issued a remarkable manifesto to the Croats, speaking as 'A Christian who recalls Christ's word, "Blessed are the Peacemakers"'. He had done all he could for peace; he would now co-operate with men who had been his allies in most critical times, and who would both respect and extend Croat interests.

CHAPTER 11

OCCUPATION AND RESISTANCE

THE INVASION, 6 APRIL 1941

Early on the morning of Palm Sunday, 6 April—only ten days after the Belgrade coup—Hitler struck. General Simović's government, apparently still hopeful that the Axis powers would not be provoked into attacking, did little to prepare for the inevitable. The weaknesses of the country's defences were soon tragically revealed; poor equipment and communications, lack of munitions, disaffection amongst some of the Croat units, and above all, an impossible strategic plan which attempted to hold the whole vast periphery instead of concentrating on strong positions in the mountainous core of the country. The Yugoslav General Staff had expected that attack would come from the north. Instead, the German armies massed in western Bulgaria, smashed the defences commanding Niš, Skoplje, and the Vardar valley, whilst another column turned the exposed left flank of the Greeks, captured Salonika, and pushed on through Bitolj to the northwest shore of Lake Ohrid where they joined up with the Italians advancing from Albania. Kragujevac was attacked from the south and fell on 11 April; Belgrade was entered the following day. In the north, the Axis advance was even swifter. Zagreb was captured on the 10th by a rapid panzer thrust, Ljubljana on the 11th by the Italians, who also overran the Dalmatian coast. The Axis satellites followed quickly, the Hungarians penetrating to Osijek and Novi Sad, the Bulgarians taking over most of Macedonia.

These military operations were accompanied by a series of merciless air attacks on Belgrade, in which a great part of the capital was destroyed and an estimated twenty thousand persons were killed. The government, rapidly losing control of the disintegrating state, withdrew first into the interior of the Šumadija, then to Sarajevo, and finally to Montenegro, whence, with King Peter, they left by air for allied territory. The Yugoslav High Command capitulated on 17 April, eleven days after the invasion had been launched. Thereafter all organized resistance ceased, though a few individuals and scattered bands sought refuge in the hills rather than surrender. Amongst them was a colonel called Draža Mihajlović, of whom the world was soon to hear more.

PARTITION

Partition followed swiftly in the wake of military defeat. Germany annexed the northern half of Slovenia, settling Austrians to replace those Slovenes who had fled or been deported, and attempting to absorb those who remained by a vigorous process of repression and germanization. Italy received Ljubljana and the rest of Slovenia, where she pursued a policy of Fascist indoctrination rather than outright denationalization. To Italy went also numerous islands and important strips of the Dalmatian littoral, including the city of Split and the naval base of Kotor, together with certain tracts of hinterland, of varying and sometimes considerable extent. She also retained the military control of a nominally independent Montenegro. Albania, likewise in her possession, was enlarged by the inclusion of the western part of Macedonia and the plain of Kosovo, whose largely Albanian population welcomed the opportunity of paying off old scores against the Serbs. Macedonia and some southern districts of Serbia were annexed by Bulgaria, who strove to settle an intricate racial problem once and for all by treating the population as Bulgars. Hungary applied a similarly brutal policy of magyarization in her share of the spoils—the rich Danubian province of Bačka, and the smaller northern districts of Medjumurje and Prekomurje.

The largest fragment of dismembered Yugoslavia was dignified by the title of the Independent State of Croatia. Though the reversion to Italy of the indisputably Croatian districts of Dalmatia was bitterly resented by those Croat nationalists who were prepared to accept 'independence' from the hand of Axis

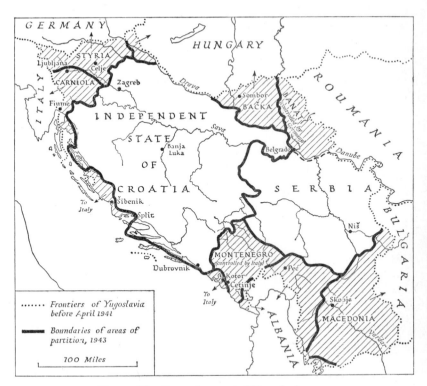

Fig. 37. The dismemberment of Yugoslavia, 1941.

protectors, compensation was offered in the form of all Bosnia-Hercegovina, with its large Moslem and Serb Orthodox communities. In theory, the Independent State of Croatia was a kingdom; but the duke of Spoleto, the Italian prince chosen to ascend the throne under the style of Tomislav II, showed a prudent disinclination to set foot in his troubled realm. Though power ultimately rested on German and Italian arms, it was exercised by the 'Ustaše', a movement taking its name from traditional Croat rebels but owing its techniques and trappings to Fascist Italy, where its leader, the 'Poglavnik' Ante Pavelić, had found asylum and received funds and facilities for terrorist action which he now proceeded to apply, on a national and horrific scale, against Jews, Serbs, and all who failed to acclaim the advent of the new puppet state.

If the Axis powers thought they could find enough support to keep the bulk of the Croats on their side, they had little such hopes of the Serbs, who had been the heart and soul of the patriotic and pro-allied sentiment which culminated in the coup of 27 March. In the Banat, the Germans sought a solution by relying on the local *Volksdeutsche* to police and administer the region. In Serbia itself, now reduced to a rump smaller than the area covered before the Balkan wars, reliable collaborators could not readily be discovered. At first, the Germans preferred to keep the country under their direct military administration. By August, however, they had found an agent in the person of General Milan Nedić, a former minister of war and commander of the southern group of Yugoslav armies, who was given limited authority to form a government of 'national salvation' and raise a small force known as the Serbian State Guard. But the latter never proved more than half-hearted auxiliaries, and the Germans could find reliable collaborators only amongst the few 'volunteers' in the service of Dimitrije Ljotić, the Serb Fascist leader. Yet another force was the official Chetnik organization, which had once done good service as irregulars against the Turks, but had gone to seed under the leadership of the superannuated hero Kosta Pećanac and was more disposed to side with the occupying authorities against the radical and desperate bands which rose in revolt throughout Serbia in the summer of 1941.

TITO AND THE COMMUNISTS

The rapidity and completeness of the catastrophe left the Serbian people prostrate and demoralized. Yet, before the summer was out, a mood of exalted optimism had kindled a revolt which all but swept the Germans out of Serbia. This reawakening of hope and national vigour was caused largely by the news that Germany had invaded Russia, for whom most Yugoslavs, particularly the Serbs, cherished feelings of Slav brotherhood and ignorant admiration. In the inter-war period, the strongly anti-

Communist Yugoslav government had maintained no diplomatic relations with the Soviet Union, but these were established in 1940 and a Treaty of Friendship and Non-Aggression was hurriedly concluded between the two countries on the very eve of the German invasion. Moscow did not, however, lift a finger to help her new ally during the latter's ensuing ordeal, and withdrew recognition from the government of the dismembered state with cynical promptness. Yet when, on 22 June 1941, the Soviet Union in her turn suffered invasion, these things were forgotten in Serbia in an upsurge of popular emotion.

The small Yugoslav Communist party, which had played little or no part in the coup of 27 March and the terrible retribution which followed, had scant cause to mourn the passing of the old Yugoslav state in which it had been outlawed and persecuted. But the invasion of the Soviet Union, 'our dear Socialist fatherland, our hope and beacon', presented it with an unparalleled opportunity which its secretary-general, the Croat metal-worker Josip Broz, better known under his conspiratorial name of Tito, was not the man to let slip. A Croat of peasant stock, he had been mobilized in the Austrian army during the First World War and sent to the eastern front where he had been captured by the Russians and converted to Communism. He had worked for a time as an official of the Comintern in Moscow before returning in 1938 to take control of the party in Yugoslavia. Amongst his closest collaborators were men of ability and resolution: Lolo Ribar, son of the former president of the Yugoslav Constituent Assembly, and Alexander Ranković, who headed the party's security apparatus; Boris Kidrič and Edvard Kardelj, from Slovenia; Milovan Djilas, from Montenegro. Some had acquired military experience in the Spanish Civil War which was to stand the party in good stead. But the Communists' first duty, as Tito saw it and expounded it at the Fifth Party Congress which met in secret in Zagreb in October 1940, was to keep Yugoslavia at all cost out of the 'imperialist' war. A radical change of policy was heralded by the arrival of fresh instructions from the Comintern when Hitler began the invasion of the Soviet Union: 'it is absolutely essential that you should take all measures to support and alleviate the struggle of the Soviet people. You must start a movement with the slogan of a united national front, indeed of a united international front, to fight the German and Italian Fascist bandits.' At one turn of fortune's wheel, the party thus found itself confronted with an imperious and exacting demand, but also with an opportunity which was to convert it from a minority group lacking popular support and aspirations, into the spearhead of a national resistance movement. For the next seven years the two currents of patriotic fervour and loyalty to a creed of social revolution directed from Moscow merged their impetus and eventually carried the Communists to victory at the head of a state reconstituted on Marxist lines.

THE RISING IN SERBIA

From his secret headquarters in a Belgrade villa, Tito directed a series of acts of sabotage and defiance, raids on German outposts and ambushes of convoys, which, by the end of July, had assumed the proportions of a general revolt throughout most of Serbia. The Politburo constituted from amongst its members a supreme headquarters with Tito as Commander-in-Chief of the 'National Liberation Partisan Detachments'. By the end of August, Tito was able to inform Moscow that 'the Germans are only holding the larger towns whilst the villages and hamlets are in the hands of the Partisans'. Tito himself left Belgrade to join the Partisans in western Serbia where his presence was urgently required. Not only had military operations reached a decisive phase, for the whole valley of the western Morava with its flourishing towns and its links with Bosnia was now open, but delicate negotiations with another resistance movement, which likewise claimed the leadership of the national rising, were called for.

This movement had crystallized round Draža Mihajlović, the officer who had refused to recognize the capitulation of the old Yugoslav army and had established his headquarters on the wooded slopes of the Ravna Gora. His followers were generally

Fig. 38. The rising in Serbia, summer 1941.

referred to as Chetniks (*četnici*) though many had served in the army and were distinct from the official organization of that name which was linked with Nedić and the Germans. The Chetniks cultivated a ferociously picturesque appearance, bristling with beards and weapons, in contrast to the Partisans, with their red star insignia and their earnest political commissars. The leaders of the two movements differed profoundly in background, character, and political outlook. Patriotic and pious, attached to the monarchy, the western allies, and the established order, Mihajlović distrusted the Croats and detested the Communists. Though personally courageous, his capacity as a resistance leader was flawed by a fatal ambivalence. He believed that, so long as the might of the Axis was unimpaired, to attempt to oppose it openly was criminal folly which could have no appreciable military effect and would only call down calamitous retribution on the civilian population who had already suffered enough. The correct policy was therefore to lie low, husband resources, and build up a force with which to strike when a more favourable moment, such as a landing by the allies, should occur. This would forestall chaos following the collapse of the occupying authorities and facilitate a restoration of the rightful power, the monarchy. There was force in this argument, but it ignored one vital factor; the irresistible urge of the people for immediate action. A guerrilla commander cannot, in fact, become stronger by indefinitely husbanding his resources. His followers simply melt away unless they grow at the cost of harrying the enemy. A resistance leader cannot retain leadership unless he actively resists.

Tito and the Communists, on the other hand, had the advantage not only of an efficient apparatus built for clandestine work, but also of a clear-cut programme of action in harmony with the popular mood. Moscow demanded unlimited sacrifice, and the people were eager to offer it. That the civil population would pay a heavy price in retribution counted for little; desperate men would be the more ready to seek desperate remedies. A passive population would suffer, in any case, from the demands made upon it by the Germans for forced labour. Armed resistance might in fact offer the best chance of survival. As for preparing to assist an eventual allied landing, such an eventuality was neither likely nor desirable, for the Communists were convinced that victory on the world scale would come not from the west but from the east. Nor were they concerned with restoring the old order but with introducing the new. But though this was the ultimate goal, instructions from Moscow warned that they should not let this prospect frighten off the more conservative-minded from co-operating with them. The same message which instructed Tito to launch an all-out campaign of resistance to the Axis urged him to 'remember that at this stage what you are concerned with is liberation from Fascist oppression and not socialist revolution'. Tito repeated the exhortation in an order of the day; 'The political line of the Partisan Detachments lays down that there must be a National Liberation Anti-Fascist Front of all the peoples of Yugoslavia regardless of party or religion. In forming Partisan Detachments it is essential not to be narrow-minded but to give wide scope to initiative and enterprise of every kind.'

Though basic differences thus divided the followers of Tito from those of Mihajlović, the former genuinely desired, for tactical reasons, at least a temporary alliance. Mihajlović, for his part, despite his fundamental disapproval of open revolt, found his hand forced by the spontaneous resolve of the Chetniks not to be outdone by the Partisans and also by the initiative of his subordinate commanders, some of whom decided to pass over to the Partisans. In mid-September the two men met to confer at the village of Struganik, at the foot of Ravna Gora. Though some agreement was reached for a limited degree of local collaboration, it proved impossible to reconcile Mihajlović's caution with Tito's insistence on all-out action and a joint command. A second meeting, held just over a month later at the village of Brajici, yielded little better results. Meanwhile, friction continued to increase between the local Partisan and Chetnik commanders in the field, to the detriment of their common action against the Germans who were massing for a decisive counter-attack. Attempts to capture Kraljevo, the key town of the area, from the Germans were frustrated by these rivalries, and on 1 November a major engagement was fought between Partisans and Chetniks, resulting in the former's capture of Požega from the latter.

The Partisans had established their headquarters in the town of Užice, where they had taken over a useful small arms factory, published their press, and set up a network of 'National Liberation Councils'. But by the end of November, dissensions with the Chetniks and mounting German pressure had fatally weakened their positions. Užice was hurriedly evacuated under heavy air and tank attack and the Partisans were forced out into the mountainous Sanjak country on the borders of Serbia and eastern Bosnia. The Germans exacted retribution by an indiscriminate massacre of the population, including the killing, in the industrial town of Kragujevac, of hundreds of school-children. The despair and horror caused by these atrocities also brought with it a deep revulsion against the Partisans whose short-lived triumphs had called down such miseries upon the people. The Chetniks, for their part, generally managed to escape German reprisals by passing into the service of Nedić with whom a tacit understanding was eventually reached that his forces should remain garrisoning the towns, whilst the Chetniks assumed virtual control of the Serbian countryside. From now on, they but rarely turned their arms against the Germans, and Mihajlović himself was left undisturbed on Ravna Gora. The Chetniks' main aim was now to hunt down the Partisan survivors. In this, with 'parallel action' if not the formal co-operation of the Germans and the Nedić and Ljotić troops, they were largely successful, and it was only in the later stages of the war that Tito was able to re-establish his influence in Serbia.

THE WAR IN MONTENEGRO

In Montenegro, where resistance to invasion was a proud national tradition, a rising had occurred with even more spectacular suddenness than in Serbia, and had ended no less tragically. On 13 July, following the proclamation of a puppet princi-pality, Partisans and Chetniks made common cause against the Italians and all but drove them into the sea. Only by mounting a major operation with reinforcements from Albania could the Italians manage to restore some measure of control. Militarily, the Montenegrins' contribution to the Partisan movement was to prove of great value, for they were a nation of fighters and provided many commanders of outstanding ability such as Peko Dapčević, a veteran of the Spanish Civil War, and Arso Jovano-vić, who became Tito's chief of staff. But politically, under the influence of Djilas and the Marxist intellectual Moša Pijade, they followed an extremist line at variance with Tito's policy of not imposing Communism or liquidating opponents. This led to many excesses and played into the hands of the Italians, enabling them to win over the 'nationalist' Chetniks, who saw no contradiction in collaborating with the Italians whilst claiming to act for Mihajlović. The Partisans managed, in the course of the winter of 1941 and early 1942, to regain some of the ground they had lost, but the fighting had now assumed the character of a Partisan-Chetnik conflict rather than a Montenegrin rising against the invader. A combined offensive of Italian and 'nationalist' troops between March and June 1942 cleared the country once more of the Partisans and left it virtually under joint Italian-Chetnik control until the collapse of Italy in the following year.

DEVELOPMENT OF THE 'NATIONAL LIBERATION MOVEMENT'

Serious as was the plight of the Serb Partisans who had been driven into Bosnia with Tito, that of the Serbs living in Bosnia itself was more desperate still. On assuming the leadership of the 'Independent State of Croatia' and after crippling the local Communist apparatus by executing the leaders of the party who had been seized in Zagreb, Pavelić set about the solution of his 'Serbian problem' by methods similar to those chosen by Hitler to deal with the Jews: mass extermination. Bands of Ustaše ruffians were sent into Bosnia with licence to burn down the Orthodox villages and cut the throats of their occupants. They fulfilled their mission with such bloodthirsty ferocity that even their Axis allies were dismayed; for rather than wait passively for torture and butchery, the Bosnian Serbs took to the forests in desperation. There, as time went on, they polarized into camps of Chetniks and Partisans. The former, in their thirst for vengeance, repaid atrocity with atrocity and made what terms they could with the occupying powers until, by an ironic necessity, they found themselves eventually fighting side by side not only with Italians and Germans, but with the Ustaše themselves against the Partisans. The latter, following the line of Tito's emissaries, insisted that Croats, Serbs, and Moslems must sink their differences in a common struggle against the occupying powers and their allies, whether Chetniks or Ustaše. The Croat peasantry at first held aloof from either side. The extreme nationalist wing of the Croat peasant party threw in their lot with the Ustaše; Dr Maček and other leaders remained neutral. A similar hesitation was shown by the Catholic Church. A few priests identified themselves wholeheartedly with the new state; others, led by Archbishop Stepinac of Zagreb, tried to moderate, and at times denounced, its excesses, and showed particular disapproval of the mass conversions which the Ustaše, when tiring of slaughter, offered the Orthodox as a condition for survival. But though there were strong pacifist tendencies in the Croat peasant movement, as represented by the teachings of the Radić brothers and the caution of Dr Maček, there was also a dormant radical and revolutionary tradition going back to the times of Matija Gubec. In the course of 1942 and 1943 these ancient revolutionary impulses were gradually re-awakened amongst the Croats who deserted in increasing numbers from the 'Domobran' conscript army or secretly left the cities to join the Partisans.

The disaster in Serbia had taught the Partisans that they could not stand against the better-equipped enemy in pitched battles, and that their survival depended on mobility and the ceaseless harassment of enemy communications and outposts. By scattering before their pursuers they could, moreover, spread the gospel of resistance wherever they went, absorb the desperate and the disaffected into their own depleted ranks, and offer a decimated population a rudimentary administration and a new creed. For the first half of 1942, Tito continued operations in East Bosnia, near the borders of Montenegro. Then, in June, he decided to make a long trek into the heart of Pavelić's state. By the end of August, most of western and central Bosnia was in his hands. Jajce was captured (25 September) and then Bihać

(5 November). In the latter town, a lull in the fighting allowed him to regroup his forces, both those under his direct control and those in other parts of the country, into eight 'divisions', each numbering between three and four thousand men, as well as the smaller Partisan units proper; the whole was given the official designation of 'The National Army of Liberation and the Partisan Detachments of Yugoslavia'. Tito also considered that the time had come to provide his movement with a more formal political and administrative framework. To this end he summoned representatives from the other liberated areas and from the towns still under enemy occupation to meet in Bihać on 26 November 1942 for an assembly to be known as the Anti-Fascist Council for the National Liberation of Yugoslavia (AVNOJ).

This gathering provided an opportunity to review developments in distant parts of the country, such as Slovenia and Macedonia, with which regular contact was difficult. In Macedonia, the population had at first welcomed the Bulgarians, but soon discovered that they had only exchanged 'Great Serb chauvinism' for its Bulgarian counterpart. The national question even divided the clandestine Yugoslav and Bulgarian Communist parties who appealed for a ruling to the Comintern in Moscow. The Comintern found in favour of the Yugoslavs, whose propaganda promising an autonomous Macedonian unit in a federal Yugoslav state gradually rallied support for the Partisans organized under Tito's emissary, Vukmanović-Tempo. In Slovenia, resistance had from the first been more widespread and effectively organized. The 'Freedom Front' had carried out a number of spectacular assassinations of prominent collaborators and controlled extensive areas of the countryside. The Italians had attempted to strengthen their hold by promoting the formation of the 'Slovene Alliance' (Zveza) composed mainly of clerical groups, with a paramilitary 'White Guard' to police the villages, whilst an equally anti-Partisan 'Blue Guard' was formed by Yugoslav ex-officers who considered themselves to be acting on behalf of Mihajlović. The Italians attempted to wipe out the Partisans by launching seven divisions against them in an offensive beginning in July 1942. But though they suffered severely, the Slovene Partisans managed to escape destruction and gradually re-established their positions.

The composition and declared aims of the Anti-Fascist Council formed at Bihać were designed to give the impression, both throughout Yugoslavia and abroad, that the 'National Liberation Movement' was no instrument of social revolution, but a broadly based expression of exemplary democratic principles. Under the presidency of Dr Ivan Ribar, the former speaker of the Yugoslav Constituent Assembly, the Council issued resolutions reaffirming its intention to prosecute the struggle against the Axis with all available means, recognizing the national rights of Serbs, Slovenes, Croats, and Macedonians, and guaranteeing 'the inviolability of private property and the provision of every possibility for individual initiative in industry, trade and agriculture'. It also proclaimed its intention of introducing 'no radical changes whatsoever in the social life and activities of the people except for the replacement of reactionary village authorities', and pledged that 'all the most important questions of social life and state organization would be settled by the people themselves through representatives who will be properly elected by the people after the war'.

ATTITUDE OF THE ALLIES

The Bihać assembly succeeded in focussing the attention of the allies on a movement which was manifestly strong enough to set up its own administration and issue defiant proclamations in the heart of Hitler's 'European fortress', and forced them to reconsider their own attitude. Since the Yugoslav collapse of 1941, the allies had retained diplomatic relations with the royal Yugoslav government in exile, which appeared to them to be fairly representative of all major national groups and political parties in the country. It contained however serious weaknesses. There was no representative in it of the one party which had still preserved its structure and was spectacularly increasing its influence inside Yugoslavia—the Communists. Indeed, its policy was becoming more and more dominated by a handful of army officers and officials fanatically opposed to permitting any replica on Yugoslav territory of the anti-German alliance between the Soviet Union and the western democracies. Worst of all, the feud between Serbs and Croats had been revived amongst the exiles by reports of the terrible massacres perpetrated by the Ustaše against the Orthodox population of Bosnia, and through the tendency of the Serbs to throw all the blame for the ignominious collapse of April 1941 on the 'treachery' of the Croats. Though Yugoslav in name, the outlook of the exiled government, which was reformed in January 1942 under the premiership of the distinguished Belgrade professor Slobodan Jovanović, became increasingly Pan-Serb. All these tendencies were strengthened by the decision to promote Mihajlović to the rank of General and to confer on him the dignity of minister of war in the reconstituted cabinet.

Within a few weeks of reaching Ravna Gora, Mihajlović had managed to convey messages to the allies declaring that he was raising the standard of revolt. These claims were eagerly pressed by the government in exile and accepted at their face value. Allied propaganda and the publicity given by the B.B.C. soon inflated the image of Mihajlović into that of a legendary hero. It seems probable that the knowledge that he had the backing of the allies and of the exiled government stiffened Mihajlović in his rejection of Tito's early proposals for military co-operation. The first British liaison officer, Captain Hudson, was sent to him in October 1941, and though little help could be given in the way of supplies the British military mission was strengthened in the course of the following year, and allied officers attached to the headquarters of other Chetnik commanders. Only gradually did the allies realize the painful truth that Mihajlović was doing little or nothing to fight the Germans but, on the contrary, was doing everything in his power to harass the Partisans. Of the latter, the western allies still knew very little (though Captain Hudson had in fact had some contact with them too).

The attitude of the Soviet Union towards events in Yugoslavia was equivocal, and betrayed a similar confusion as to what was going on. Though Moscow had, from the outset, been in touch with the Partisans through the secret radio link with the Yugoslav Communist party, the Soviet attempted to give no military assistance or supplies, despite Tito's pressing requests, and were liberal only with support through the broadcasts of a station calling itself 'Free Yugoslavia', believed to be located in or near Tiflis, and with advice, often tactlessly given. At the same time, Moscow seems to have believed that Mihajlović could, after all, turn out to be the leader of the national resistance, whereas Tito's followers might be liquidated militarily or prove a political embarrassment by creating discord, both inside Yugoslavia and amongst the allies themselves through the untimely advocacy of social revolution. In the spring of 1942 the royalist government, with whom the Soviet Union had re-established relations after the Germans began their invasion of June 1941, protested energetically to Moscow against the activities of the 'international brigands' and 'Trotskyists' in Yugoslavia, and demanded that they be called to heel. Though Tito was ready enough to accept Comintern advice, which coincided with his own convictions, about subordinating eventual revolutionary aims to the necessities of all-out struggle against the Axis in which all patriots could join in, he resented the failure of the Russians to send in even token aid to his hard-pressed forces, and protested bitterly against Moscow's seemingly gratuitous slight in raising the legation of the royalist government to the rank of Embassy (August, 1942). But though the Russians were thus maintaining correct relations with the exiled government, they had begun to denounce the growing evidence of Chetnik collaboration with the enemy and to show signs of giving more open backing to the Partisans.

THE AXIS OFFENSIVES OF 1943

To Hitler, the pretensions of the Bihać assembly appeared as an intolerable provocation, and the activities of the 'National Army of Liberation' a continued threat to his important rail communications with Split, Fiume, and Belgrade which must be removed at all costs. A campaign of serious proportions was concerted between the Axis military leaders. It aimed at the encirclement and destruction of the Partisan forces, the Germans and Pavelić units operating from the north and north-east, the Italians from the south and west. During the campaign, which lasted between January and March (referred to by the Partisans as the Fourth Enemy Offensive), Tito fought his way doggedly back into east Bosnia towards Montenegro. The Montenegrin Chetniks, some twelve thousand strong, had taken up strong positions along the Neretva river, confident of barring his way, whilst Mihajlović himself moved up from Serbia to take personal command of the operations on this sector. Handicapped by a train of some three thousand sick and wounded, and suffering heavily from enemy artillery and air attack, the Partisans broke through the Neretva line in a desperate battle, routed the Chetniks, and regained the mountainous soil of Montenegro.

They were not however left long undisturbed. Confident that they could here be more ineluctably destroyed, the Germans and their allies, now including Bulgarian troops, prepared for a fresh drive for encirclement. Here the very difficulties of the terrain, as Tito himself wrote, 'proved a disadvantage to us, and an advantage to the enemy. They restricted our manoeuvring power and very nearly prevented our main striking force in Montenegro from breaking out of the enemy's encirclement. Great technical superiority, long-range guns, numerous aircraft and special units trained in mountain warfare gave the enemy for his part a definite advantage over us by helping him to surmount these difficulties.' The new tactical methods applied by the Germans proved particularly dangerous. The Germans 'now turned some of the Partisans' own weapons against them, in particular mobility and surprise. They no longer advanced solely along the main lines of communication, but...sent specially trained mobile shock units ahead. They were also quicker to seize any point of vantage and dig themselves in; better, too, at preparing ambushes...Finally, realising the dependence of the Partisans on the civil population, the Germans forcibly

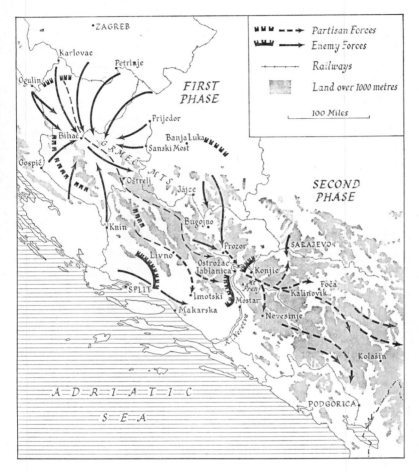

Fig. 39. The Fourth Enemy Offensive against the Partisans.

mobilized every civilian they could lay hands on in the whole area. Their instructions were clear enough; "Every Partisan found is to be shot. If the local inhabitants are hostile to the German forces, treat them with the greatest possible brutality and severity. If they are friendly, harness them in the struggle against the Partisans."[1]

[1] Fitzroy Maclean, *Disputed Barricade* (London, 1957), pp. 221-2.

225

This 'Fifth Enemy Offensive' lasted through May and June 1943, and proved the Partisans' greatest military ordeal. Only after suffering incredible hardships and heavy casualties—Tito himself was wounded and one of the two British liaison officers sent in by parachute to join the Partisans was killed—did they succeed in crossing the Sutjeska gorge and escaping into north-east Bosnia. But their morale was unimpaired and within the next six months they recovered sufficiently to take full advantage of the opportunities offered by a sudden change in the fortunes of war—the capitulation of Fascist Italy.

THE CAPITULATION OF ITALY

The Italian capitulation at the beginning of September 1943 was the signal for a race between the Germans and the Partisans to accept the surrender of the Italian troops and take over the positions and military equipment held by them in Slovenia, Dalmatia, and Montenegro. Tito, who had just received a fully constituted British military mission headed by Brigadier Maclean at his headquarters and resented the allies' failure to give him advance information of this important development, nevertheless managed to seize the lion's share. His forces took over most of the islands and the coast of Dalmatia, including the city of Split which they held for nearly three weeks; most of Italian-held Slovenia, except for Ljubljana; even more significant, for its later territorial implications, the greater part of Venezia Giulia (Primorje); also most of Montenegro. The Italian surrender brought the collapse of the various Yugoslav auxiliaries dependent on them; the White and Blue Guards in Slovenia, some Chetnik groups in Dalmatia, and larger units in Montenegro, where they attempted to hold out under General Djukanović and Colonel Stanišić at Ostrog Monastery but were forced to surrender (mid October). Though most of the Partisans' territorial gains were abandoned sooner or later, the Army of National Liberation was immensely strengthened with the spoils of ten Italian divisions.

Confident of increased strength and prestige as the result of

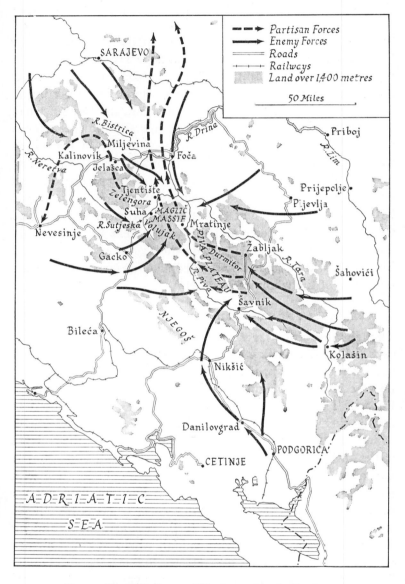

Fig. 40. The Fifth Enemy Offensive against the Partisans.

the collapse of Italy, Tito convoked a second session of the Anti-Fascist Council at Jajce, at the end of November 1943. He judged the time ripe for an important political advance. The Council, transformed into a Praesidium of sixty-seven members, representing the different ethnic and to some extent political groups of the country, assumed new legislative and administrative functions, whilst its executive organ, the Committee of National Liberation, took upon itself virtually the character of a provisional government. Tito, whose identity as Josip Broz was now officially disclosed, was dignified with the rank of marshal of Yugoslavia and the office of premier. The Council proclaimed the decision to reconstitute Yugoslavia on a federal basis, with the inclusion of certain territories held by Italy, and warned that King Peter and the government in exile should not return to Yugoslavia, since 'the question of King and Monarchy will be settled by the people of its own will after the liberation of the whole country'.

ALLIED SUPPORT WITHDRAWN FROM MIHAJLOVIĆ

Though the Germans managed to make good many of the losses caused by the defection of Italy and continued their pressure against the Partisans, the latter had now shown themselves to be a factor of major military and political importance in eastern Europe. The allies were accordingly faced with the need to modify their policy in two related aspects; their relations with Mihajlović and with the government in exile. With the collapse of the Italians, many of Mihajlović's subordinate commanders had either perished or passed over to open collaboration with the Germans. But in Serbia itself the Partisans had not yet recovered much of their earlier influence, whereas Mihajlović was still thought to be a force to be reckoned with, and his Chetniks were certainly giving valuable help to allied airmen who had been shot down and managed to reach the areas under his control. But was he really an asset against the Germans? The allied commanders, conscious that the Germans would be compelled to withdraw their forces from the Balkans to avoid being cut off by the advance of the Red army, resolved to put him to a final test by inviting his co-operation in certain specific operations. Though his men did succeed in destroying a bridge over the Lim near Višegrad (October 1943) they evaded or refused action against the more vital railways running through Serbia.[1] In January, Mr Winston Churchill announced that allied supplies would in future be sent only to Tito, and in the following May, the British liaison officers were withdrawn from Mihajlović. In explaining this change of policy in the House of Commons, Mr Churchill declared: 'The reason why we have ceased to supply Mihajlović with arms and support is a simple one. He has not been fighting the enemy, and, moreover, some of his subordinates have made accommodations with the enemy, from which have arisen armed conflicts with the forces of Marshal Tito...We have proclaimed ourselves the strong supporters of Marshal Tito because of his heroic and massive struggle against the German armies.'[2]

Britain's policy aimed at bringing about some sort of compromise between Tito, whom military expediency compelled her to support, and the royalist government to whom she felt bound by legal and moral ties. Professor Jovanović, whose government had included Mihajlović as minister for war and who had been unduly influenced by the fanatical anti-Partisan and anti-Croat intrigues of an unconstitutional 'military cabinet', resigned in June 1943. There was little change in the outlook of the succeeding governments until mid-May 1944, when King Peter invited Dr Ivan Šubašić, the former Ban of Croatia and a man of recognized good will, to form a government with the aim of co-operating, and ultimately merging, with Tito's

[1] H. Seton Watson, *The East European Revolution* (London, 1947), p. 129.

[2] A curious indication of the complexities of the situation is the fact that after the British had decided to withdraw support from Mihajlović, the Russians seriously considered the advisability of *establishing* a mission with him. Their motives are obscure, but may have included a lingering belief that the Chetnik leader might somehow after all manage to take over power when the Germans pulled out, and that it would be useful to have a rival leader to play off against Tito, if the signs of national independence which the latter had already begun to show should prove a serious embarrassment.

Committee of National Liberation. The king also agreed not to return to Yugoslavia, as stipulated by the Anti-Fascist Council, until a plebiscite had been held, and broadcast an appeal to his people to rally to the Army of National Liberation. On 26 August the king recognized Marshal Tito as the sole military leader of the Yugoslav forces of resistance. By the end of the year, he had reluctantly consented to transfer his royal powers to a three-man regency, under whose shadowy and short-lived auspices a 'United Government' was formed, in which Dr Šubašić was given the post of foreign minister under the premiership of Marshal Tito (7 March 1945). Thus did the allies succeed in effecting the nominal merging of the exiled royalist government with the new Communist masters of Yugoslavia, who thereby gained a triumph in the political field no less valuable than their hard-won victories in forest and mountain-side.

The Germans, in the meanwhile, planned a new stroke against the Partisans aiming at crippling them by the capture of Tito and his chief associates. On the night of 24 May 1944 they launched a sudden air-borne attack against his headquarters at Drvar. The Partisan leaders had just time to make their escape, and after a forced march reached an airstrip where they were picked up and flown to Italy. It was a sign of the important role which the Soviet armed forces, whose mission had been with Tito since the end of February, were now to play in the Yugoslav theatre of war, that the aircraft which took them out (though operating from an allied base) was a Russian one. From Italy, Tito set up fresh headquarters on the Dalmatian island of Vis, under the joint protection of Partisan and British forces. The following August he returned to Italy to confer with the Supreme Allied Commander in the Mediterranean and with Mr Churchill. Amongst the matters discussed were plans for increased military co-operation between British and Partisan forces in the impending withdrawal of the Germans from the Balkans, the possibility of an allied landing in Istria with the aim of striking through to Vienna, and Tito's determination to recover control of Serbia, where the British prime minister feared that the royalist and conservative sympathies of the peasantry might lead to bitter bloodshed.

THE LAST PHASE OF THE WAR

Serbia

After their expulsion from Serbia in 1941, the Partisans had only been able to maintain themselves there in small, isolated detachments. But in the course of 1944, the switch of allied support from Mihajlović to Tito, the advance of the Red army, and a growing awareness that the days of enemy occupation, Nedić collaboration, and Chetnik control of the countryside were numbered, began to have their effect. In the spring of that year, Tito sent one of his ablest commanders, Koča Popović, to start a fresh drive in Serbia. At the same time, the defection of Major Djurić, Mihajlović's commander for central and south-east Serbia, speeded the process of Chetnik disintegration in those areas, whilst, a few months later, strong forces under Peko Dapčević began to fight their way back into Serbia from east Bosnia and Montenegro. By the end of September, the Germans had begun a general withdrawal from the Balkans, Bulgaria had gone over to the allies, and the Partisans were within twenty miles of Belgrade. Tito flew to Moscow to conclude an agreement inviting the Red Army to enter Yugoslav for joint military action with his own troops, but also providing—and this stipulation was a significant portent—that the areas liberated should be placed under Yugoslav administration and that the Red Army should withdraw as soon as military operations were over.

General Nedić, seeing the approach of inevitable disaster, held that his only hope lay in reaching some agreement with Mihajlović. Relations of a sort existed indirectly between the two men since Mihajlović's Chetniks had melted into the Nedić forces to avoid German reprisals at the end of 1941. Now Nedić, who claimed to be no Quisling but a trustee for the king operating in exceptionally difficult circumstances, needed Mihajlović

231

and could offer him the arms and supplies necessary if the Chetnik leader was to make good his claim that he would launch a rising when the Germans began to weaken. The two leaders met to confer at Ražana, Mihajlović sent his representative to Belgrade to arrange the equipping of his men, and at the beginning of October, Mihajlović accepted the offer to take over what remained of the Serbian Quisling forces, many of whom had already gone over to the Partisans. But Mihajlović had made one fatal miscalculation; it was not an Anglo-American force, which might even at this eleventh hour have shown some sympathy for him, but the Red Army which was driving back the Germans in the Balkans. When, in a few parts of eastern Serbia, his commanders did manage to take over from the retreating Germans, they were swept aside by the advancing Russians who promptly handed them over to the Partisans. Mihajlović himself was soon forced to abandon his headquarters at Ravna Gora and to escape with the motley forces now under his nominal command into north-east Bosnia. But his cause was now hopeless and there was no escape. His followers dwindled to a handful. Reduced by sickness and hunger, he was finally hunted down the following March in the mountainous country round Višegrad and brought back to Belgrade to face trial and execution. Tito, his victorious rival, had been installed in the capital since the Partisans and Red Army units fought their way into it on 20 October of the previous year. Though they still had to undergo six months of hard fighting, in which Tito's Army of National Liberation suffered its heaviest losses in the rigours of regular warfare, their ultimate and complete victory was no longer in doubt.

Croatia

The collapse of Italy had brought both advantages and disadvantages to the 'Independent State'. It was a blow to the regime's prestige, for the Duce had been the Poglavnik's early patron and Fascism the model for the Ustaš movement. But some of Pavelić's lieutenants, such as 'Marshal' Slavko Kvaternik, had always looked primarily to Germany, which was henceforth to assume the exclusive protection of the puppet state. Moreover, Italy's occupation of part of Dalmatia, an intolerable affront to Croat nationalists, was now a thing of the past, and so far as the Germans could regain those areas from the Partisans they were handed over to Ustaš administration. But there were some in the Independent State who believed that it should follow Italy's example and defect whilst there was still time; victory seemed certain for the allies, who might be prepared to sponsor the survival of an independent Croat state rather than see it form part of a Communist-dominated Yugoslavia. A conspiracy to this effect was detected in the summer of 1944 and its ring-leader, foreign minister Lorković, executed. But a few months later, an Ustaš envoy was sent to Italy to negotiate terms with the allies on much the same lines. His advances were not entertained, but in Zagreb the Ustaše did negotiate with representatives of their old enemy the Chetniks, who saw their last hope of survival in passing through Croatia in order to make a final stand with the Germans in Venezia Giulia before seeking internment in Italy. But before they in turn fled from Bosnia before the advance of Tito and the Red Army, the Ustaše vented their rage in a final spate of atrocities against the Orthodox population. At the beginning of May, Pavelić accompanied the remnants of the Ustaš forces in their retreat to the Austrian border and the Partisans entered Zagreb.

Slovenia and the Primorje

Tito's troops did not cease their pursuit of the Quisling forces at Yugoslavia's pre-war boundaries. They drove them into Austria and occupied Klagenfurt and Villach which they had claimed after the 1914–18 war but been forced to surrender as the result of a plebiscite (see page 168). Once more they were obliged to withdraw on the peremptory demand of the Anglo-American authorities. The latter also aroused Partisan resentment by accepting the surrender and arranging the internment of some 20,000 Quisling troops. Tito's main effort, however, was directed

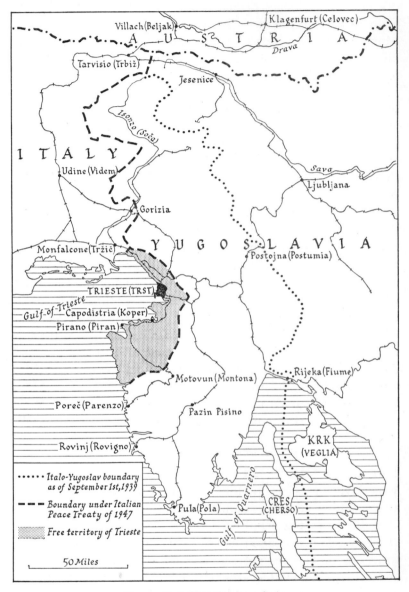

Fig. 41. Italo-Yugoslav boundaries.

against Trieste, which Yugoslav propaganda had been claiming with growing insistence since the Anti-Fascist Council's Jajce resolution. Not only had Partisan detachments succeeded in seizing control of the great part of the Primorje (Venezia Giulia) but they were fighting in Trieste itself when the Second New Zealand Division entered the city on 3 May and received the Germans' surrender. For the next forty days, a tense situation developed, British and Yugoslav troops both occupying Trieste, with the Yugoslavs setting up a civilian administration. Under strong allied pressure, Tito finally withdrew his troops, and agreement was reached in June by which the city itself and a strip of territory to the west (Zone 'A') were to be under the military administration of the allies, whilst the rest of the disputed territory (Zone 'B') remained in Yugoslav hands. The resentment caused by this dispute dissipated much of the good will created by the wartime co-operation between the Partisans and the British. Nor was Tito's bitterness directed solely against the British. He had looked in vain for support from the Russians, with whom he had signed a Treaty of Friendship in Moscow only a few weeks before. But the Soviet Union had no wish to risk a major clash with the western allies by championing Yugoslav interests at the expense of the Italians, thereby also alienating sympathies from the Italian Communist party which otherwise stood a good chance of being carried to power. The Trieste problem thus not only put a heavy strain on Yugoslavia's relations with the West, but was to prove a serious irritant in her relations with the Soviet Union.

CHAPTER 12

THE POST-WAR PERIOD

FOUNDATION OF THE REPUBLIC

The end of the war found Tito and other Communist leaders of the Partisan movement in control of all power, civil and military, throughout Yugoslavia. There was no organized political opposition, and most people were preoccupied with the basic tasks of keeping alive in the chaotic aftermath of war. Soon after Belgrade was liberated, the provisional government consisting of twenty representatives of the Anti-Fascist Council (AVNOJ), three representatives of the royalist government in exile, and five representatives of Yugoslavia's pre-war political parties, proceeded to summon a provisional assembly. Though this included a number of representatives of the pre-war political parties in addition to members of the Anti-Fascist Council, the power and influence of the Communist party remained overwhelming in the provisional assembly, as in the country at large. Local government organs were still largely in the hands of the Partisans. The army remained in being, its hard core consisting of some 350,000 men, most of them Communists or Communist supporters, and comprising a total of around 800,000 men and women in uniform, engaged in the multitudinous military, semi-military and civilian tasks required for the preservation of order, the guarding of property, and the supply of food and essential services for the population in the anarchic conditions resulting from the passage of occupying or liberating foreign armies. To consolidate support for their seizure of power, and also for the coming elections, the Communists began in August 1945 to organize a political movement called the People's Front (Narodni Front). This was conceived as a monolithic organization in which political parties were to merge their identities and programmes, and work together under Communist leadership for a common programme to deal with the many urgent economic and political problems demanding solution.

One of these was the reform of the currency. In April 1945 war-time and pre-war currencies were called in and replaced by a new dinar with an exchange rate of one new to ten old dinars, and a foreign exchange rate of fifty new dinars to one U.S. dollar. Middle-class people in the towns, rich peasants and all who had accumulated savings during the war were hard hit (as they were meant to be) by this reform. Their position was made worse by strict control over rents of house property. The effect of these changes was to impoverish, and virtually eradicate, the small class of town bourgeoisie which had played such an important part in political life in Yugoslavia between the two world wars.

These classes were further weakened by the legislation introduced by the provisional assembly confiscating the property of collaborators and Volksdeutsche, limiting the amount of land that might be owned by individuals and institutions, and nationalizing most industrial property. Some 80 per cent of all industry thus passed into state hands. The assembly also passed an electoral law disenfranchising all deemed to have collaborated with the enemy and extending the vote to all citizens over the age of eighteen, and to all enlisted men and women regardless of age. The law provided for a two-chamber parliament; a Federal Council composed of 319 members (one member for every 40,000 voters), and a Council of Nationalities (twenty-five members for Serbia, Croatia, Slovenia, Macedonia, Montenegro, and Bosnia-Hercegovina respectively, and fifteen for each of the two special regions, Vojvodina and Kosovo-Metohija (Kosmet)).[1]

Members of the pre-war political parties saw clearly the way events were developing, but found they could do little against the Communists' control of power and popular support. They complained that they were not allowed freedom for election

[1] The population and area of these administrative divisions were estimated (1953) and are shown overleaf.

campaigning, and resigned from the provisional government. Thus no opposition condidates were put forward. There was a single list of People's Front candidates, all pledged to support the official, in effect the Communist party's, political programme. Polling took place on 11 November 1945, and results indicated 90·48 per cent votes for, and 9·52 per cent against, the People's Front in respect of the Federal Council, and 88·68 per cent for, with 11·32 per cent against, the People's Front, for the Council of Nationalities.

Although heavy pressure and persuasion had been exercised in favour of the official list, majority backing for Tito and the Partisans appears to have been genuine at this time. Only in Serbia was there any considerable support for the king. In the rest of the country the Serbian family which had provided a king for the Yugoslav kingdom, had never been popular. King Alexander and Prince Paul had identified themselves more with Serbian than Yugoslav aims. Tito had led the people to victory; he was already a legendary hero and there was no other political leader among Yugoslavs within or without the country of comparable stature. He had demonstrated that he could unite people from different parts of the country; pre-war political parties were largely discredited by the fact that many of their leaders had been in exile, and had continued during the war the regional disputes and personal feuds that had ruined Yugoslav political life between the wars. Above all, Tito had won the support of the peasants, especially of those peasants from the many arid districts of the country which had suffered

	Population	Area in sq. miles
Serbia	4,460,000	55,700
Croatia	3,914,000	56,300
Bosnia-Hercegovina	2,843,000	51,600
Vojvodina	1,714,000	22,200
Slovenia	1,463,000	20,000
Macedonia	1,304,000	26,500
Kosmet	809,000	10,300
Montenegro	420,000	15,800
Total	16,927,000	256,400

238

conditions of intolerable poverty during the inter-war years. These peasants had been the backbone of the Partisan movement and Communist indoctrination had merely confirmed in them a radical desire for social change, which was the natural peasant reaction to generations of exploitation by feudal landlords or governments whose policies had favoured the town dwellers. For these people the war had been fought to throw out occupying armies and also to achieve an improved social order. Tito was unique amongst Communist leaders in post-war Europe in having peasant support, in facing no considerable bourgeois opposition, and in being a genuinely popular national leader.

ORGANIZATION OF THE NEW STATE

The new parliament met on 29 November 1945. It abolished the monarchy and proclaimed a new state based on federal and democratic principles to be known as the Federal People's Republic of Yugoslavia. It ratified earlier legislation of the three sessions of AVNOJ, and on 31 January 1946 enacted a new constitution. This constitution (of 138 articles) was based on the 1936 constitution of the Soviet Union.[1] It defined state authority as belonging to the people and proclaimed equal rights for all citizens, including freedom of religion, speech, association and assembly. It specified the organs of government from the bi-cameral legislature to elected assemblies for local government in the federal republics. These were to be the same as those established for the provisional government—Serbia, Croatia, Slovenia, Montenegro, Macedonia and Bosnia-Hercegovina. Serbia was to include the autonomous province of Vojvodina and the autonomous region of Kosovo-Metohija. The constitution specified matters which were to be the responsibility of the central government; these included matters of finance, economic planning, foreign policy, defence, communications and law. It was clear that although the federated republics might be the organs through which executive action was taken,

[1] Constitution of the Federative People's Republic of Yugoslavia, Belgrade, 1947, pp. 86 (in English translation).

they would have little power to follow independent policies in any matters of major importance.

A section dealing with 'Socio-Economic Organization' placed the means of production and all foreign trade in the hands of the state (art. 14) and placed restrictions on the owning and inheritance of private property. 'The land belongs to those who cultivate it' was laid down as a principle, and it was stated that no large landholdings would be allowed to private ownership (art. 19). Legislation putting these principles into effect resulted in the nationalization of mining, industry, banking, insurance, wholesale trade and eventually (April 1948) all foreign-held property. Land and house property was not nationalized, but the earlier law limiting landed property to 35 hectares (87½ acres) for individuals, 10 hectares (25 acres) for institutions, was confirmed.

LAND REFORM

Land expropriated or sequestrated from collaborators and Volks-deutsche totalled about 1·6 million hectares. A quarter was forest and came under state ownership and a further quarter was kept by the state to be developed as state farms or as property of public institutions. 792,000 hectares of land were redistributed; of this, 407,000 hectares were distributed amongst 263,000 peasant families who were landless or had holdings too small for subsistence. 385,000 hectares were given to peasant families from Bosnia, Montenegro and other poor regions who were settled on sequestrated land in the Vojvodina and Sava valleys. 47,000 hectares were given to groups of peasants to form 72 'working co-operatives'. These were to be the nucleus of the collectivization of agriculture which according to Communist policy was to be carried through gradually by getting peasants to pool their smallholdings into agricultural co-operatives. But in 1945–6 it was not possible to carry this doctrinaire policy very far: it was necessary to get the peasants to till the soil to provide food for townspeople and industrial workers, and not to antagonize them by too hasty schemes of collectivization.

Land reform, in so far as it meant nationalization and redistribution to poor peasants of large estates formerly owned by a few individuals, by the Roman Catholic Church, by banks and other institutions, was a popular measure which had long been advocated by peasant parties in Croatia and Slovenia as well as in Serbia, where there had been few such large estates. But the policy of collectivization by forcing peasants to pool their smallholdings was most unpopular. The government's policy of enforced purchase of agricultural produce at fixed low prices, and the policy of taxing the (during years of scarcity of food, quite high) profits was also very unpopular. Many peasants saw Communist policy as an attack on the traditional independent way of life and means of livelihood of the small landholders who formed the bulk of the Yugoslav population.

Dragoljub Jovanović, former leader of the Serbian Peasant party, one of the few pre-war politicians who had won universal respect, was the spokesman in the first post-war parliament of this opposition. He criticized government policies and maintained that peasants were insufficiently represented in public life: he was only silenced when in 1947 he was tried on charges of treason and imprisoned for nine years.[1] Jovanović was only one of very many Yugoslavs imprisoned by the regime in the years 1945–8 because of their political opinions or because they failed to co-operate wholeheartedly with the new economic and political measures. State security, and the government Department of the Defence of the People (OZNA), based on Soviet models, were draconian in their activities. This situation did not improve until after 1950.

RELIGION

Opposition to the Communist government also came from some of the religious communities, especially from the Roman Catholic Church (predominant in Croatia and Slovenia) which was bitterly hostile to the new regime. In the 1948 census (in which people stated their religion) the percentages of different religions were as follows: Orthodox 49·53 per cent; Roman Catholic

---

[1] Dragoljub Jovanović was released in 1955 and died soon afterwards.

36·7 per cent; Moslem 12·52 per cent; other Christian churches 1·14 per cent; Jews 0·04 per cent; other religions 0·07 per cent.[1]

Article 25 of the new constitution guaranteed freedom of conscience and of religion to all citizens, and declared the separation of church and state. It stated that there should be freedom for religious communities to engage in religious activities for the purposes of religion; schools for the training of priests were to be allowed. The misuse of religion for political ends, and the formation of political organizations on a religious basis were specifically forbidden. It declared that the state might give financial support to any religious community. The interpretation of this clause was to remain a source of bitter conflict between the Roman Catholic Church (to a less extent, and for a shorter period, also the Orthodox Church) and the Communist regime for many years.

Relations with the three major communities (Orthodox, Catholic and Moslem) had already been much embittered at the end of the war by the trial (often summary) and execution or imprisonment of priests or officials who had collaborated with the enemy during the war. The trial that received most publicity outside Yugoslavia was that of Archbishop Stepinac of Zagreb who was tried in 1946 on charges of having collaborated with the Pavelić regime in Croatia, and condemned to sixteen years' imprisonment. He was released from prison in December 1951 but confined to his village outside Zagreb and was forbidden to resume his archiepiscopal duties.[2]

The regime was determined to break the great political power and influence which through material possessions (land, banks, industries, newspapers, etc.) and by means of spiritual, educa-

[1] As these official figures total 100 per cent of population it must be assumed that they include Communists or others who had renounced their religion but had been included under the heading of the religious group into which they had been born. A person's religion (Orthodox, Catholic or Moslem) was often traditionally used as an alternative description to an ethnic group; thus Serb and Orthodox, Catholic and Croat or Slovene, were often and still are used by the people of Yugoslavia as synonymous.

[2] He was made a Cardinal in 1952 but refused to go to Rome to receive his Cardinal's hat, because government permission to go was conditional on his not returning to Yugoslavia. He died of leukaemia in 1960.

tional and confessional pressure, the churches had exercised in the past. The greater part of the material possessions of the churches had already been nationalized. Many schools, colleges, newspapers, etc., were now forcibly closed down. Churches, however, still remained open and were freely used and many leaders of all three faiths continued to wage their battle against communism.

The Orthodox Church was the first to begin to accept the limited conception of the role of the church in national life which the new regime was prepared to offer. But agreement between the churches and the state was reached only slowly. A number of the more rigid Moslems who were not prepared to accept the new ideas fled to Turkey, but gradually the Moslem community in Yugoslavia accepted many of the new social and political concepts of the Communist regime. In 1950 the veil for Moslem women was officially abolished, and the ideas of equality of education and of opportunity for boys and girls came to be accepted as inevitable even by the traditionalists.

The Catholic Church alone remained totally opposed to communism and relations with the state improved little until after Archbishop Stepinac's death in 1960. In November 1952, after a complaint by the Yugoslav government that the Vatican was interfering in internal affairs in Yugoslavia and making impossible a settlement between church and state, relations deteriorated, and in December of that year Yugoslavia broke off diplomatic relations with the Holy See.

In May 1953 a new law was passed clarifying the legal position of religious communities and restating the principles enacted in the articles of the 1945 constitution. Priests, church officials and their families came to be included in the state system of insurance and the state made grants to Orthodox, Moslem and Roman Catholic communities for the maintenance of their schools for theological study, for the repair of church buildings and, in the case of the Orthodox and Moslems, for the payment of salaries and church expenses. In spite of Communist party opposition to political aspects of organized religion the churches in Yugoslavia continued to be active and well supported, though their political and temporal power was much curtailed.

THE FIRST FIVE-YEAR PLAN

Whilst the basis of the new state was being formulated by the executive and enacted by parliament, the main tasks in the winter of 1945–6 were to provide food and shelter for the population and get essential services and communications in working order throughout the country. Devastation caused by the war had been on a gigantic scale. Yugoslavia had lost 1,700,000 people, among them a high proportion of the trained and industrial personnel whose numbers in pre-war days had not been very high. Material losses were calculated at 46·9 thousand million dollars, a figure which cannot convey the real picture of appalling destruction that was present in towns, villages, communications, industry, farming and every other aspect of civilized life. The first task of the government was to repair and reconstruct; for this work the United Nations Relief and Reconstruction Administration provided $425 million in aid. Most important among the many items on which this money was spent were food, medical supplies, rolling stock and lorries, industrial plant, farm stock and seeds. By the end of 1946, as a result of tremendous efforts by the whole Yugoslav people, this phase of reconstruction was finished. The government was determined to make an immediate start on implementing its ambitious plans for a fundamental reconstruction of the Yugoslav economy.

A Five-Year Plan for the development of the country's resources was introduced in mid-1947, although production in agriculture and industry had not yet been restored to pre-war levels. Its general aim was to raise the standard of living by developing the country's rich and largely unexploited economic resources. It aimed to change the backward condition of the country with its melancholy history of underdeveloped industry and rural unemployment and poverty by a rapid programme

244

of industrialization. It hoped by this means to strengthen the regime against its internal and external critics (of whom there were many) and thus prevent 'a return to the old unjust political and social order'.

National income (1939) level was to be doubled by 1951; the plan aimed to increase pre-war industrial production by nearly 300 per cent. Industry's share of total production was to increase from 45 per cent in 1939 to 64 per cent in 1951. Special emphasis was laid on the development of heavy industry, especially iron and steel and non-ferrous metals. General targets in agriculture were less specific, the overall aim being a return to pre-war levels, modernization of farming methods by mechanization and the 'socialization' of agriculture by increasing the number of co-operative (collective) farms. About 70 per cent of the total population of the country was still peasant, and independent peasants were responsible for the greater part of agricultural production. Although many of them had been in favour of radical social change which they hoped would improve their lot, few other than Communist supporters among them wished for a 'socialization' of agriculture.

The plan provided for investment of over a third of national income over the five years. For its realization considerable foreign credits and capital would have been necessary, and Yugoslavia hoped a great part of this would come from eastern countries. Although the Soviet Union did not approve of the plan, it had promised loans and credits for the purchase of capital equipment (for mines, steel works and electric power stations) and some armaments to a total of over $300 million. Russian technicians were sent to Yugoslavia and two joint Yugoslav-Soviet companies were formed for Danube shipping (JUSPAD) and for air lines (JUSTA). Trade agreements were signed with the Soviet Union and all eastern European Communist states. In 1947 49 per cent of Yugoslavia's exports and 51 per cent of her imports were with Communist countries which were to supply most of the capital goods and raw materials necessary for realization of the industrial plan.

Critics both in and outside Yugoslavia condemned the plan as too ambitious. In the event, although the government forged ahead with many of its industrial projects, the plan itself was never put to the test for in 1948 a major politica. quarrel with Soviet Russia resulted in a rupture of relations with that country and subsequently with all other Communist countries of eastern Europe.

THE COMINFORM DISPUTE

The expulsion of Yugoslavia from the Cominform (an organization of the Communist parties of six countries of eastern Europe, the Soviet Union, Italy and France) startled public opinion in Yugoslavia and throughout the world when it was suddenly announced on 28 June 1948. This was because the frictions and disputes between the Yugoslav and Soviet leaders which had led up to it had not been made public. The many and diffuse reasons given for this dramatic action of the Soviet leaders narrowed down to four major charges: that the Yugoslav Communist leaders had followed an un-Marxist line on major questions of home and foreign policy; that they had shown an unfriendly attitude to the Soviet Union and its Communist party; that they had treated the Yugoslav peasants as one class, not discriminating against rich peasants, and had not collectivized the land; and that they had subordinated the Yugoslav Communist party to the People's Front and kept the activities of that Communist party secret as if it were still an underground organization. These charges were accompanied by attacks on individual Yugoslav Communist leaders for their 'petty-bourgeois nationalism', their 'boundless ambition, arrogance and conceit' and their 'belligerence and hostility' when taxed with error by the Soviet Communist party. The situation was made worse when the two major supporters of the Soviet point of view among the Yugoslav leaders, Hebrang and Žujović, were arrested by the Yugoslav government.

The crux of the whole matter lay in the independence of the Yugoslav leaders, in their insistence, against Soviet advice, on

246

following policies which they believed were best suited to conditions in Yugoslavia, and calculated to further the end of their own interpretation of Communist aims, by methods that were most likely to keep Tito and his supporters in power. Collectivization of the land which the Soviet leaders advised would have meant an open conflict with more than half the total population. The cessation of food supplies that would have resulted could have brought the economy to a standstill and resulted in the overthrow of Tito's government. This situation would have suited the Soviet leaders who hoped to be able to replace Tito and his loyal supporters by the kind of stooge regimes that had been installed in other Communist countries of eastern Europe.

An appeal of the Soviet Union to Yugoslav communists to overthrow Tito met with very little response. Most of the Yugoslav Communist party and the greater part of the nation rallied behind Tito in the face of the Soviet threat. It was demonstrated clearly that the Partisan movement during the war had bred a strong nationalist feeling which provided the strongest basis for Tito's regime.

A break with the Cominform countries on whom more than half of Yugoslavia's foreign trade, and all the aid and credits for the Five-Year Plan depended, seemed likely to spell calamity for Yugoslavia whose relations with the West were also very poor at this time. Steps were taken to meet some of the Soviet criticisms. A public congress of the Communist party was held in July 1948. It was decided that the central committee was henceforth to be elected, its work to be less clandestine, and an attempt was made to take more workers into the party. Harsher measures against the peasants began in 1949 and by 1951 about two million peasants had been coerced into the semi-collectivization of their land in over 6,500 co-operative farms. The folly of this policy was immediately demonstrated in a critical drop in agricultural production, which reached its lowest level since 1920 after the disastrous harvest of 1952. The policy of coercive collectivization was abandoned in 1953 and the majority of the co-operatives were disbanded.

In the meantime, the break with the Cominform had become absolute. A Cominform economic blockade of Yugoslavia resulted in the stoppage of trade, credit and, most serious of all, heavy industrial imports from eastern Europe and Russia. These included coal and coke, plant for steel mills, power stations, etc., on which depended the development of industry projected in the Five-Year Plan. Trade with eastern Europe had come to a standstill by the end of 1949. The joint Yugoslav-Soviet companies were dissolved.

The break with the Cominform lasted until after Stalin's death. In a visit to Belgrade in 1955 Kruschev admitted the error of Russia's attitude to Yugoslavia in 1948, blaming it on Stalin and Beria. He made a clumsy attempt to effect a reconciliation with the Yugoslav leaders and began a new phase in Yugoslav-Soviet relations. The new relationship remained an uneasy one and the Yugoslav Communists continued to follow an independent national policy which was still not wholly accepted by the Russian leaders.

REORIENTATION OF POLICY AFTER 1948

The break with the Cominform had a profound influence on the evolution of Tito's Yugoslavia. It demonstrated clearly the dangers of relying solely on economic relations with the Soviet Union and other Communist countries. Yugoslavia was forced to accept aid from the West and to reorientate her trade. This inevitably resulted in a breach in the 'iron curtain' that had cut Yugoslavia off from non-Communist countries since the end of the war. It also resulted in Yugoslav Communists reappraising the fundamental bases of their own Communist state. These had been taken ready-made from the Soviet Union. From now on, the Yugoslavs were to evolve their own form of Communism, sometimes called Titoism. The results were important changes in economic planning, a less rigid form of Communist government in Yugoslavia, and the evolution and practice of a policy of non-alignment in foreign policy.

To avoid economic collapse, Tito accepted aid from the West.

This was slow in coming because of the mutual suspicions of both western and Yugoslav leaders. Western countries were unwilling to see Tito's government destroyed by economic blockade for fear that it would be followed by Yugoslavia being dominated by the Soviet Union. Tito would not accept aid with any political strings attached, and was determined to remain free to develop his own Communism. Immediately after the Cominform blockade, Yugoslavia began to export strategic metals and minerals to the West. This was followed by the U.S.A. lifting its embargo on the export of industrial equipment to Yugoslavia. Trade treaties and agreements between Yugoslavia and eastern Europe had lapsed. They were replaced by trade agreements with Great Britain, West Germany and other countries of western Europe.[1] Short- and medium-term credits were made available and from 1949 Yugoslavia was receiving loans from the Export-Import Bank of the U.S.A. and from the International Bank for Reconstruction and Development.

Although it was clear that the Five-Year Plan could not be realized, it had still not been abandoned, and credits and import facilities were still being used for raw materials and industrial equipment needed for the ambitious expansion of industry envisaged in the plan. Threats from the Communist bloc and the deteriorating international situation after the outbreak of the Korean war had also induced Yugoslav leaders to attempt rapid expansion of their armaments industry and military equipment. Her foreign indebtedness was rising steeply.

A severe drought in 1950 reduced the harvest to half that of a normal year and precipitated an economic crisis which in the long run had fortunate results for Yugoslavia. In that year the U.S.A., Great Britain and France instituted a programme of tripartite aid, first started to avert starvation and economic crisis, and later evolving into a programme of aid designed to assist the Yugoslavs to develop their economic resources and

---

[1] Agreement with western Europe was delayed for some time by negotiations over compensation for foreign assets nationalized by the Yugoslav government. Agreement about compensation was reached in 1949.

achieve economic viability. It was hoped this would be achieved by 1954. U.S.A. aid was to be spent on food and raw materials. Britain allowed her aid to be spent additionally on investment materials for agriculture. There were no restrictions on the small amount of French aid. Tripartite aid to Yugoslavia continued until 1958, and totalled $2,517 million including aid for military supplies.

CHANGES IN ECONOMIC PLANNING

In spite of the break with the Cominform and the reorientation to western aid and trade, Yugoslav leaders did not abandon the programme of industrialization which was the basic aim of their economic planning. The Five-Year Plan was extended for a year to 1952. The industrial programme of the Five-Year Plan was scaled down to a number of key projects, and it was accepted that these would not be completed by 1952. Among these projects were the steel industry (including armaments), coal, metal and mineral mining, non-ferrous metallurgy, electric power, machine tools, oil, textiles, and a number of industries connected with building programmes. Industrial production had risen up to 1948, by 1950 it was stagnating; but after the injection of foreign aid it rose steadily, and by 1953 most of the key projects were virtually completed. From 1953 to 1956 there were only annual plans. Long-term planning was resumed with the 1957–61 plan (completed by 1960) and a further plan was projected for 1961–5. By 1963 Yugoslavia had made striking progress in industrial development and production. Exports of manufactured goods rose by over 100 per cent between 1954 and 1960. During the early 1960's production slowed down and measures had to be taken to curb inflation.

CHANGES IN AGRICULTURE

Changes in agriculture were less striking. In the early years, lack of investments, bad harvests in 1950 and 1952, and the policy of enforced collectivization had brought disastrous results.

Agricultural production (still below pre-war levels) had seriously declined, and Yugoslavia was only saved from starvation by food imports from the U.S.A. under the aid programme.

Big changes in agricultural policy and treatment of peasants were introduced from 1953. A decree of 30 March 1953 permitted peasants to withdraw land and livestock from co-operatives; by the end of the year, more than three-quarters of co-operatives had been disbanded or completely reorganized. Though the government had not abandoned its theoretical belief that co-operatives were the ideal 'socialist' system for agriculture they did not (up to 1965) attempt again to enforce it. In 1958 there remained 507 working co-operatives with 216,000 hectares of land. Official policy was now to encourage peasants to join General (buying and selling) Co-operatives through which increased aid to agriculture (cheap seed, fertilizers, breeding stock, use of machines, etc.) was channelled. By the beginning of the 1960's it was claimed that more than 90 per cent of all private peasants belonged to such organizations.

Investment into agriculture was increased (643 thousand million dinars over ten years[1] compared with 19 thousand million in the first Five-Year Plan) but was still insufficient for effective modernization. Much-needed machinery, fertilizers, and breeding livestock were allowed to be imported. An attempt was made to eliminate waste by improved marketing, installation of refrigeration plant and improving road and transport communication in rural areas. A start was made on bringing abandoned land back into cultivation and reclaiming land by irrigation and draining.

The confidence of the independent peasants in the government had to be restored to gain their co-operation in increasing production. The system of enforced sales at fixed low prices (OTKUP) was abolished. The arbitrary taxation system was changed; taxation was to be fixed in advance on an agreed estimate of yield, and improvements were not to be subject to

[1] During 1952–6 annual plans were adopted but ten year programmes were prepared for each sector of the economy to indicate the general lines of future plans.

taxation. Agricultural production showed a steady increase in the second half of the 1950's and reached its peak in the good harvests of 1958 and 1959. The drop in production between 1960 and 1962, though attributable to bad weather, was greater in the private sector than on state and co-operative farms. The maximum holding of arable land had been reduced again to allow only 10 hectares (25 acres) to a private owner, and in many cases this was too small for highly productive farming. Although pressure on the peasants to collectivize their farms was not resumed, it seemed likely that the government would follow a policy of increasing state farms by purchasing land whenever possible and especially from the increasing number of peasants who left the land to become industrial workers.

DECENTRALIZATION

Reforms in the policy towards the peasants were only part of far-reaching changes introduced in the 1950's into most aspects of the political and economic organization of the state. The highly centralized form of economic planning copied from Stalinist Russia and expressed in the first constitution and the Five-Year Plan was abandoned in favour of political and economic decentralization. The state, though federal in theory, had during those years allowed only very limited powers to the six federal republics. Their powers were now increased. All ministries in Belgrade were abolished with the exception of those for Foreign Affairs, Interior (Security) and Defence. Their functions were taken over by corresponding departments set up for the purpose in the six federal republics. In Belgrade, committees of permanent officials, much reduced in numbers and powers, were instituted to co-ordinate activities and establish general lines of policy. Executive responsibility lay with the republics. Economic planning and control were also decentralized. Most of the functions of the Ministry for Economic Planning were transferred to small planning institutes at Federal level as well as at the level of the regional republics. Emphasis was placed on the importance of local government in political and economic decisions and increased powers were given to People's Committees in local government districts. The Commune was taken as the basic unit in local self-government and given increased powers especially in relationship to industries and other economic enterprises in their areas.

On 26 June 1950 a law was passed handing over management of all economic enterprises to the workers.[1] Workers' Councils were to be elected bi-annually in all enterprises, factories and workshops and they were given by law considerable powers over internal administration, conditions of work, distribution of capital and income, and over the decisions as to what products an enterprise should make and how and where it should market them.[2] At the same time, centralized control of prices was largely abolished and prices (for most, but not all products) were allowed to regulate themselves by the law of supply and demand. Centralized control of foreign trade was abandoned in 1951.

The political and economic principles behind these changes were incorporated in a new constitution issued in 1953. Government was still to be (at both federal and republican level) on a bi-cameral basis. The Federal Council, which was to be elected by direct suffrage as before, was now to include a number of representatives for each republic and region (the former Council of Nationalities) who would be summoned only when regional matters were under discussion. The new second chamber was the Council of Producers, elected by indirect suffrage from local Councils of Producers in which each industry was represented according to its contribution to the national income. Thus workers, but not private peasants and individuals, were represented in both houses. Tito became president of the Republic

[1] The principle of self-management through Workers' Councils was also extended to virtually all groups of workers, including universities, schools, hospitals, civil service, transport, foreign trade, etc.

[2] The freedom of Workers' Councils has been limited by various regulations stipulating compulsory payment of taxes, savings from investment, salary payments, etc. but the tendency of recent regulations has been to increase rather than diminish the powers exercised by the Workers' Councils. See below, page 257.

as well as head of the government;[1] he was elected by the Federal Parliament, which also elected a Federal Executive Committee to replace the ministers whose departments had been abolished.

LIBERALIZATION

Political and economic changes in the 1950's were accompanied by a marked liberalization of life for the ordinary people in Yugoslavia. The number of people arrested and detained on political grounds was greatly reduced, and the powers of the secret police curbed. Literature and ideas from the West were allowed to enter the country, more (but not all) Yugoslavs were allowed to travel abroad, and tourists from the west were encouraged to visit Yugoslavia. Conditions of life for the ordinary people began to improve slowly as the new industrial enterprises, freed from control, began to produce many of the much-needed consumer goods that had been so conspicuously lacking in earlier years. Quality goods began to be imported from abroad and there was a marked improvement in social services, health, education and cultural matters.

Increased quality goods in the shops stimulated both townspeople and peasants to greater productivity to make money to buy the goods they had been denied for so long. In many cases (since wages were still low) people were unable to pay for them out of income. In the towns people worked overtime, or doubled their jobs; many peasants began to undertake part-time work in industry and a general improvement in standards of living resulted in both town and country.

The new system was subject to considerable changes and modifications throughout the 1950's and early 1960's. One problem that received constant attention was that of striking a balance between too much and too little decentralization. The central government intended that two principles should continue to operate even with the increased participation of ordinary people in management and local and central government.

1 Under the old constitution he had been president of the Praesidium.

These were that there should be continuous economic growth and that the Yugoslav Communist party's conception of the socialist state should continue to be put into practice in all aspects of public life. In 1965 the Yugoslav Communist party numbered 1,018,331 members. These were clearly insufficient to fill all the many public functions in political and economic life throughout the country, and it meant that the policy had to have the support of great numbers of people both from the Socialist Alliance (the new name for the reorganized People's Front) and from every walk of life.

A number of modifications in the Workers' Councils were introduced from 1954 onwards. These were aimed mainly at regulating the Councils' financial activities—new forms of taxation were introduced and some form of federal price control was reinstituted. Credit and investment were again brought under some kind of central control. With the reintroduction of overall planning in 1957 (five-year plans were introduced for 1957–61 and 1961–5), general objectives were laid down and there was some movement away from decentralization. But no attempt was made to go back to the highly centralized state of the period before the break with the Cominform.

Liberalization in all aspects of life did not mean that there was any fundamental change in the basic limitations on political freedom inherent in the Yugoslav Communist system. The state remained a Communist one. All elections, for government and local government and for Workers' Councils were still held on the one-party system. No one was allowed in high office in political, economic, administrative or cultural life who was not a supporter of the regime. Freedom of expression was allowed in a limited field. It was now possible to criticize the way the government policies were being carried out—even to query some of the policies themselves; but it was not permitted to question the basic principles on which the state was founded, nor to advocate any alternative form of government.

This was exemplified by the case of Milovan Djilas, a personal friend and Communist colleague of Tito throughout the Partisan warfare, and a prolific polemicist for the Communist government in the post-war years. His outspoken criticism of Stalinism had earned him bitter hatred from the Russian side but this did not undermine his position as one of the four most important Yugoslav leaders. But when he turned to querying basic concepts of Yugoslav communism and began to advocate a more democratic form of government, he was first warned, then summoned before the party and condemned by it, and finally tried on charges of subversive activity.[1] In 1957 he was condemned to imprisonment for three years (increased later to seven years) but was given provisional release in 1961.[2] When he continued political writing which he allowed to be published abroad, he was again tried and condemned to imprisonment in 1962. Djilas's fate illustrated not only the strength of the determination of the Communists to keep power in their own hands, it showed also their conviction—openly expressed by Tito himself—that a western democratic system would again produce the political chaos and regional quarrels that had ruined the pre-war state in Yugoslavia and would nullify the progress that had been made since the war.

Although opposition political writing was thus proscribed, literature of a non-political kind flourished under the new liberalization. More books, in much greater variety, were imported from the West, more were translated, and renewed cultural contacts were accompanied by great literary, academic and scientific activity. Throughout the post-war years, Yugoslav writers were prolific in publications of prose and poetry inspired

[1] Vladimir Dedijer, also a pre-war Communist, friend of Tito and distinguished Partisan, supported Djilas when he appeared before the party in 1957. Dedijer, like Djilas, was thrown out of the party, but he was not imprisoned, and after a time was allowed to go abroad to work, and later to return to Yugoslavia.

[2] The book which occasioned the increased sentence was *The New Class*, first published in U.S.A. in 1957. It was a detailed attack on the kind of government, political élite and arbitrary exercise of power which Djilas thought had developed with Communist government in Yugoslavia. The book which caused his imprisonment in 1962 was *Conversations with Stalin* also published in the United States. As the book was not an attack on communism or communists in Yugoslavia it appears that Djilas was imprisoned for repeatedly refusing to accept the limitations imposed on his own freedom of thought and expression.

by the tragic and heroic experiences of the Partisans and of the whole nation during the Second World War. But the work of the outstanding Yugoslav writer in these years, Ivo Andrić, who was awarded the Nobel Prize for literature in 1962, dealt mainly with the experiences of his native Bosnia in earlier periods of South Slav history.

In art, too, liberalization allowed Yugoslav artists to turn away from 'socialist realism' to experiment (at least for a time) in abstract and other forms of modern art in vogue in the non-communist world. Thus Yugoslav cultural life ceased to be cut off from the main stream of western civilization with which it had had such fruitful connections for so many centuries. Culture in Yugoslavia still remained very regional—Serbian, Croatian, Slovene, Macedonian, Bosnian, etc.—as it had been in the past, but the best-known names in science and the arts were beginning to be known in all parts of the country—a trend resulting from the process of unification which the revolutionary political and economic changes were bringing to the country.

THE 1963 CONSTITUTION

By 1962 so many changes had taken place in every aspect of social, political and religious life that it was thought necessary 'to sanction the changes by a single constitutional act'.[1] A new constitution was passed in April 1963. This differed considerably from those of both 1946 and 1953 and introduced many new and unusual features. An important part of the constitution dealt with economic affairs and incorporated principles (of workers' management and participation in the profits of their work) and institutions (such as Workers' Councils and the local government unit, the Commune) which had already been tried out in the preceding years during the period of liberalization.

The new political provisions were both complicated and original. They limited and defined the field of central, federal

[1] The quotations are from the 'Report on the Principles of the Preliminary Draft of the New Constitution of Socialist Yugoslavia', by Edward Kardelj. Edition Yugoslavia, Belgrade, October 1962.

government,[1] greatly increased the legislative independence (additional to the considerable executive powers which they had had before) of the republics, and gave much wider powers to the smaller units of government within the republics—the Communes. Republics and Communes were to have their own elected assemblies with powers to decide many matters (political, social and economic) that had hitherto been dealt with by central government. A special fund was set up to finance the economic growth of insufficiently developed republics and areas. The Council of Producers was abolished and replaced by four councils, each dealing only with a special aspect of government—education and culture, economics, social welfare and public health, political administration. The Federal Assembly remained as before the general political body with defined legislative powers; the four councils were to have deliberative and advisory powers and to be associated with the Federal Council when laws in their field of activity were passed. A novel section of the constitution contained detailed provisions designed to ensure that as many people as possible should get experience of government at all levels by serving on the local republican and federal assemblies. Another unusual feature was a section defining the fundamental principles on which Yugoslavia's foreign policy should be based. This laid great stress on the need to work for regional and international co-operation and emphasized the principles of equality of peoples, of non-interference in the internal affairs of other countries, and adherence to the principles of the charter of the United Nations.

FOREIGN RELATIONS

After the end of the war, relations between Tito's government and the west had deteriorated rapidly.[2] This was partly because of western disapproval of the Soviet type of communism Tito's

---

[1] These included security, foreign policy, protection of the 'socialist order of the republics, of the unified base of the socio-economic and political system', foreign trade, international traffic, etc. The name of the state itself was changed from the 'People's' to the 'Socialist' Federal Republic of Yugoslavia.

[2] See above, page 235.

government was introducing so rapidly; it was also exacerbated by the nationalization (without immediate compensation) of foreign-held property and industries in Yugoslavia, and by sympathy of western people with the Yugoslav middle classes, who seemed hardest hit by the new reforms. At the same time, Yugoslav Communists reacting sharply to this hostility, and, filled with the first flush of enthusiasm for their own and Soviet successes during the war, were very pro-Russian and anti-western. As the cold war developed between 1945 and 1948 Yugoslavia was at first wholeheartedly behind Stalin. Relations with the West were made worse by the long-drawn out dispute over Trieste and its hinterland[1] and because Yugoslavia was giving aid (arms, medical assistance and refuge on Yugoslav territory) to the Greek Communists who were in revolt in the districts of Greece adjacent to the Yugoslav-Greek border.

The sudden break between Yugoslavia and Russia that came with the Cominform quarrel in 1948 forced the Yugoslav government to make dramatic changes in its foreign policy. The result was a reappraisal of the fundamental bases of Yugoslav foreign policy, changing it from one that was aligned with the Communist countries of Russia and eastern Europe, to a policy that took more account of national interests and was more independent and uncommitted in the international field. At the United Nations[2] Yugoslavia began to play a more active independent part and her relations with the West slowly improved. Relations with Russia and the Cominform countries remained uneasy (or in varying degrees hostile) until after M. Kruschev's visit to Belgrade in 1955. With Albania in particular relations remained especially embittered. Yugoslav aid, which had been given to Albania in the immediate post-war period, was now denounced by Albanians as having been characterized by imperialistic motives, and throughout the 1950's and early

[1] See above, page 235.
[2] Yugoslavia had supported the USSR and the Eastern Bloc in the United Nations between 1945 and 1948. In 1949 Yugoslavia was elected a member of the Security Council of the United Nations in spite of the opposition of the Eastern bloc.

1960's Albania remained the only Communist country, beside China, to continue its intransigent hostility to the Tito regime.

One immediate result of the Cominform quarrel was that in 1949 Yugoslavia stopped the aid she had been giving to Greek Communists. The revolt was put down by the Greek government, and improved relations with Yugoslavia made possible the signature of a Balkan Pact (1953) between Yugoslavia, Greece and Turkey. Although this never developed into a close relationship, it helped to give an atmosphere of greater security and showed that Yugoslavia could have at least a general alliance with two countries, members of NATO.

Increased relaxation of relations with the West and the need for settlement of her northern frontiers also led towards a solution of the Trieste problem. In this, Tito, backed by the whole Yugoslav nation, took a strong line against any solution greatly adverse to Yugoslav interests, and eventually (1954) secured a settlement on the lines of Yugoslavia retaining Zone B (with certain frontier rectifications in her favour) and Italy keeping Zone A which included the port of Trieste.[1] Though this fell short of Yugoslav claims it was rapidly followed by improved relations with Italy which led to an increase in trade between the two countries and to the acceptance by Yugoslavia of considerable technical assistance from Italy.

Improved relations with other countries in the West also brought increased trade especially (after the settlement of reparations claims) with West Germany, and with the three countries involved in the major aid programmes—France, Great Britain and the U.S.A.[2]

Relations with Russia were more complex. Rapprochement with Yugoslavia was initiated by Russia after the death of Stalin, and Kruschev and Bulganin visited Belgrade in 1955. Kruschev's apology for Soviet mistakes in their relations with Yugoslavia did not have the immediate effect of bringing the Yugoslavs

[1] See above, page 235.
[2] In 1961 imports totalled $910 million, exports $569 million. Of these exports $261 million were to western Europe, $43 million to north America, $175 million to eastern Europe and the U.S.S.R., and $90 million to the rest of the world.

back into the Soviet camp, but it led for a short time to close relations between Tito and Kruschev in which Tito made strenuous efforts to get his ideas of communism accepted in eastern Europe. On his insistence the Cominform was disbanded (17 April 1956), and he pressed for removal of Stalinist leaders in the satellite states, especially of Rakosi in Hungary. The 1956 rising in Hungary put an end to this brief period of Tito's influence on Russian policy. Escalation of the Hungarian revolt into counter-revolution put the whole Communist position in jeopardy. The brutal suppression of the revolt by the Soviet Union brought Russian tanks near the Yugoslav frontier and underlined the anomalies and weaknesses of the Yugoslav position. Relations between Yugoslavia and Russia deteriorated with mutual recriminations about which one was responsible for the Hungarian revolt. Yugoslavia again was isolated from the rest of the Communist world, but this time the situation was not so serious or prolonged, and as before it was mitigated by continued aid from the U.S.A.

At the end of 1957 as a gesture towards Russia (and probably with a miscalculation of consequences) Yugoslavia recognized East Germany, resulting in a rupture of diplomatic but not trade relations with Western Germany. These had not been restored by 1966. Yugoslavia was still not prepared to abandon attempts to influence the evolution of communism in eastern Europe. In Communist meetings summoned by Kruschev (1957, 1959 and 1960) Yugoslav delegates continued to speak and vote against the organization of a Communist bloc in international affairs and a Russian bloc against China in the Communist world. Yugoslav leaders' new ideas about the 'independent roads to socialism' were clarified and redefined for the benefit of Yugoslav and other Communists. These were announced at the seventh congress (1958) of the Yugoslav Communist party (which changed its name to League of Communists). They emphasized non-alignment and co-existence in the international field, and in internal communism ideas of decentralization and participation of people in government through Workers' Councils, Communes, etc. They also recommended some limitation of Communist party privileges and leadership. Most important was the emphasis on independence from outside (meaning Russian) interference in national Communist policies. This Yugoslav challenge was strongly disapproved of by Russia and violently denounced by China. But Yugoslav leaders continued to support, if no longer actively to lead, the controlled liberalization of communism that was taking place in most satellite countries.

Relations with Russia did not improve until the early 1960's when the overt Chinese challenge to Soviet leadership of the Communist world forced Russia to look for allies. In spite of Chinese hostility to Titoist communism Yugoslavia refused to become totally committed to Russia, though improved relations did follow Tito's visit to Russia in 1962, and were cautiously maintained after Kruschev's fall in 1964.

An important basic principle of Yugoslav foreign policy which emerged after 1950 was that of non-alignment. Begun to gain friends and support in Yugoslavia's first period of isolation, it evolved into a movement to organize small, weak or non-committed countries so that jointly their views on international issues would have more weight in world affairs. Between 1958 and 1966 Tito visited many Afro-Asian and South American countries to get support for the movement, his greatest successes being with Nasser in Egypt, and with Nehru in India.

Yugoslavia organized two conferences of non-aligned nations, the first in Belgrade (September 1961) attended by twenty-three Afro-Asian countries, the second in Cairo (October 1964) attended by forty-seven nations. Yugoslavia remained the only European, and only Communist state in the movement. By 1966 Tito had not had much success in leading non-aligned nations to greater influence. This was mainly due to world conditions beyond his control and also to divergence of aims among the Afro-Asian nations participating. But Tito's international prestige had been increased and he continued to lead non-aligned nations in pressing for limitation of nuclear armaments, for peace in Vietnam and for detente between East and West—including admission of China to membership of the United Nations.

By the mid 1960's Yugoslavia's position between East and West was more stable than at any previous time. It was aided by developments in east European and Soviet communism which brought them nearer to Titoist concepts of communism. In economic matters Yugoslavia continued to have relations with both East and West but preferring co-operation with Western economic organizations (including a cautious approach to the Common Market) as long as these required less political alignment than was exacted from members of the COMECON which Yugoslavia still treated with suspicion. Although trade with Communist countries increased in the 1960's Yugoslavia continued to cultivate a trade pattern which covered most of the world.

The rapid rate of economic growth of the late 1950's slowed down in the early 1960's resulting in recurrent cycles of inflation which in 1965 led to drastic economic reforms and currency devaluation and, in 1966, to the issue of new currency. Considerable external debts, an adverse balance of payments and mounting unemployment showed that Yugoslavia's combination of Communist and Western economic measures had not yet solved her economic problems. This economic dilemma was not unique to Yugoslavia, and the overall picture showed that since 1945 there had been a substantial rise in the general standard of living that was especially noticeable in the traditionally more backward areas. An economic revolution had taken place that was rapidly transforming Yugoslavia into a modern industrialized state.

CONCLUSION

Thus after nearly twenty years of Communist rule under Tito's leadership great changes had taken place in Yugoslavia. Her population (over 19 million in 1966) had far surpassed pre-war levels. In spite of increased industrialization about half of the working population was still employed in agriculture, of whom the majority were independent peasants owning their own smallholding, but the second largest occupational group was in the manufacturing industries and this was rising by 7 per cent annually whilst employment in agriculture was falling. More important as a sign of change was the fact that industrial production contributed about half of total output, whilst agriculture, in spite of the number of people employed, only contributed about one-quarter. Yugoslavia had shown a rapid rate of economic growth and a substantial improvement in standards of living. In spite of considerable external debts and an adverse balance of payments, Yugoslavia in 1966 was in a better economic situation than at any time in pre-war years.

Politically, Tito's government had proved itself strong enough to remain in undisputed power, but not secure enough to allow organized opposition. Strong government, regional autonomy and the national policy of the Communist party had left no room for racial disputes of the kind that had ruined pre-war Yugoslavia. But considerable regional rivalry still remained. Whether this would again be strong enough to challenge the unity of the state it was still impossible to say. The testing time for Yugoslav national unity and for the results of the Communist state which owed so much to Tito himself would be likely to come when the question of a succession to President Tito had to be settled in the future.

SHORT BIBLIOGRAPHY

The following is not a source bibliography, but a list of books in English which will be useful for further reading:

GENERAL AND EARLY HISTORY

Auty, P. *Yugoslavia* (London, 1965).
Dvornik, F. *The Slavs; their Early History and Civilisation* (Boston, 1956).
Kerner, J. (ed.). *Yugoslavia* (University of California, 1949).
Pribichevich, S. *Living Space; the Story of South-eastern Europe* (London, 1940).
Stavrianos, L. S. *The Balkans since 1453* (New York, 1958).
West, R. *Black Lamb and Grey Falcon* (2 vols) (London, 1942).
Woodford, D. McClellan. *Svetozar Marković and the Origins of Balkan Socialism* (Princeton University Press, 1964).

SLOVENIA

Čermelj, L. *The Life and Death Struggle of a National Minority* (Ljubljana, 1945). Tr. by F. S. Copeland.
Moodie, A. E. *The Italo-Yugoslav Boundary* (London, 1945).
Vosnjak, B. *A Bulwark against Germany* (London, 1917).

CROATIA

Eterovich, F. H. (ed.). *Croatia; Land, People, Culture* (Toronto, 1964).
May, A. *The Hapsburg Monarchy 1867–1914* (Cambridge, Mass. 1951).
Seton-Watson, R. W. *The Southern Slav Question and the Habsburg Monarchy* (London, 1911).
Taylor, A. J. P. *The Hapsburg Monarchy 1809–1918* (London, 1948).

DALMATIA

Gardner Wilkinson, J. *Dalmatia and Montenegro* (London, 1848).
Hodgkinson, H. *The Adriatic Sea* (London, 1955).
Jackson, T. G. *Dalmatia, the Quarnero and Istria* (3 vols) (Oxford, 1887).
Villari, L. *The Republic of Ragusa* (London, 1904).
Voinovitch, L. *Dalmatia and the Yugoslav Movement* (London, 1920).

BOSNIA AND HERCEGOVINA

Evans, A. J. *Through Bosnia and Hercegovina on Foot* (London, 1877).
Mariott, J. A. R. *The Eastern Question* (Oxford, 1925).
Obolensky, D. *The Bogomils* (Cambridge, 1948).

MONTENEGRO

Djilas, M. *Land without Justice* (New York, 1958).
Stevenson, F. S. *History of Montenegro* (London, 1914).

THE INTER-WAR PERIOD

Graham, S. *Alexander of Yugoslavia* (London, 1938).
Hoptner, J. B. *Yugoslavia in Crisis, 1934–41* (New York, 1962).
Lodge, O. *Peasant Life in Yugoslavia* (London, 1942).
Seton-Watson, H. *Eastern Europe between the Wars, 1918–41* (Cambridge, 1945).
Tomasevich, J. *Peasants, Politics, and Economic Change in Yugoslavia* (Stanford, 1954).

THE SECOND WORLD WAR

Clissold, S. *Whirlwind; an Account of Marshal Tito's Rise to Power* (London, 1949).
Dedijer, V. *Tito Speaks* (Weidenfeld and Nicolson, 1953).
Maclean, F. *Disputed Barricade* (London, 1957).
Maclean, F. *Eastern Approaches* (London, 1949).
Rootham, J. *Miss Fire* (London, 1946).

SERBIA

Laffan, R. G. D. *The Guardians of the Gate* (Oxford, 1918).
Ranke, L. *History of Serbia* (London, 1874).
Remak, J. *Sarajevo* (New York, 1959).
Seton-Watson, R. W. *Sarajevo* (London, 1926).
Temperley, H. W. V. *History of Serbia* (London, 1917).
Vucinich, W. S. *Serbia between East and West; the Events of 1903–8* (Stanford, 1954).

MACEDONIA

Barker, E. E. *Macedonia; its Place in Balkan Power Politics* (London, 1950).
Brailsford, H. N. *Macedonia; its Races and their Future* (London, 1906).

THE POST-WAR PERIOD

Avakumović, I. *History of the Communist Party of Yugoslavia*. Vol. 1. (Aberdeen University Press, 1964).
Djilas, M. *The New Class; an analysis of the Communist System* (London, 1957).
Hoffman, G. W. and Neal, F. N. *Yugoslavia and the New Communism* (New York, 1962).

SOURCES OF THE MAPS

1. **The Socialist Federal Republic of Yugoslavia.**
   Religious faiths based on a folding map in *Résultats préliminaires du Recensement de la Population dans le Royaume des Serbes, Croates et Slovènes du 31 Janvier 1921, publié par la direction de la Statistique d'Etat, Belgrade* (Beograd, 1924).

2. **Zones of cereal production.**
   Based on R. Bičanić, 'The effects of war on rural Yugoslavia', *Geographical Journal*, vol. 103, p. 42 (London, 1944).

3. **The Balkan peninsula about A.D. 800.**
   Based on R. Lane Poole, *Historical Atlas of Modern Europe*, plate 4 (Oxford, 1902).

4. **The territories of Samo and Ottokar.**
   Based on (i) J. W. Thompson, *Feudal Germany*, p. 496 (Chicago, 1928); (ii) W. R. Shepherd, *Historical Atlas*, p. 7 (9th ed., New York and London).

5. **The Slovene lands (pre-1918 frontiers).**
   Based on *Northern Italy: Ethnographical Map* (1918), 1:1,500,000. G.S.G.S. No. 3703A.

6. **Roman frontiers and the Eastern Church.**
   Based on *The Cambridge Medieval History*, vol. 1, maps 1, 2, 8, and vol. 6, map 57 (Cambridge, 1911 and 1929).

7. **Croatia about A.D. 1070.**
   Based on S. Stanojević, *Istoriski Atlas*, plate 45 (3rd ed., Beograd, 1934).

8. **The northern frontiers of the Ottoman Empire, 1699–1739.**
   Based on W. R. Shepherd, *op. cit.* pp. 125 and 133.

9. **The 'military frontier' of Austria and Hungary.**
   Based on *The Cambridge Modern History Atlas*, map 111 (2nd ed., Cambridge, 1924).

10. **The ethnography of Croatia-Slavonia, 1910.**
    Based on the map in *The Peoples of Austria-Hungary*, vol. 1, *Hungary* (N.I.D., London, 1919). Compiled from the Hungarian Census of 1910.

11. **Venice in Dalmatia.**
    Based on the *Enciclopedia Italiana*, vol. 12, p. 252 (Milano, 1931).

12. **The territory of Ragusa.**
    Based on S. Stanojević, *op. cit.* plate 52.

13. **The Illyrian Provinces, 1809–14.**
    Based on C. Grant Robertson and J. G. Bartholomew, *An Historical Atlas of Modern Europe*, plate 8 (2nd ed., Oxford, 1924).

14. **Medieval Bosnia.**
    Based on S. Stanojević, *op. cit.* plate 47.

18-2

15. **The growth of Montenegro.**
Based on (i) E. Hertslet, *The Map of Europe by Treaty*, vol. 4, p. 2782 (H.M.S.O., London, 1891); (ii) *Enciclopedia Italiana*, vol. 23, p. 744.

16. **The Balkan peninsula, A.D. 910–1265.**
Based on (i) E. A. Freeman, *Atlas to the Historical Geography of Europe*, maps 34–7 (London, 1903); W. Miller, *The Latins in the Levant*, p. 81 (London, 1908); (iii) W. R. Shepherd, *op. cit.* pp. 59, 67 and 89.

17. **The Balkan peninsula, A.D. 1340–55.**
Based on (i) E. A. Freeman, *op. cit.* maps 40 and 41; (ii) W. R. Shepherd, *op. cit.* p. 89.

18. **Serbia in the tenth and eleventh centuries.**
Based on S. Stanojević, *op. cit.* plate 46.

19. **Serbia under the Nemanjid dynasty.**
Based on (i) S. Stanojević, *op. cit.* plate 48; (ii) H. W. V. Temperley, *History of Serbia*, p. 60 (London, 1919).

20. **Serbia under Prince Lazar (1371–89).**
Based on S. Stanojević, *op. cit.* plate 51.

21. **The ethnography of the Vojvodina, 1910.**
Based on (i) J. Cvijić, 'Carte ethnographique des régions septentrionales Yougoslaves', 1:1,000,000 (1919), as drawn in I. Bowman, *The New World*, p. 360 (4th ed., New York, 1928); (ii) the folding map in J. Cvijić, J. Radonić, S. Stanojević and H. Zeremsky, *Le Banat* (Paris, 1919). Compiled from the Hungarian Census of 1910.

22. **Serbia under George Branković (1427–56).**
Based on S. Stanojević, *op. cit.* plate 51.

23. **The patriarchate of Peć, 1557.**
Based on S. Stanojević, *op. cit.* plate 50.

24. **The growth of Serbia, 1817–1913.**
Based on C. Grant Robertson and J. G. Bartholomew, *op. cit.* plates 23–5.

25. **The Balkans in 1878.**
Based on (i) *The Cambridge Modern History Atlas*, map 119; (ii) C. Grant Robertson and J. G. Bartholomew, *op. cit.* plates 23–5.

26. **The 'contested zone', 1913.**
Based mainly on *Report of the International Commission to inquire into the Causes and Conduct of the Balkan Wars*, p. 45 (Carnegie Endowment, Washington, 1914).

27. **The Balkans in August 1913.**
Based on C. Grant Robertson and J. G. Bartholomew, *op. cit.* plate 25.

28. **Conflicting claims in Macedonia, 1912.**
Based on (i) P. Dehn, *Die Völker Südeuropas und ihre politischen Probleme* (Halle, 1909); (ii) A. Oakes and R. B. Mowat, *The Great European Treaties of the Nineteenth Century*, p. 315 (Oxford, 1918).

29. **The Bulgarian exarchate, 1870–1912.**
Based on D. Rizoff, *Die Bulgaren in ihren historischen, ethnographischen und politischen Grenzen*, map 31 (Berlin, 1917).

30. Yugoslavia in relation to Austria-Hungary.
Based on C. Grant Robertson and J. G. Bartholomew, *op. cit.* plates 21 and 40.

31. The Treaty of London, 26 April 1915.
Based on I. Bowman, *op. cit.* pp. 350 and 358.

32. The territorial formation of Yugoslavia.
Based on (i) Anon., 'The new boundaries of Bulgaria', *Geographical Review*, vol. 9, pp. 299–305 (New York, 1920); (ii) C. Grant Robinson and J. G. Bartholomew, *op. cit.* plates 25 and 40.

33. Istria: languages and frontiers.
Based on *Northern Italy: Ethnographical Map* (1918), 1:1,500,000. G.S.G.S. No. 3703A.

34. The Klagenfurt plebiscite, 10 October 1920.
Based on H. W. V. Temperley (ed.), *A History of the Peace Conference*, vol. 4, p. 370 (London, 1921).

35. Albania and the Albanian minority in Yugoslavia, 1913–43.
Based on (i) E. P. Stickney, *Southern Albania or Northern Epirus in European International Affairs, 1912–23*, pp. 96, 108 and 109 (Stanford, Cal., 1926); (ii) H. W. V. Temperley, *A History of the Peace Conference*, vol. 4, p. 338; (iii) Yugoslav Census, 1921.

36. The boundaries of the *banovine*, 1929–41, and the boundaries of the autonomous *banovina* of Croatia, 1939–41.

37. The dismemberment of Yugoslavia, 1941.

38. The rising in Serbia, summer, 1941.
Based on F. Maclean, *Disputed Barricade* (London, 1957).

39. The Fourth Enemy Offensive against the Partisans.
Based on F. Maclean, *op. cit.*

40. The Fifth Enemy Offensive against the Partisans.
Based on F. Maclean, *op. cit.*

41. Italo-Yugoslav boundaries.
Based on J. Kerner (ed.), *Yugoslavia* (University of California, 1949).

INDEX

Abdul Hamid, Sultan, 150
Adam, Archbishop, 95
Adrianople (Edirne), 99, 120
Adriatic, 1, 8–9, 15, 23–4, 26, 32, 43–57, 61, 63, 73, 78–9, 83, 86, 91, 130–1, 140, 160, 173
Afro-Asian countries, 261–2
Agram, see Zagreb
Agram Treason Trial, 41, 130
Agrarian party, 172, 191
Agrarian Reform, 67, 170, 240–1
agriculture, 173, 178, 185–6 240–1, 244–5, 250–2, 264
Akerman, Convention of, 120
Albania, 9, 63, 67, 74, 79, 81–2, 84, 86, 94, 96, 131, 159, 209, 259–60
Albanians, 8, 12, 76, 98–100, 109, 116, 135–7, 141–53, 165, 168–9, 175, 209, 217
Alexander (Karageorgević), King, 164, 171–89, 194, 238
Ali Pasha, 142
Almissa, see Omiš
Andrássy, Count, 36, 68, 126
Andrić, Ivo, 257
d'Annunzio, Gabriel, 167
Anti-Fascist Council (AVNOJ), 220–1, 227, 230, 235–6, 239
Antivari, see Bar
'Argosy', 51
Arsenije, Patriarch, 109
Assling, 16
Aurelian, Emperor, 9
Ausgleich, 21, 36, 55, 122
Austerlitz, 52
Austria, 2, 4, 13–22, 30–42, 52–7, 65–72, 77–80, 83, 85–6, 106, 109–10, 113–34, 138, 145, 148–9, 154–69, 187, 196
Avars, 11, 13
Axis, 196–207, 208–36
Axis pact, 200–7

Bach, Alexander, 21, 35–6
Bačka, 35, 103, 122, 166, 209
Balkan Entente, 187, 200, 202

Balkan pact, 260
Balkan wars, 22, 41, 56, 72, 85–6, 130–3, 152–3, 157
Balša family, 73–4, 85, 99
Ban, 25, 31, 33, 35, 37–8, 41, 55, 59–60, 190, 200
Banat, 35, 103, 110, 166, 211
Banja Luka, 64
Banovine, 178, 190, 193, 198–200
Bar (Antivari), 73, 81–2, 84–5, 95
Baranja, 103–4, 122, 166
Barthou, Louis, 188
Baši-knez, 108
Beg, 64, 141
Belgrade, 6, 40, 85, 101, 106, 108–10, 113, 115–18, 124, 127, 129, 133–4, 164–5, 170–1, 173–5, 178, 182, 188, 191, 194, 196, 200–8, 213, 223, 232, 252, 259–60, 262
Beneš, E., 160
Berat, 98
Berchtesgaden, 203
Beria, 248
Berlin Memorandum, 68
Berlin, Treaty of, 68, 83, 125, 143–5, 148, 151, 202
Beust, Chancellor von, 36
Bihać, 219–21, 223
Bileća, 82
Biograd, 23
Bitolj (Monastir), 90, 131, 135, 145–6, 148–9, 152, 202
'Black Hand', 72
Bleiweis (Blajvajs), J., 19
'Bloc of National Agreement', 172
'Blue Guard', 220, 226
Bobovac, 61
Bodin, 90
Bogomils, 26, 46, 58–60, 62–4, 93, 105
Bohorič, Adam, 15–16
Bojana, R., 84
Boris, King, 187, 202
Borojević, Marshal, 161
Bosanius, R., see Bosna R.
Bosante R., see Bosna R.
Bosiljgrad, 166

Bošković, R., 51
Bosna R., 58, 60
Bosnia, 2–3, 22, 26–7, 40, 42, 47–9, 55, 58–72, 74, 82, 85, 90, 93–4, 97, 100, 102–5, 113, 126, 129–30, 132, 144–5, 155–8, 170, 175–6, 183, 193, 199, 210, 213, 217–19, 224, 226, 232–3, 237–9, 240, 257
Brač (Brazza), 61
Brailford, H. N., 146, 148
Brajici, 216
Branković, George, 101, 104–5
Brda, 77, 79, 80, 82
Brdo, 206
Bribir, 26
British (see also Great Britain), 54, 78, 82, 120, 149, 235
Broz, Josip, see Tito
Bucharest, Treaty of, 115, 120, 145
Budapest, 34, 112, 133, 159, 163, 190, 202–3
Budva, 73, 79
Bulganin, Marshal, 260
Bulgaria, 59, 85–6, 89–90, 93–5, 98, 103, 125–6, 129–31, 135–53, 159, 162, 169, 179, 183, 187, 196, 201–3, 208–9, 220, 222, 224
'Bulgarian atrocities', 144
Bulgarian exarchate, 142–5
Bulgarian language, 12, 135–6
Bulgars, 11, 58, 68, 98, 100, 124, 139
Bunjevci, 104, 122
Burian, Baron, 70, 159
Burma, 261
Byzantine empire, 23, 26–7, 43–8, 58, 61, 87–91, 93, 95–8, 113, 138–41

Cairo, 261
Campo Formio, Treaty of, 52
Carantania, 13
Caribrod, 166
Carinthia, 14–15, 18–22, 53, 154, 165, 168
Carlowitz, Treaty of, 30, 49, 66, 109
Carniola, 13–22, 53, 154, 160, 165
Caporetto, 162
Catherine, Empress, 113, 219
Catholic Church, 2, 10–11, 13, 16, 23, 58–60, 63–6, 72, 86, 89, 93, 105, 109–10, 143, 155, 157–8, 168, 192, 194–5, 241–4

Cattaro, see Kotor
'Centralism', 170–9
Cetinje, 73–6, 78–9, 84–5
Charlemagne, Emperor, 13, 43
Charles IV of Austria-Hungary, 159
Chetniks, 211, 214–33
China, 260–3
Churchill, Mr Winston, 201, 207, 229–30
Ciano, Count, 196
Cincar-Marković, 200, 202–4
Claudius, Emperor, 9
Clissa, see Klis
Code Napoléon, 18
collectivization, 240, 245–6, 252
COMECON, 263
Cominform, 246–50, 259–61
Comintern, 212, 220, 223
Comitadjis, 147
Common Market, 261, 263
Communists, 3, 171, 177, 179, 182, 212–35, 236–64
Concordat, 157, 192, 194–5
Constantine, Emperor, 9
Constantinople (Istanbul), 11, 24, 63, 65–7, 91, 96–8, 106, 111, 113, 115, 120, 140, 143
Constituent Assembly, 170
constitutions (1921), 170, 171–6
(1931), 181–4
(1946), 239–40
(1953), 253–4
(1963), 257–8
'Contested Zone' (Macedonia), 128, 131
co-operatives, 240, 245–6, 251
Corfu, Declaration of, 162
Corinth, Gulf of, 98
Corvinus, Matthias, 103
Council of Nationalities, 237–8, 253
Council of Producers, 253, 258
Crete, 49, 68, 113, 147, 149
Crimean War, 80–1, 123
Crna Gora, see Montenegro
Crnička, 79
Crnojević family, 74–5
Croat Peasant party, 4, 170–207
Croat Separatists, see Ustaše
Croatia, 2, 4, 15, 18–19, 23–42, 47, 55–7, 58–72, 89, 109, 120, 128, 132, 154–68, 170–207, 208–12, 218–21, 232–3, 237–9, 241–3
Croats, 11, 18, 22–42, 43–57, 58–72, 100, 122, 154–69, 208, 241–2

Crusade, First, 90
  Fourth, 45, 47, 94, 140
Cumans, 140
currency reform, 237, 263
Curzola, see Korčula
Cvetković, Dragiša, 197–206
Cyprus, 113
Cyrillic alphabet, 12, 15, 23, 40, 74, 119
Czechoslovakia, 163, 187, 196, 203, 205, 207
Czechs, 12, 17, 33, 70, 119, 160, 165, 198–9

Čačak, 216
Čaršija, 173
Časlav, 89
Čifliki, 141

Dalmatia, 2–3, 8–9, 11–12, 15, 17–19, 23, 27, 37, 40–57, 60, 62–3, 78, 83, 89, 103–4, 113, 132, 154–5, 160–8, 182–3, 193, 199, 208–9, 226, 233
Dalmatin, J., 15
Danilo I, 75–6
Danilo II, 80–1
Danilov Grad, 82
Danube R., 1, 9, 11, 35, 66, 93–4, 99, 103, 109–10, 116–17, 122–3, 139, 143
Dapčević, Peko, 217
Davidović, L., 172
Debar (Dibra), 94, 131, 145
decentralization, 252–4, 261
Dedijer, V., 256
Democrat party, 170–3, 175, 191
dictatorship, royal, 176–84
Dinaric Alps, 1, 4, 8
Dioclea, see Zeta
Diocletian, Emperor, 9, 13
Djakovo, 38
Djilas, M., 212, 218, 255–6
Djukanović, General, 226
Djurić, Major R., 231
Domobran, 219
Dráma, 149
Drang nach Osten, 70, 126, 131, 134
Drava R., 1, 12, 24, 27, 35, 193
Drim R., 95
Drina R., 24, 115
Drvar, 230
Dubrovnik (Ragusa), 4, 18–19, 43, 46–7, 49–54, 58, 61, 63, 94–8

Dulcigno, see Ulcinj
Durazzo, 94, 98
Dušan, Stephen, 47, 60, 73, 87, 91–2, 96–9, 130–1, 141

Eastern Church, see Orthodox Church
Eastern empire, see Byzantine empire
'Eastern Question', 68, 85, 87, 128, 157
economic questions, 3–6, 16, 22, 25–6, 51, 70–1, 84, 95–6, 152, 173–4, 177, 181, 185–6, 244–6, 248–58, 263–4
Edward VII, King, 150
Egypt, 262
Enos–Midia line, 86, 131
Enver Bey, 150
Epirus, 99, 140–1
Eugene, Prince, 110

Fascism, 168, 232
'February Patent', 36
Federal Council, 237–8, 253, 258
Federal Executive Committee, 254
Federal Parliament, 254, 258
Federalism, 170–1, 192–4, 252–4
Ferdinand of Austria, 27, 29
'Fifth Offensive', 224–7
Filov, 203
Fiume, see Rijeka
Fiume, Resolution of, 41, 56, 155
Five-Year Plan, 244–8, 250–2
'Fourteen Points', 162–3
'Fourth Offensive', 224–5
France, 17–18, 33, 52–4, 82, 113, 160, 179, 181, 187, 201, 249–50, 260
Francis Ferdinand, Archduke, 72, 133
Francis Joseph, Emperor, 55–6, 133, 159
Franciscans, 59, 65, 104
Franks, 13, 23
Frederick III, Emperor, 62
'Free Yugoslavia' Radio, 223
'Freedom Front', 220
Fremantle, Admiral, 78
French Revolution, 17–18
Friedjung, Dr, 41
Fruška Gora, 205

Gabrovo, 141
Gaj, Ljudevit, 33–4, 154
Garašanin, Ilija, 157
Gavrilo, Patriarch, 206
Geneva Conference, 164
Genoa, 46

Germans, 4, 13–22, 30, 38, 56, 85, 95, 112, 122, 165, 168
Germany, 16, 68, 70, 129–30, 134, 159, 177, 185, 187–8, 195–207, 208–33, 249, 260–1
Gipsies, 135, 137
Glagolitic script, 15
Goethe, 19, 119
Göring, General, 188
Gorizia (Görz), 18–19, 22, 53, 154, 160
Gospoda, 186
Gospodar, 80
Gottschee, *see* Kočevje
Gradisca, 22, 154
Grahovo, 81
Graničari, 161
Gravosa, *see* Gruž
Graz, 18
Great Britain, 113, 160, 174, 179, 201, 203–5, 207–8, 222, 228–35, 248–9, 260
Greece, 67, 85–6, 98, 130–2, 135–53, 200–4, 259–60
Greeks, 8–10, 65, 93, 98, 106, 111–12, 119, 132, 135–53, 260
'Green Bands', 163, 187
'Green International', 172
Gregory VII, Pope, 24, 90
'Grimani Line, 49
Grimm, J., 19, 119
Gruž, 70
Gubec, Matija, 25–6, 219
Gundulić, Ivan, 51
Gusinje, 84, 86

Habsburg dynasty, 14, 20, 30–2, 34–6, 42, 110, 112, 133, 160, 170, 187
Hajduk, 103, 115
Hatt-i-Sherif, 142
Hebrang, A., 246
Heraclius, Emperor, 87
Hercegnovi (Castelnuovo), 52
Hercegovina, 2–3, 22, 24, 48, 55, 58–72, 81–2, 85, 90, 113, 129–32, 144, 155, 158, 166, 176, 193, 199, 237–9
Hilmi Pasha, 148–9
Hinković, H., 160
Hitler, Adolf, 197–207, 208–35
Hlum, *see* Hum
Holy Roman empire, 14
Honorius III, Pope, 93
Horvati (Hrvati), *see* Croats

Hoste, Captain, 54
Hranić, Sandalj, 62
Hrebeljanović, Knez Lazar, 60, 99–100, 106
Hudson, Captain, 222
Hum, 60, 62, 90, 94
Hungarians (Magyars), 4, 12–13, 21, 31–42, 58–72, 94, 100, 122, 165
Hungary, 2, 4, 12, 19, 21–2, 25–42, 44, 46–7, 55–6, 59–72, 89, 95, 97, 102–4, 109–10, 112, 116, 122–3, 125, 128, 132, 154–69, 176, 187–90, 201, 203, 208, 261
Huns, 11
Hunyadi, John, 101–2, 105
Hussein, Aga, 67
Hvar (Pharos, Lesina), 8, 51, 54, 61

Ibar R., 89, 95
Illyria, 9, 11, 19, 20, 35
Illyrian Provinces, 18, 33, 53–4, 154
Illyrians, 8, 9, 12
Independent Democratic party, 173
Independent Croat State (*see also* Ustaše), 209–33
India, 262
International Bank, 249
Ipek, *see* Peć
Issa, *see* Vis
Istria (*see also* Primorje), 15, 18–19, 22, 40, 53–4, 160, 165, 167, 230
Italians, 12, 43, 56, 58, 84–5, 149, 165
Italy, 16, 18, 22–3, 52, 54, 86, 95, 130–1, 160, 162, 164, 167, 176, 180, 182, 184, 187, 196, 201–3, 208–35, 260
Ivan the Black, 74

Jajce, 63, 219, 228, 235
Janina, 142
Janissaries, 64, 108, 111, 113, 115–16
Janjici, 60
Janka Puszta, 190
Japan, 203, 207
Jassy, Treaty of, 77, 113
Jauerburg, 16
Jedinstvo, 174
Jelačić, Ban, 35, 79
Jesuits, 16, 109
Jevtić, B., 189–91, 194
Jews, 71, 135, 137, 165, 211, 242
JNS, 184

Joseph II of Austria, 16–17, 32, 113
Jovan II, Patriarch, 106
Jovanović, Arso, 217
Jovanović, Dragoljub, 190, 241
Jovanović, Jovan Zmaj, 112
Jovanović, Slobodan, 206–7, 222, 229
JRZ, 192, 194, 197
Julian Alps, 167
Justinian, Emperor, 11, 43

Kadis, 108, 114
Kallay, Baron, 69–70
Kapetans, 64, 67
Kara Dagh Mts, 135
Karadžić, Vuk, 19, 118–20, 154
Kara George, 114–18, 120
Karageorgević, Alexander (Prince of Serbia), 121, 127
Karageorgević, Peter (King of Serbia), 127–34, 157
Karawanke Mts, 168
Kardelj, E., 212
Karlovac, 30
Karst, 4
Kidrič, Boris, 212
Khuen-Héderváry, Count, 38, 40
Kiepert, geographer, 144
Klagenfurt (Celovec), 168, 203–4
Klek, 50
Klis (Clissa), 48, 63
Knez, 60, 100, 118
Kočevje (Gottschee), 15
Koloman, King, 25
Konariotes, 141
Kopaonik Mts, 95
Kopitar, J., 19, 154
Korčula (Korkyra nigra, Curzola), 8, 51, 54, 61
Korošec, Msgr, 160, 163, 175, 183, 190
Kosovo, Battle of, 27, 62, 74, 81, 100, 103, 109, 131, 141
Kosovo-Metohija (Kosmet), 95, 135, 146–8, 151–2, 168–9, 209
Kossuth, 34
Košutić, Ing. A., 179
Kotor (Cattaro), 43, 47, 52, 61, 78, 91, 95, 163, 199, 209
Kotromanić, Stephen, 60
Kragujevac, 116, 124, 208, 217
Kraljević, Marko, 99–100
Kraljevo, 116, 216
Kratovo, 131

Krek, Msgr, 160
Krešimir, Peter, 24
Krnjević, Dr J., 179
Kruschev, N., 259–62
Kruševac, 100
Kulin Ban, 58–9
Kumanovo, 95, 131
Kupa R., 65
Kustendil, 94
Küstenland (see also Primorje), 154
Kvaternik, Slavko, 232

Ladislas I of Hungary, 25
Ladislas of Naples, 47
Lagosta (Lastovo), 54, 168
Laibach, see Ljubljana
Lastovo, see Lagosta
Lazar, knez, see Hrebeljanović
League of Communists, 261
League of Nations, 180–1, 189–90
Legions, Yugoslav, 159
Leopold I, Emperor, 31, 109
Leopold II, Emperor, 32
Lepanto, 48
Lesina, see Hvar
Leskovac, 106
Lewis, Emperor, 14
liberalization, 254–7
Lika, 6, 182
Lim R., 89, 229
Lissa, see Vis
Little Entente, 187–8, 196
Ljotić, D., 211, 217
Ljubljana (Laibach), 15, 17–19, 21–2, 205, 207–9, 226
London, Treaty of (1913), 86, 131, 152 (1915), 160–3, 167
Lorković, M., 233
Lovćen, Mt, 74
Lucio, Giovanni, 46

Macedonia, 3, 87, 97, 99, 109, 126, 129–30, 135–53, 175, 179, 183, 193, 208–9, 220–1, 237–9
Macedonian Internal Revolutionary Organization (VMRO), 146, 148, 187
Macedonian language, 11, 135–6
Maček, Dr V., 174–207, 219
Maclean, Brig. F., 226
Mačva, 59
Madrid, Treaty of, 48

Magyars, see Hungarians
Mahmud II, 67
Mali, Stephen, 77
Manuel, Emperor, 91
'March Laws', 34
Marchfeld, 14
Maria Theresa, Empress, 16–17
Maribor, 182
Marić, General, 194
Marinković, Dr V., 182
Marmont, Marshal, 54
Marseilles, 188, 190
Martinuzzi, Cardinal, 103
Marulić, Marko, 51
Marxism, 261
Masaryk, T. G., 160,
Mavrovlachs, see Vlachs
Maximilian, Emperor, 9
Medjumurje, 166, 209
Medun, 82
Mesta R., 135
Meštrović, Ivan, 160
Metković, 70
Metohija, 95, 168–9, 209
Michael, Prince of Raška, 90
middle class, 237, 259
Mihajlović, Draža, 209, 213–18, 220,
    222–4, 228–32.
'Military Frontier', 19, 27–31, 33, 37–
    8, 110
Mitrovica, 149
'Mocenigo Line', 50
Mohacz, 27, 29, 48
Mohammad II, 63, 65
Moldavia, 67
monarchy, Yugoslav, 228–30
Monastir, see Bitolj
Montague, Lady Mary Wortley, 111
Montecuculi, General, 108
Montenegrins, 6, 53, 65, 73–86, 103,
    129, 164, 175
'Montenegrin Vespers', 75
Montenegro, 2, 4, 68, 73–86, 89–90,
    102–3, 113, 124–5, 128–32, 151,
    153, 155, 157–9, 163–5, 193, 209,
    212, 217–19, 224, 226, 237–9,
    240
Morava R., 1, 90, 95, 101, 110, 115,
    130, 213
Morea, 49–50, 113
Morlacchia, 12
Morlachs, see Vlachs

Moscow, 201, 223
Moslem organization, 183
Moslems (see also Turks), 63–72, 86,
    165, 170, 172, 175, 192–3, 210,
    219, 242–3
Munich Agreement, 197
Mürzsteg Programme, 149
Mussolini, 183, 196, 199

Nagoda, 36–42, 55
Nahies, 108, 120
'Nani Line', 49
Napoleon, 17–19, 33, 52–4, 78, 115–17,
    154
Nasser, President, 262
Natalie, Queen, 127
National Liberation, Army of, 213, 220,
    223, 226, 232, 236
National Liberation, Committee of,
    228, 230
National Liberation Movement (see
    also Partisans), 213–35
NATO, 260
Nedić, General M., 202, 211, 214–17,
    231–2
Nehru, President, 262
Nemanja, Stephen, 47, 90–1, 93
Nemanjid dynasty, 87–96, 99, 141
Neretva R., 24, 44, 47, 60, 94, 224
Neumarktl, 16
Nevesinje, 68
Nevrokop, 145
Nicholas I, Czar, 138
Nicholas II, Czar, 150
Nicholas I of Montenegro, 81–6, 126,
    129, 157, 164
Nikšić, 82
Nin (Nona), 23, 106
Niš, 94, 143, 208
Njegoš, see Peter II, Vladika
Njeguši, 75
Nona, see Nin
non-alignment, 261–3
Novasella, 82
Novi Pazar, Sanjak of, 68, 86, 90, 108,
    126, 130, 132, 149, 168–9, 217
Novi Sad, 112, 208
Novo Brdo, 96

Obod, 74, 85
Obor-knez, 108, 116
Obradović, Dositej, 112, 118

Obrenović family, 114
 Alexander, 127
 Michael, 121, 124
 Milan, 82, 121, 124–7, 145
 Miloš, 116–18, 120–4
'October Diploma', 36
OECD, 262
Ohrid, 89, 93–4, 98, 106, 131, 135,
 140, 142, 145–6, 208
Omer Pasha, 67
Omiš (Almissa), 47
Orseolo II, Peter, 44
Orthodox (Eastern) Church, 2, 10–11,
 23–4, 54, 58–60, 63, 65–72, 86, 89,
 93, 105–6, 110–12, 1 9–20, 142–
 53, 155, 157–8, 165, 194–5, 204,
 206, 241–4
Osijek, 208
Ostrog, 226
Ostrogoths, 11
Otto I, Emperor, 13
Ottokar of Bohemia, 14
Ottoman Empire, see Turkey
OZNA, 241

Pančevo, 112
Paris, 34, 185, 188
Paris, Treaty of (1856), 80, 123
Parliament, Yugoslav, see Skupština
Partisans, 3–7, 213–35, 238 247
Partition of Yugoslavia, 200–11
Pashaliks, 107–8
Passarowitz, Treaty of, 28, 30, 50, 66,
 110
Pastrović clan, 79
Pašić, N., 160, 162–4, 170, 173
Patarenes, see Bogomils
Patzinaks, 140
Paul, Prince, 189–207, 238
Pavelić, Dr A., 179, 188, 193, 210, 232,
 233, 242
Peasant Movements, 4, 6, 15, 25–6, 170,
 179–80
Peć (Ipek), 75, 86, 93, 95, 98, 105–7,
 109, 111, 142
Pečanac, Kosta, 211
People's Federal Republic of Yugo-
 slavia, 239–40
People's Front, 236–7, 246, 255
Perčec, G., 179
Perović, Dr, 189, 206
Pešić, General, 202, 204

Peter II, King of Yugoslavia, 189, 209,
 228–30, 238
Peter I, Vladika, 77–8
Peter II, Vladika, 78–9
Peter the Great of Russia, 76, 113
Peter III of Russia, 77
Petrinja, 30
Petrović, Danilo, see Danilo I
Petrović, George, see Kara George
Petrović-Njegoš, see Peter II, Vladika
Phanariotes, 111
Pharos, see Hvar
Piave R., 162
'Pig War', 129
Pijade, Moše, 218
Pirot, 125, 143
Plav, 84, 86
Plevlje, 68
Podgorica, 82, 84–5
Poglavnik, 210, 232
Poles, 12, 33, 70, 119, 165
Pomaks, 144
population, 263
Požarevac, 115–16
Požega, 12, 31, 116
Pragmatic Sanction, Croatian, 31
Prague, 40, 197
Prečani, 173–4, 176–7, 181–2, 192–3,
 197
Prekomurje, 22, 166, 209
Pressburg, 33–4
Pressburg, Treaty of, 52
Prešern, F., 19, 21
Pribičević, Svetozar, 172–3, 175–6
Priboj, 68
Prijepolje, 68
Prilep, 94, 99–100
Primorje (Venezia Giulia), 180, 226,
 233–5
Princip, Gavrilo, 72, 183
Prizren, 94, 109
Probus, Emperor, 9
Protestantism, 15–16, 71, 165
Protić, S., 170–1
'Proveditore Generale', 51

Račić, Puniša, 174
Rački, Franjo, 38
Radić, Stephen, 4, 164, 170–4, 219
Radić, Pavle, 172, 174
Radical party, Serbian, 158, 162–4,
 170–4, 183–4, 189–92

Ragusa, *see* Dubrovnik
Raja, 3, 64, 106, 114
Rakosi, 261
Ranković, Alexander, 212
Rapallo, Treaty of, 167
Raš, 95
Raška, 87–91, 95
Ravna Gora, 213, 216–17, 222, 232
Razana, 232
Reformation, 15–16
Regency, 189–207
Reichsrat, 21
Resana, 146, 150
'Reval Programme', 150
Rhodope Mts, 130
Ribar, Dr Ivan, 221
Ribar, Lolo, 212
Ribbentrop, J., 203
Rijeka (Fiume), 1, 22, 32, 35–6, 42, 160, 163, 167, 223
Romans, 9–10, 23–4, 43, 48, 139
Romantic Movement, 17, 33, 119
Rome, Pact of, 162–3
Roumania, 86, 104, 132, 137–8, 153, 187, 200
Roumanians, 122, 145, 165, 196, 201
Rudnik, 116, 201
Rudolf II, Emperor, 31
Rudolf IV, Emperor, 14
Rumelia, 120, 145–6
Russia, 53, 68, 70, 76–8, 80–3, 85, 113–34, 138, 160, 162, 201, 207, 211–16, 222–3, 229–30, 235, 239, 245–63
Russians, 12, 18, 35, 52–3, 78, 165, 211, 232
Ruthenians, 70, 122, 165

Sabor, 31, 33, 37–8, 200
St Cyril, 23, 89
St Gothard, 108
St Hermagor, 21
St Methodius, 23, 89
St Sava, 62, 93, 106
Salona, 8
Salonica, 1, 97, 126, 129–30, 135, 139, 141, 146, 148, 150, 152, 159, 202, 208
Samo, 13–14
Samuel, Emperor, 89, 140
San Stefano, Treaty of, 68, 82, 124–5, 144
Sanjak, *see* Novi Pazar

Sanjak-beg, 48
Sarajevo, 67, 72, 133, 209
Sava R., 1, 10, 12–13, 27, 66, 70, 94, 110, 240
Sava, Vladika, 77
Saxons, 95–6
Sazonov, S. D., 160
Schacht, Dr, 195
Sclavinia, 139
Scutari (Skadar, Skodra), 9–10, 73–4, 79, 82, 84, 86, 90–1
Sebenico, *see* Šibenik
Segna, *see* Senj
Semenderia, *see* Smederevo
Senj, 48, 63
Serbia, 2–4, 8, 15, 22, 26, 41–2, 47–8, 59–66, 68, 70–3, 82, 84–134, 137–53, 154–69, 170–207, 208–16, 219, 228–9, 231–2, 237–9, 241–2
Serbs, 11, 18, 22, 30, 33, 35, 38, 40–2, 51, 54, 56, 58–62, 65–72, 79, 86–134, 135–53, 154–69, 209, 209–18, 242
Serbo-Croat language, 11–12, 19, 37, 56, 118, 135–6
Seres, 98, 142, 149
Simeon, Emperor, 89, 140
Simović, General, 206–9
Sistova, Treaty of, 66, 77, 113
Skadar, *see* Scutari
Skoplje (Skopje, Üsküb), 94–5, 98, 100, 109, 125, 131–2, 136, 141, 145, 149, 151, 208
Skupština, 115–18, 121, 123–4, 127, 171–2, 174, 176, 182, 190–1, 194, 200
Slavonia, 4, 19, 26, 29–30, 35, 65–6, 103, 193, 199
Slavs, 4, 8, 11–14, 17–18, 21, 36, 43, 58, 87, 139
Slovaks, 122, 165
Slovenes, 11, 13–22, 26, 33, 54, 122, 154, 168, 170, 172, 176, 180, 190, 192–3
Slovenia, 2–3, 11–22, 42, 120, 158, 175, 182, 193, 209, 212, 220–1, 226, 233, 237–9, 241–2
Smederevo (Semenderia), 101–3, 106, 115
Sofia, 147, 183, 202
Sokolović, Grand Vizir, 106
Sokols, 179
Sombor, 112

Spahi, 106
Spaho, Dr, 183, 191, 197
Spalato, *see* Split
Spanish Civil War, 212, 217
Spić, 79, 82–3
Split (Spalato), 8, 46, 48, 55, 60, 62,
  173, 209, 223, 226
Sporazum, 199–200, 204–5
Spuž, 82
Srebrnik, 63
Srem (Srijem, Syrmia), 27, 31, 158,
  193, 199
Srškić, Dr, 182
Stalin, 7, 256, 259–60
Stambuliski, 172
Stambuloff, 145
Stanišić, Col., 226
Stanković, Dr, 189, 206
Starčević, A., 38
Stari Vlah, 12
Stephen 'the First-Crowned', 93
Stephen, knez, 100
Stepinac, Archbishop, 219, 242–3
Stojadinović, M., 190–7, 204
Stone, Miss, 148
Strossmayer, Bishop, 38–41, 154
Struganik, 216
Struma R., 130
Strumica, 145, 166
Styria, 13, 15, 18, 20, 22, 154, 165, 168
Subotica, 104, 165, 205
Sumner Welles, Mr, 207
Supilo, F., 160
Sutjeska, 61, 226
Sutorina, 50
Syrmia, *see* Srem

Šabac, 115
Šar Mts, 130, 135
Šibenik (Sebenico), 51
Škoda, 201, 205
Šokci, 104, 122, 154
Šubašić, Dr I., 200, 229–30
Šubić family, 26, 59, 60
Šumadija, 113, 115–16, 118, 208

Taaffe, Count, 21
Takovo, 116
Tamerlane, 101
Tara R., 89
Tartars, 93
Tchermen, Battle of, 99

Temesvar, 35, 66, 110, 205
Tempo, *see* Vukmanović
Tetovo, 95
Thessaly, 99, 141
Thrace, 139, 144
Tilsit, Treaty of, 53, 78
Tito, Marshal (Josip Broz), 3, 7, 211–
  35, 236–64
Tomašević, Stephen, 63
Tomislav, King, 23
Tomislav II, Duke of Spoleto, 210
Tommaseo, 55
Trabunja, 61, 90
Transylvania, 27–8, 66
Traù, *see* Trogir
Travnik, 64, 67
'Trialist Solution', 157
Trieste (Trst), 1, 15, 21–2, 154, 180,
  235, 259–60
Trogir (Traù), 8, 51, 183
Trubar, P., 15
Trumbić, Ante, 160, 162, 173
Turin, Congress of, 47
Turkey, 2, 27–30, 48–50, 63–72, 73–86,
  99–134, 135–8, 141–53, 187, 200,
  202–3, 205, 243, 260
Turks, 3–4, 15, 25, 87, 165, 211
Tvrtko, Stephen, 27, 47, 60–2, 100

Ulcinj (Dulcigno), 82–3, 96
Uniate (Greek Catholic) Church, 71,
  110, 143, 165
United Nations, 258–9, 263
United States, 84, 162, 174, 179, 249–
  50, 256, 260
UNRRA, 244
Uroš, Simeon, 99
  Stephen I, 96
  Stephen II, 94
  Stephen III, 94
  Stephen IV, *see* Dušan, Stephen
  Stephen V, 99
Uskoks, 48, 63
Ustaše (*see also* Independent Croat
  State), 179, 188, 210, 222, 232–3
Uzes, 140
Užice, 115, 216–17
Uzunović, 189

Vali, 64
Valona, 98
Valvasor, Freiherr von, 16

Varaždin, 30
Vardar R., 1, 8, 95, 130, 152, 208
Vardariotes, 140
Vasilije, Vladika, 77
Vatican (*see also* Catholic Church),
    Concordat, 243
Veles, 131, 145
Venezia Giulia, *see* Primorje
Venice, 2–4, 23–4, 27, 43–57, 60, 62–3,
    66, 74–6, 89, 97–8, 113, 141
Versailles, Treaty of, 164–9
Victoria, Queen, 85
Vidin, 106
Vidovdan, 100, 171, 179
Vienna, 14, 21, 32, 34–6, 41, 49, 54–5,
    65–6, 71, 109, 126, 133, 149, 158,
    163, 176, 203, 230
    Treaty of, 18, 53
    Congress of, 18, 78, 116
Vietnam, 263
Villach, 233
Vinica, 147
Virovitica, 31
Vis (Lissa), 8, 54, 230
Višegrad, 229, 232
Visigoths, 11
Vlachs (Mavrovlachs, Morlachs), 12,
    48, 65, 135–8, 140, 145
Vladikas, 74–80
Vlastimir, 89
Vodnik, V., 17
Vojislav, Stephen, 90
Vojvoda, 109–10
Vojvodina, 3–4, 35, 103–4, 112, 155,
    166, 168, 175–6, 183, 193–4, 199,
    237–9, 240
Volksdeutsche, 211, 237, 240
Vrhbosna, 64
Vučić, 121
Vukašin, Despot, 99–100
Vukčić, Stephen, 62–3
Vukičević, 174
Vukmanović-Tempo, S., 220

Wallachia, 110
'White Guard', 220, 226
William of Tyre, 90
Wilson, President, 162–3, 167
Workers' Councils, 253, 257, 262
World War I, 134, 153, 157, 159, 212
    II, 208–35

'Young Turks', 150
'Yugoslav Idea', 19–22, 38–40, 119–20,
    154–9
Yugoslav Committee, 160, 164
    National Council, 163–4
    National party, 184
    Peasant Radical Democratic party,
    182
    Radical Union, *see* JRZ

Zadar, *see* Zara
Zagreb (Agram), 22, 25, 29, 32, 37–40,
    159, 164–5, 170, 174–5, 180, 191–2,
    200, 205–8, 212, 218, 233, 242
    Manifesto, 183–4
Zapolya, John, 27, 29
Zara (Zadar), 23, 41, 43, 46–7, 51, 55,
    57, 61, 167, 182
    Resolution of, 56, 155
    Treaty of, 47
Zemun, 112
Zeta, 73–4, 87–91, 94, 96, 99
Zois, Baron, 17
Zrin, 26
Zrinski, Nicholas, 31
'Zveza', 220
Zvonimir, King, 24–5

Žablak, 74, 79
Žiča, 93
Živković, General, 178, 182, 190–1
Župan, 23, 87, 89–91
Župe, 58
Žujović, Sreten, 246